Sacco and Vanzetti

Sacco and Vanzetti

THE ANARCHIST BACKGROUND

Paul Avrich

PRINCETON UNIVERSITY PRESS

PRINCETON, NEW JERSEY

Copyright © 1991 by Princeton University Press
Published by Princeton University Press, 41 William Street,
Princeton, New Jersey 08540
In the United Kingdom: Princeton University Press, Chichester, West Sussex

Library of Congress Cataloging-in-Publication Data

Avrich, Paul
Sacco and Vanzetti : the anarchist background / by Paul Avrich
p.   cm.
Includes bibliographical references and index.
ISBN 0-691-04789-8
ISBN 0-691-02604-1 (pbk.)
1. Sacco, Nicola. 1891–1927. 2. Vanzetti, Bartolomeo. 1888–1927.
3. Anarchists—United States—Biography. 4. Anarchism—United States—History.
5. Sacco-Vanzetti case. I. Title.
HX843.7.S23A97 1991
364.1'523'09227447—dc20
[B]   90-40838

This book has been composed in Linotron Primer

Princeton University Press books are printed on acid-free paper and meet the
guidelines for permanence and durability of the Committee on Production
Guidelines for Book Longevity of the Council on Library Resources

Third printing, and first paperback printing, 1996

Printed in the United States of America

10 9 8 7 6

Contents

Illustrations

Acknowledgments

THIS BOOK could not have been completed without assistance from so many colleagues and friends that it is impossible to mention them all by name. A few, however, have gone to special lengths in providing me with materials and information, and I owe them particular thanks: Valerio Isca, Professor Nunzio Pernicone, Charles Poggi, and Sebastiano Magliocca, who, though he did not live to see the book in print, was an inestimable source of encouragement and advice.

It has been my good fortune to have spoken to a number of men and women who were personally acquainted with either Sacco or Vanzetti, or both, and who gave me the benefit of their recollections: Beltrando Brini, Gemma Diotalevi, Sara Ehrmann, Joseph Moro, Jenny Paglia, Frank Paradiso, Luigi Paradiso, Ralph Piesco, Bartolomeo Provo, Harry Richal, Fiorina Rossi, the late Art Shields, Concetta Silvestri, and Lefevre Brini Wager.

The following individuals were good enough to place at my disposal documents and photographs that could not be obtained elsewhere: Federico Arcos, Maria Teresa Ciaccio, Herbert and Roberta Feuerlicht, Elisabeth Giansiracusa, Professor David E. Kaiser, Victoria Thompson Murphy, Febo Pomilia, Siphra Rolland, Elide Sanchini, Professor James A. Sandos, Professor James E. Starrs, and George Vaux.

Others who have aided me in important ways are Professor Abraham Ascher, Attilio Bortolotti, Robert S. Calese, Robert D'Attilio, Emilio Diotalevi, Jr., Professor Richard Drinnon, Dr. George Esenwein, Oreste Fabrizi, Vincenzo Farulla, Professor Pietro Ferrua, Stewart Freilich, William Gallo, Audrey Goodfriend, Professor George T. Kelley, Aurora Magliocca, Arnold Paglia, Lena Paglia, Paolo Paolini, Maria Rando, Spencer Sacco, Jenny Salemme, Aurora Sallitto, Dominick Sallitto, Edwin Shapiro, Professor Marshall Shatz, Louis Tarabelli, Galileo Tobia, John Vattuone, Stewart Weinstein, and Diva Agostinelli Wieck.

I am particularly indebted to Charles Poggi, Professor Nunzio Pernicone, and Professor Richard Polenberg for reading the entire manuscript and offering suggestions by which I have greatly profited. My thanks are due also to Gail Ullman and Alice Calaprice of Princeton University Press for their valuable editorial advice.

The quest for pertinent material has taken me to many libraries and archives, in Europe as well as in America. To the staffs of these institutions, which are indicated in the notes and bibliography, I am much indebted for assistance. I owe special thanks in this regard to the following individuals: Dr. Laura Monti and Dr. Giuseppe Bisaccia of the Boston Public Library; Judith Mellins and Bernice Loss of the Harvard Law School Library; Alice M. Neary and Irma Jackson of the Immigration and Naturalization Service; David G. Paynter of the National Archives; Roger Ritzmann of the New York State Archives; Jennifer Burlis-Freilich of the Missouri State Archives; and Barbara Rivolta of the Paterson Museum.

To the individuals listed above, and to the many others who have helped me in various phases of my work, I tender my heartfelt thanks. My examination of the relevant sources was facilitated by a fellowship from the National Endowment for the Humanities, for which I am deeply grateful. The responsibility for this book, however, remains my own.

New York City
August 23, 1990

Sacco and Vanzetti

Introduction

SEVENTY YEARS have passed since the arrest of Nicola Sacco and Bartolomeo Vanzetti, sparking one of the most controversial episodes in American history. On April 15, 1920, a paymaster and his guard were shot to death during a robbery of a shoe factory in South Braintree, Massachusetts. Three weeks later, Sacco, a shoe worker, and Vanzetti, a fish peddler, both Italian immigrants and anarchists, were charged with participating in the crime. The following year they were brought to trial.

According to the prosecution, Sacco did the actual killing (at least of the guard) and Vanzetti was one of four accomplices. The evidence against them was contradictory. On the one hand, a number of witnesses identified them as members of the holdup gang. Both were armed on the night of their arrest, Sacco with a .32-caliber Colt automatic, Vanzetti with a .38-caliber Harrington & Richardson revolver. Both told lies when they were questioned by the police. Their weapons, moreover, seemed to fit the circumstances of the crime, and this weighed heavily against them in the minds of the jurors. On the other hand, both men had substantial alibis, neither had been convicted of any previous crime, and witnesses for the prosecution altered the stories they had told the police and private investigators after the holdup. Furthermore, no information was presented to the jury about the other bandits, who were never apprehended, and the authorities were unable to connect the stolen money, nearly $16,000, with the defendants or their anarchist associates.

The trial, occurring in the wake of the Red Scare, took place in an atmosphere of intense hostility towards the defendants. The district attorney, Frederick G. Katzmann, conducted a highly unscrupulous prosecution, coaching and badgering witnesses, withholding exculpatory evidence from the defense, and perhaps even tampering with physical evidence. A skillful and ruthless cross-examiner, he played on the emotions of the jurors, arousing their deepest prejudices against the accused. Sacco and Vanzetti were armed; they were foreigners, atheists, anarchists. This overclouded all judgment. The judge in the case, Webster Thayer, likewise revealed his bias. Outside the courtroom, during the trial and the appeals which followed, he made remarks that bristled with animosity towards the defendants ("Did you see what I did with those anarchistic bastards the other day? I guess that will hold them for a while.")[1] When a verdict of guilty was returned, many believed that the men had been convicted because of their foreign birth and radical beliefs, not on solid evidence of criminal guilt.

In the aftermath of the trial, as legal appeals delayed sentencing, a mounting body of evidence indicated that the wrong men had been apprehended. Key prosecution testimony was retracted and new evidence produced that was favorable to the defendants. Herbert Ehrmann, a junior defense attorney, built a strong case against the Morelli gang of Providence, which specialized in stealing shipments from shoe manufacturers.[2]

All this, however, availed nothing. For the attitude of the authorities had become so rigidly set against the defendants that they turned a deaf ear to contrary views. As a result, a growing number of observers, many of whom abhorred anarchism and had no sympathy with radical propaganda of any kind, concluded that the accused had not received a fair trial. The judge's bias against the defendants, their conviction on inconclusive evidence, their dignified behavior while their lives hung in the balance—all this attracted supporters, who labored to secure a new trial. At the eleventh hour, Governor Alvan T. Fuller conducted a review of the case, appointing an advisory committee, headed by President A. Lawrence Lowell of Harvard, to assist him. The Lowell Committee, as it became known, though finding Judge Thayer guilty of a "grave breach of official decorum" in his derogatory references to the defendants,[3] nevertheless concluded that justice had been done.

As events moved towards a climax, the case assumed international proportions, engaging the passions of men and women around the globe. Anatole France, in one of his last public utterances, pleaded with America to save Sacco and Vanzetti: "Save them for your honor, for the honor of your children and for the generations yet unborn."[4] In vain. On August 23, 1927, the men were electrocuted, in defiance of worldwide protests and appeals. By then, millions were convinced of their innocence, and millions more were convinced that, guilty or innocent, they had not received impartial justice.

This, then, was no ordinary case of robbery and murder. Other factors, as yet imperfectly understood, propelled it into international prominence. Set against the background of the Red Scare and its aftermath, it highlighted some of the major issues of the day: mass immigration, labor militancy, repression of radicals. Like the Haymarket affair of the 1880s, it was an episode that divided the nation, arousing deep-seated emotions, defining loyalties, and spawning a literature of criticism and protest. No other case of the period attracted more widespread attention, for it had a significance that made it symbolic of its time and place, elevating it to the level of tragedy and uncovering an aspect of American society that would not otherwise have been so nakedly exposed. "It revealed," wrote Edmund Wilson in 1928, "the whole anatomy of American life, with all its classes, professions, and points of view and all their relations, and it raised almost every fundamental question of our political and social system."[5]

Not surprisingly, then, it is a case that refuses to die. So many forces were at work, so many issues and principles at stake, that for more than six decades it has remained the subject of controversy. In 1947, twenty years after the executions, a group of prominent citizens, including Eleanor Roosevelt, Albert Einstein, and Herbert Lehman, offered the state of Massachusetts a bas-relief plaque of Sacco and Vanzetti by the sculptor of Mount Rushmore, Gutzon Borglum, only to have it rejected by the governor. In 1959 a resolution in the state legislature to exonerate the defendants, as had been done for the "victims of the witchcraft hysteria who were hanged in Salem,"[6] failed of adoption. More recently, however, Governor Michael S. Dukakis marked the fiftieth anniversary of the executions by proclaiming August 23, 1977, "Nicola Sacco and Bartolomeo Vanzetti Day." Dukakis, while sidestepping the issue of innocence or guilt, declared that "the atmosphere of their trial and appeals was permeated by prejudice against foreigners and hostility toward unorthodox political views."[7]

In the sixty-odd years that have passed since the execution of Sacco and Vanzetti, a substantial literature about them has accumulated. Most studies, however, whatever their merits, suffer from two defects. First, the authors have not availed themselves of materials in the Italian language, which shed light on virtually every aspect of the case, if not resolving all its mysteries and ambiguities. Second, few writers have consulted the anarchist sources, with their wealth of information about the movement to which Sacco and Vanzetti belonged. A deeper knowledge of the anarchist dimension—of the social, political, and intellectual world in which the defendants lived and acted—would go far to explain their behavior on the night of their arrest.

To explore this dimension, including some of the darker corners of the movement, is one of the objects of the present volume. The primary focus, however, is on the lives of the two men, beginning with their childhood in Italy. Why did they emigrate to the United States? What were their experiences after arriving in this country? Why did they become anarchists? In what radical activities did they engage? Such are the questions that this book attempts to answer. It makes no pretense, however, of settling the issue of whether Sacco and Vanzetti were guilty of the crimes for which they were executed. Nearly seven decades after their trial, the case against them remains unproved. Nor, on the other hand, can their innocence be established beyond any shadow of doubt.

In coming years, one hopes, new evidence will be discovered and deeper understanding obtained. In the end, however, we may never succeed in resolving the controversy. As the biographer of the Lowells remarked, immortality would almost be desirable so as to "get at the truth of the Sacco-Vanzetti case."[8] Yet even immortality might not suffice. For time is working against us. Memories fade; people die. As the months and years roll by, chances diminish of learning "the truth" about Sacco and Vanzetti. It is frustrating to ponder that there are still people alive—the widow of Sacco among them—who might, if they chose, reveal at least part of the truth. The issue of guilt or innocence awaits definitive treatment, but, alas, it may never receive it.

PART ONE

Immigrants

CHAPTER ONE

Italian Childhoods

IN 1908 MORE than 130,000 Italians emigrated to the United States. Among them were Nicola Sacco and Bartolomeo Vanzetti. They came from opposite ends of Italy and did not meet until 1917. After that, however, their fates were inseparably linked.

Sacco and Vanzetti hardly seemed destined for immortality when they arrived on America's shores. In most respects they differed little from the millions of their fellow Italians who entered the country during the early years of the century, when immigration was at flood tide. Both, typically, were single young men of adventurous spirit in search of wider opportunities. Both came from peasant families, deeply rooted in the Italian soil. Though Sacco was from the south and Vanzetti from the north, both had grown up in small, remote towns, largely sheltered from the outside world. On reaching America, both abandoned their agrarian heritage for the career of an urban worker. Their lives, moreover, were compounded of the usual struggles, disappointments, and successes that fell to every new arrival.

In all this their experiences were unexceptional. What distinguished them from the ordinary lot of Italian immigrants was that both became militant anarchists who followed a course of clandestine insurgency. More than that, they became the defendants in one of the most celebrated trials in American history.

.   .   .

Sacco began life in Torremaggiore, a quiet southern town in the foothills of the Apennines, inland from the Adriatic spur of Italy's boot. Remote from urban civilization, Torremaggiore was more than an hour's journey to the nearest city, the provincial capital of Foggia, a bustling market for the wool, wheat, vegetables, olives, and grapes of the Puglia region, of which the province of Foggia forms a part. Torremaggiore, surrounded by vineyards and olive groves, took its name from the ancient castle, long since transformed into a tenement, that surmounted the hill on which the town was perched. Below the castle ran a maze of narrow streets with two-story mud-and-stone houses, whitewashed to shield them from the sun. Wide doorways, garlanded with vegetables and fruits, led directly into the living quarters or opened into courtyards cluttered with farm implements, chickens, and goats.[1]

In such a house, on April 22, 1891, Nicola Sacco was born, the third son in a family of seventeen children. Nicola was not his original name; he was baptized Ferdinando. Not until 1917, the year in which he met Vanzetti, did he adopt the first name by which he became generally known. To his family, however, he remained Ferdinando, or simply Nando, the nickname of his youth.

Nando grew up in comfortable circumstances, at least by the standards of a southern Italian community at the turn of the century. Though Puglia was a region in which rural destitution was endemic,[2] there were no extremes of wealth and poverty in Torremaggiore, and the Saccos, while far from being affluent, were among the more prosperous of the town's ten thousand inhabitants. The father, Michele, thirty years old at the time of Ferdinando's birth, was a substantial peasant who had married Angela Mosmacotelli, the daughter of an olive oil merchant. Shortly after the wedding, Michele took charge of the business, which prospered under his supervision. Outside the town, in addition, he owned a plot of land for the cultivation of fruit and vegetables, as well as an extensive vineyard, one of the largest in Torremaggiore, from which he produced and sold wine. This enterprise, too, flourished under his direction, so that he hired a number of laborers to assist him.[3]

As property owners and employers, firmly rooted in the local soil, the Saccos were a respected family who played a role in public affairs. Ferdinando's older brother Sabino later became the mayor of Torremaggiore, and several uncles served on the town council. At home, Nando grew up in a happy environment, surrounded by affection and love. Years later, when his life took a darker turn, he recalled with nostalgia his "sweet youth" in Torremaggiore, secure within the bosom of his family.[4] Though devoted to his father, a model of sobriety and good sense, Nando was especially attached to his mother, to whom he bore a striking physical resemblance. A woman of kindly and generous temper, it was to her that he invariably turned when feeling ill or out of sorts, and she always lent a sympathetic ear.[5]

Happily such moments were rare. For Nando was blessed with excellent health and with a buoyant and genial disposition. He was less given to moping than many boys his age, and illness or moodiness seldom intruded. To be cheerful, he afterwards noted, "is my nature, because I remember my dear and poor mother when she use to say that not matter if you work hard the smile shining always on your face."[6]

And work hard he did, even in his tender years. A child of nature, who loved the outdoor life, he did not take eagerly to classroom learning. Alert and intelligent though he was, he never liked school, as he later confessed, judging himself a "little thick."[7] According to some accounts, he received no formal education at all and was unable to read and write when he came to America. Sacco himself, testifying at his trial, claimed to have attended school for seven years, quitting at the age of fourteen. The truth, however, lies in between, namely that he completed the third grade; and it can be shown that he was literate in Italian when he arrived in the United States.[8]

Dropping out of school at the age of nine, Ferdinando went to work in his father's vineyard, a twenty-minute walk from the town. There he performed a variety of chores, from weeding and hoeing to planting and picking. Another of his duties was to see that animals pasturing on adjacent land did not wander into the vineyard. To accomplish this, he often remained overnight, sleeping on a hayrick he had built with his father and brothers. Rising before dawn, he watered the vegetables, flowers, and fruit trees grown by the Saccos alongside their vineyard. The sun would be coming up when Ferdinando completed this work. Returning to the center of the vineyard, he would jump up on a wall surrounding the well and survey the "enchanted scene." "If I was a poet," he wrote from prison in 1924, "probably I could discribe the red rays of the loving sun shining and the bright blue sky and the perfume of my garden and flowers, the smell of the violet that was comes from the vast verdant prairies, and the singing of the birds, that was almost the joy of deliriany." After such interludes Nando would return to his chores, singing a favorite song. In the evening, just after dusk, he would return to the garden. If going home for the night, he would fetch the baskets of fruit and vegetables that he had gathered for his mother during the day, along with "a bunch of flowers that I used make a lovely bouquet."[9]

Throughout these years in Torremaggiore, Ferdinando's closest companion was his brother Sabino, seven years his senior. Despite the difference in their ages, the pair were steadfast friends. They worked together, played together, and shared each other's innermost dreams. In 1904, however, Sabino, now twenty, was conscripted into the army, obliged to serve for three years. This left Ferdinando, at thirteen, the oldest son remaining at home. (Nicola, the first Sacco son, had already married, set up house, and begun a family. Ferdinando would later assume his name.)

A trustworthy boy, mature for his years, Nando began to take on new responsibilities. Sometimes his father sent him around in a mule-drawn cart to pay the hired hands or buy supplies. These were enjoyable interludes, a break from the usual routine. More than any-thing else, however, Nando was fascinated by machines. In summertime, when there was nothing that needed tending in the vineyard, he liked to stoke the big steam-powered machine that threshed all the wheat of the district. Better than farming or helping his father, Nando liked working around engines; and in the fall of 1907, after the harvest was in, he quit the vineyard and went back to town to learn to be a mechanic.[10]

He did not remain long at this trade. By now Sabino had returned from military service, burning with new ambitions and ideas. Army life, narrow though it was, had broadened his horizons. Politically he had moved to the left. In contrast to his father, a Mazzinian republican of long standing, he had come to consider himself a socialist. Soon after his return he began to frequent the socialist club in town. Whether any of this rubbed off on Ferdinando—barely sixteen when Sabino came home—it is difficult to say, but probably not a great deal. If the youth had any political sympathies at this time, they leaned towards the republicanism of his father rather than the socialism of his brother.[11]

Ferdinando was enthralled, however, by quite another of his brother's preoccupations. Since his return from the army, Sabino had talked incessantly of going to America, the shining land across the sea. Not that he felt driven by economic necessity, as there was ample place in his father's business for both him and his younger brother. But now twenty-three, a veteran of military service, he longed for a wider world than that of the backwater in which he had been reared. Nor was this feeling unique; the same quest for a new life was driving millions of young men across the Atlantic. America, for Sabino, was the land of freedom, opportunity, and adventure. It was all that was modern and enlightened in the world.

Ferdinando shared his brother's excitement. No less than Sabino he yearned to go to America, the country "that was always in my dreams."[12] Given his love of machines, it offered him boundless possibilities and aroused his most thrilling expectations. He was "always a dreamer," his father later recalled, "though he worked hard, too. I can see him among the vines there on the hillside, a robust youngster, and good-hearted." But it was also the promise of freedom that lured the youngster to America. "I was crazy to come to this country," he declared at his trial, "because I was liked a free country, call a free country," the country on which he fastened his hopes.[13]

Michele Sacco, who loved his sons dearly, had counted on their remaining in Torremaggiore and joining him in his business. But, unable to dissuade them, he wrote to an old friend, Antonio Calzone, from the nearby town of Casalvecchio, who had several years before emigrated to the United States, settling in Milford, Massachusetts. Calzone replied with enthusiasm, urging the boys to come as soon as possible. So it was that, in April 1908, Sabino and Ferdinando Sacco left their father's house and set out to realize their dream. From the vineyards and olive groves friends and neighbors came to the road to embrace them in farewell. There were tears in many eyes. Two more young Italians were off to America.[14]

· · ·

Two months later, in June 1908, yet another young Italian, Bartolomeo Vanzetti, started on his journey to America. Three years older than Ferdinando Sacco, he had been born, the son of a farmer, in the picturesque town of Villafalletto, high in the hills of Piedmont in the northwestern corner of the country. Some twenty miles to the south lay the provincial capital of Cuneo, a market for chestnuts, silk, and grain. Turin, to the north, was the principal city of the region, a center of industry and trade. The nearest port was Genoa, half a day's journey to the east, from which the products of Piedmont and adjacent regions were shipped all over the world.

Villafalletto, nestled in the Alpine foothills, sat on the right bank of the Maira River, amid orchards, woods, and fields rising gently towards the mountains on the horizon. The houses, adorned with pastel colors and red tile roofs, formed a chain of connected dwellings with interior courtyards. A piazza, decorated with a fountain, stood at the center of the town, dominated by the campanile of a church. From the hills above the town there were magnificent views of the river, meandering through the valley below.[15]

Villafalletto gained its livelihood primarily from agriculture, raising hay, wheat, beans, clover, and silkworms (mulberry trees lined a corner of every field). In the surrounding hills grew a variety of fruits—apples and cherries, pears and grapes, peaches and plums—in addition to berries, mushrooms, and nuts. Dairy products, too, were an important part of the economy. The larger farms boasted as many as three hundred cows, to say nothing of chickens and hogs, and a factory in town produced several tons of cheese every week.[16]

The principal crop, however, was hay, which grew in such abundance that seasonal labor had to be hired to harvest it. Every May a legion of mountaineers, equipped with sacks and scythes, descended into Villafalletto in mule-drawn carts to carry out the task. As they entered the town they would begin to sing, "throatfull, with stentorean voices their rough songs."[17] Halting in the piazza, they would negotiate their wages with the local farmers—Vanzetti's father among them—before camping out for the night. By dawn the next day they were deployed in the meadows, ready to begin their work.

Nor was their labor completed with the mowing of the hay. They returned in June to pick the mulberry leaves and in July to harvest the wheat, and yet again in late autumn, when heavy snowfall began in the mountains. Leaving the older folk behind, they brought their furniture, cows, and sheep down into the valley and took shelter on the farms where, having toiled in spring and summer, they were permitted to pasture their herds. Vanzetti's father gave space to such a family, three unmarried brothers and a sister ("very clean and decent persons," Vanzetti recalled), who spent the winter in one large room.[18]

As far back as Vanzetti could trace them, his forebears had been farmers in Villafalletto. His grandfather, apart from tilling the soil, had been a dealer in agricultural products, and his father, following this tradition, traded in wine, fruit, and grain. The Vanzettis, like the Saccos in Torremaggiore, were modestly prosperous by the standards of the region. They had a sizeable parcel of land, a beautiful garden, and a comfortable house near the center of town, whose well-wrought old furniture later impressed an affluent visitor from Boston, who had journeyed there to see Vanzetti's kinfolk.[19] The Vanzettis, again like the Saccos, were among the most highly regarded families of the community, hard working and respected by their neighbors. "There is not at present, nor ever was, a more honorable family in that little town, pious, honest, and just," wrote a friend of Vanzetti's father. "Never has the slightest blemish ever tarnished the name of this good family."[20]

It is a little-known fact that Vanzetti's father, Giovan Battista Vanzetti, like his son after him, had gone to seek his fortune in America. This occurred in 1881, when he was thirty-two and still unmarried. Traveling as far as California, he was quite dazzled by what he saw and might have remained had his father, with four daughters to marry off, not written him to come home. Deferring to his father's wishes, he returned to Villafalletto in 1883, scarcely two years after his departure. Four years later, having taken charge of the family business, he married Giovanna Nivello, a twenty-five-year-old widow with a young son, who was sent to live with an uncle.[21] Without delay (Giovan Battista was now thirty-eight) the couple began a family of their own. Bartolomeo, the oldest child, arrived on June 11, 1888, barely a year after the wedding. Next came Luigia, in 1891, then Spirito—who died in infancy—in 1899. Four years later Vincenzina was born, followed by Ettore in 1905.[22]

For the first thirteen years of his life Bartolomeo remained in Villafalletto, a happy and contented child. His earliest memories were of his father planting fruit trees in the garden and of his mother giving him honey from a beehive.[23] Like Sacco, he inherited from his ancestors an abiding passion for the land. As a boy he loved to work in the garden, whose birds, insects, and flowers he later described in idyllic detail. "You ought to see the king wasps," he wrote, "big, velvety, lucid, ravishingly forcefully on these flowers' calices, and the virtuous honeybees—the wasp, the white, the yellow, the forget-me-nots, the hedge's butterflies and the variated armies of several genuses of grass eaters, the red conconcinas, the meadows gri-gri. Each of your step would arise from the ground a rainbow cloud of these creatures, with a multiphoned vibration of wings."[24]

So "unspeakably beautiful" was the scene, Vanzetti remarked, that to do it justice would require "a poet of the first magnitude." Small wonder that, in later years, he should have looked back on Villafalletto with profound longing—the "most loved place" in all the world. During the 1920s, at the darkest moment of his life, he could conjure up out of the past vivid pictures of his native town, with its majestic valley and hills. "Can you see from your home," he wrote an American friend, "mountain peaks eternally covered by snow? If so, your place is like mine."[25]

There was little in Bartolomeo's upbringing that foreshadowed his future radical activities. Both his parents were devout Catholics, without a hint of the anticlerical republicanism discernible among the Saccos in Torremaggiore. Devoted to his father, and still more to his mother, whom adored with a passion that never abated, Bartolomeo took his religious faith for granted, as part of an established and unchallengeable way of life. He showed not the slightest inclination to question the values, religious or otherwise, on which he was nurtured. He exhibited, on the contrary, a distinct spiritual cast, which manifested itself at an early age. Once while at play, his sister relates, a group of children erected an altar, and Bartolomeo, pretending to be the priest, led his congregation in the mass.[26] It was a role to which he seemed perfectly suited.

Under other circumstances, the thoughtful, introspective boy might have developed into a teacher or scholar, if not indeed a friar or priest. William G. Thompson, who became Vanzetti's counsel in 1924, thought him one of the most gifted men that he had known. With an education, Thompson felt, he might have been a Harvard professor, rather than the fish peddler and casual laborer that he was.[27] But such was not to be. To Vanzetti's father, a practical-minded farmer, there was little profit in excess learning. Besides, he was shortly to open a café in Villafalletto, where his son could cook pastry and tend bar. For a time he was undecided whether to apprentice Bartolomeo to a baker or to let him continue his studies and train for a profession. While considering the matter, however, he read in a newspaper that in

Turin forty-two lawyers had applied for a position paying thirty-five lire a month. This sealed Bartolomeo's fate. Education was a waste of money, his father decided. Better that his son should learn a trade and assist in the new café.[28]

Bartolomeo's life now took a somber turn. In 1901, when he was thirteen years old, he was apprenticed to Signor Comino, the owner of a pastry shop in Cuneo. His father conducted him to the place and left him, as Vanzetti later put it, "to taste for the first time the flavor of hard, relentless labor." He worked for fifteen hours a day, from seven in the morning until ten at night, seven days a week, with only a three-hour respite every other Sunday. Scarcely out of his childhood, he found it hard to adjust to such a routine. He was always on his feet, so that his shoes quickly wore out, and he had to write home for a new pair.[29] A dutiful son, he did not complain, but his once idyllic life was at an end.

After nineteen unhappy months, Bartolomeo moved to the town of Cavour, in Turin province, where he worked in the bakery of a Signor Goitre, with whom he remained for two years.[30] Conditions here were no better than in Cuneo, except that he had ten hours off a month instead of six. There were times, however, when he was compelled to work for eighteen hours a day, rather than the usual fifteen, after which his feet burned as if on hot coals. "I did not like the trade," he writes, "but I stuck to it to please my father and because I did not know what else to choose."[31] As an apprentice he led a solitary life, work occupying most of his time. As in Cuneo, he was lonely and homesick. "To tell the truth," he wrote his parents on the eve of his fifteenth birthday, "I am tired of this miserable life."[32]

In the fall of 1904, Bartolomeo, now sixteen, abandoned Cavour for Turin, seeking a different line of work. After searching for several weeks, he was offered a job as a bartender at twenty lire a month, but the offer fell through. Discouraged, Bartolomeo left Turin to work as a confectioner in Cuorgnè, a town some thirty miles to the north. But by May 1906, after seven or eight months, we find him back in Turin, employed as a caramel maker, first by a Signor Prandis and then by a Signor Abraria.[33]

Nine months later, however, Bartolomeo's health broke down. In February 1907, while working for Signor Abraria, he suffered an attack of pleurisy that landed him in bed. In great pain, he was confined indoors, like a "sad twilight flower," he recalled.[34] Despite the attentions of Signor Abraria, his condition failed to improve, and his father had to be summoned from Villafalletto to bring him home. Bartolo (as he was called) was then eighteen. "And so I returned," he later wrote, "after six years spent in the fetid atmosphere of bakeries and restaurant kitchens, with rarely a breath of God's air or a glimpse of His glorious world. Six years that might have been beautiful to a boy avid of learning and thirsty for a refreshing draught of the simple country life of his native village. Years of the great miracle which transforms the child into the man."[35]

The bitterness of these words is apparent. Torn from his family at a tender age, deprived of his friends, his school, his mother's love, compelled to slave in kitchens to learn a trade that he loathed, he could not conceal his resentment, above all against his father, on whom he fixed responsibility for his fate. Small wonder that hints of estrangement would appear in his future relations with Giovan Battista (he later wrote that Eugene Victor Debs, the American socialist leader, "loved me more than my own father"). Nevertheless he continued to treat him with filial respect, calling him an "honest and good man."[36]

As for his mother, "my good, my best-loved mother," Bartolo worshipped her as fervently as in the past. She, for her part, was relieved to have her son home. She put him to bed ("I had almost forgotten that hands could caress so tenderly," he wrote) where he remained for a full month. For two more months he went about with the aid of a walking stick as he gradually recovered his health. Remaining in Villafalletto, he made new friends, worked in the garden, and wandered through the woods beside the Maira. He was later to call his convalescence, amid the tranquillity of his native town, one of the happiest intervals of his life.[37]

And yet his years away from home, hard and lonely as they had been, had not been wasted. Bartolomeo had grown up. He had learned a good deal about life. He had also learned a trade that would prove useful in later years. Though taken out of school, he had studied on his own whenever the opportunity afforded. During his years in Cavour, for instance, he encountered "a certain learned person" who supplied him with newspapers and books. In addition, his employer, Signor Goitre, subscribed to a religious publication in Genoa, which "was lucky because I was then a fervent Catholic."[38]

Afterwards, in Turin, his fellow workers, boys of his own age, ridiculed his devotion to the church. They called him "a hypocrite and bigot."[39] Some, considering themselves socialists, quoted from radical and anticlerical pamphlets, which circulated in Turin in great quantities. Bartolo, however, resisted. On one occasion, he tells us, he defended his faith with his fists. Yet the seeds of doubt had been planted, and in time his religious ardor began to cool. With mounting skepticism he looked back on the values that he had absorbed as a child. "To my parents," he later wrote, "to my mother especially, I owe not only my life that she gave me by birth and cares, but all that is good in me.

Yet, even my parents, in spite of their love and good-will, they teach me many wrong ideas, false principles, and a false divinity."[40]

In place of religion, Bartolo found himself drawn to new, more radical currents of thought. About this time, on the eve of his illness, the first glimmerings of socialism appear in his thinking, mingled with the sentimental humanism of Edmondo De Amicis, whose *Cuore*, written in the form of a schoolboy's diary, aroused his deepest emotions. As a result, he writes: "The principles of humanism and equality of rights began to make a breach in my heart."[41]

Now in Villafalletto, during his months of convalescence, Bartolo's ideas assumed a clearer form. With ample time to read, he plunged into a work of St. Augustine, from which a single sentence—"The blood of martyrs is the seed of liberty"—remained indelibly printed on his mind. Twice he read *I Promessi Sposi*, Manzoni's great romantic novel, before attempting *The Divine Comedy*, a dusty copy of which he came upon in the house. "Ah, me!" he writes, "my teeth were not made for such a bone; nevertheless I proceeded to gnaw it desperately, and I believe not uselessly."[42]

His health once restored, Bartolo sought new friends among the educated element of Villafalletto's inhabitants—the physician Dr. Francia, the pharmacist Scrimaglio, the veterinarian Bo—whose secularist views swept away the lingering traces of his Catholicism. "Already I began to understand that the plague which besets humanity most cruelly is ignorance and the degeneracy of natural sentiments," he wrote. "My religion soon needed no temples, altars and formal prayers. God became for me a perfect spiritual Being, devoid of any human attributes." His father countered that the church was necessary in order "to hold in check human passions, and to console the human being in tribulation." Yet, try as he might, he failed to rekindle his son's religious faith.[43] Bartolo, avoiding family disputes, received his father's arguments with a smile. Nor did he seek to influence his sister Luigia, then sixteen, who remained forever faithful to the church. Happy to be home, amid the serenity of his native town, he preferred to keep his heresies to himself.

The serenity, however, was soon disturbed. No sooner had Bartolo recovered his health than his mother, aged forty-five, was stricken with cancer. For three months her illness kept her in agonizing pain. In the final weeks, Vanzetti tells us, her suffering became so intense that not even her husband could bear the horror of the sickroom. It remained for Bartolo himself to care for her, just as she had earlier cared for him. He remained at her bedside day and night, tortured by the sight of her distress. Towards the end of 1907 she died in his arms. It was he who laid her in her coffin and threw the first handful of earth over her bier. "And it was right that I should do so," he noted, "for I was burying part of myself."[44]

The tragedy hit the family very hard. Giovan Battista, now fifty-eight, grew grey within a few months. The children, the youngest ones barely two and four, were left without a mother. Bartolo, although the oldest, was nevertheless the most deeply affected. His mother was the one person to whom he had been truly close, and her death left a void that was never filled. It was the saddest experience of his life, he later remarked, sadder than being imprisoned. He described it in highly emotional terms and in later years was greatly upset whenever his thoughts turned to his mother. "I hold my mother's memory as the sacrest thing to me," he wrote. "My heart is the tabernacle in which my mother, and she was brave, lives."[45]

Following his mother's death, Bartolo became silent and morose. The joy of life had left him. He went for days without speaking, wandering in the forests along the Maira. He even considered suicide, so unbearable was his grief. "Many times," he wrote, "going to the bridge, I stopped long and looked down at the white stones far below in a bed of sand, and thought of them as a bed where there would be no more nightmare."[46]

In this agitated state of mind, his thoughts began to turn to America. After the death of his mother, he said, "there was nothing for me to do but come away. I had to put the seas between me and my grief."[47] In America, a place of refuge for the suffering, the tragedies of his youth might be forgotten. Perhaps, too, he could find a new life, freer and happier than in the past. Financial hardship played no role in his decision to leave. As with Sacco, he forsook a comfortable home and a good living amid surroundings that he genuinely loved. "There was no economic necessity for either of us to come to this country," he wrote to Governor Fuller before his death. "We came because we heard that it was a land of freedom—freedom not merely to gain wealth, for which we cared little, but freedom of the mind and of ideas. We always think that a natural right, and in that is our happiness."[48]

Vanzetti's father, though he himself had gone to America as a young man, did not want his son to leave. Having lost his wife only months before, he was loath to lose his oldest child as well. Besides, his café had prospered. Should the boy's training as a pastry maker and confectioner go to waste? Far better that he should remain in Villafalletto, help in the business, and marry and raise a family. But Bartolo was determined to go. He needed a change. He did not want to work for his father. He was desperate to get away.

On June 9, 1908, two days before his twentieth birthday, Bartolo took leave of Villafalletto. The parting was tearful. His family wept as in mourning. The neighbors consoled his father, "speechless in his sorrow."[49] Friends offered Bartolo their blessings. Then, in a group, they followed him out on the road, comforting and lamenting. The scene resembled that in Torremaggiore when, two months before, Sacco had made his departure. Neither he nor Vanzetti was ever to return. Italy, in the years ahead, would seldom be far from their thoughts. But they had gone to America to stay, to "this free country," as Sacco called it, "the country that was always in my dreams."[50]

CHAPTER TWO

Free Country

IT WAS IN EARLY April 1908 that Sabino and Ferdinando Sacco left Torremaggiore for America. By cart they traveled to Foggia, and then by train to Naples, from where they sailed for Boston on a ship of the White Star Line. The voyage was uneventful, although Nando got seasick and Sabino took him to the ship's doctor, who "ordered for me a good purge and for my brother that felt fine . . . a good soup."[1] They landed in Boston on April 12, ten days before Nando's seventeenth birthday, and proceeded at once to Milford.

In Milford, a town of fifteen thousand inhabitants on the approaches to the hill country west of Boston, the brothers received a warm welcome. Ever since the 1880s, Italian immigrants had been arriving there in growing numbers, settling mainly in the Plains section, which, with its Naples Street, Genoa Street, and Columbus Avenue, comprised one of the numerous "Little Italys" in America. Many of these immigrants, moreover, were *paesani* of the Saccos, coming not merely from the province of Foggia but from a cluster of towns north of the capital—Casalvecchio, Castelnuovo, Sansevero, and Torremaggiore itself—in which their parents had relatives and friends. Milford, in short, was a veritable Little Foggia in Massachusetts, where Sabino and Ferdinando could feel at home. To make things even easier, they moved in with the family of Antonio Calzone, their father's friend from Casalvecchio, whose house at 17 Mount Pleasant Street stood amid a colony of Foggian immigrants, including a barber, a baker, and an undertaker, in addition to shoe workers, laborers, and mill hands.

In one respect their arrival was inauspicious. A period of economic prosperity had given way to a depression, and jobs were hard to find. The brothers, however, were fortunate. Sabino almost immediately got work in a foundry; and before long, with Mr. Calzone's help, Ferdinando was hired by the Cenedella Construction Company, which was doing paving work in Milford. At first he labored as a water boy at $1.15 a day.[2] It was menial work, but he liked it. He liked the sizzle of the tar being poured, the sense of useful labor being done, the banter with his workmates, mostly Italians recently arrived like himself. Above all, he liked it when the engineer let him help with the steam roller and he could stand beside the hot, wheezing engine, oiling it from a long-nozzled can or stoking it with coal, as he had stoked the big wheat thresher in Torremaggiore.[3]

Never one to shirk hard labor, Sacco was regarded with favor by his employers. After three months as water boy, he was transferred to pick-and-shovel work ("born with a shovel in one hand and a pickaxe in the other," the immigrants joked). He now received $1.75 a day, a raise of sixty cents. This work lasted only three more months, until November of 1908, when winter set in and it became too cold for outdoor labor. Mr. Calzone then got him a job at his own place of employment, the Draper Company, a large manufacturer of textile machinery in neighboring Hopedale. There Ferdinando (called "Freddy" by his workmates) labored in the foundry, trimming the slag from pig iron. He remained there for almost a year.[4]

Meanwhile, the pace of American life had proved too hectic for Sabino. Towards the end of 1909, after a year and a half of assorted jobs, he went back to Italy, to the olive oil and wine business of his father. Within a few years he was married and had a family; in 1920 he was elected mayor of Torremaggiore on the socialist ticket. He never returned to the United States, not even when his brother was arrested, but spent the rest of his life in his native town, where he died at the age of ninety-two.

Ferdinando, however, remained. Brimming with energy and determination, he did not give up so easily. Now eighteen years old, he knew that if he returned to Italy he would soon have to enter the army, a prospect he was loath to face. Come what may, he resolved to stay on. To better himself, however, he would have to learn a trade. As an unskilled laborer, wielding shovel and pick, he would remain at the bottom of the heap. With proper training, on the other hand, he might rise to a position of prosperity and carve a niche for himself in the Milford community.

His choice of a trade came almost by accident. In the fall of 1909, Sabino, about to return to Italy, introduced him to Henry Iacovelli, a fellow Foggian who lived in the neighborhood. Four years older than Ferdinando, Iacovelli, like the Calzones a native of Casalvecchio, had come to America as a child in 1893 and was now a skilled worker at the Milford Shoe Company, employed as an edge-trimmer.[5] Iacovelli sent Sacco to Michael F. Kelley, superintendant of the factory, who conducted a training program for recent immigrants. For a fee of fifty dollars Kelley taught them edge-trimming, lasting, stitching, and other skills of shoe manufacturing, then sent them "out into the world as real mechanics." It was not exactly a school, said Kelley, but a mixing of the beginners with the older hands, who could teach them "how to get ahead."[6] Sacco, having saved a little money from his previous job, immediately enrolled in the course. The training involved three months of work without pay, something he could ill afford. But the rewards were soon apparent. Instructed by Iacovelli, under Kelley's general supervision, Ferdinando caught on quickly. By the beginning of 1910 he had emerged as a qualified edge-trimmer.

By that time the depression had faded. Eastern Massachusetts being the center of the nation's shoe industry, jobs were again plentiful and skilled workers were drawing attractive wages. Sacco soon found employment in a factory at Webster, some twenty miles west of Milford. In a short time, however, he grew lonely. He missed his *paesani* in Milford—the Calzones, the Iacovellis, the rest of the Foggian community—who had lightened the burdens of his immigration. After seven months, therefore, he returned to his American "hometown" and was hired by the Milford Shoe Company as a regular employee. He worked there steadily from September 1910 to May 1917, operating an edging machine. During this time he mastered the techniques of his craft, becoming one of the best edge-trimmers in the business.

In Sacco's absence, his room at the Calzones had been rented to another young immigrant, but he found a place with Henry Iacovelli's parents, whose house at 11 Pond Street was in the same neighborhood. The atmosphere was homelike and congenial. "All the single men from Foggia ate there," a relative of Sacco's recalled, "even those who did not live there, a sizeable group around a big table."[7]

Such was Sacco's home for the next year and a half. Happy to be back in Milford, he plunged into his new job with all his customary energy, earning the superior wages of a skilled craftsman. He worked hard. He was steady and reliable, well liked by both his employers and his workmates. His foreman, John J. Millick, who supervised his shop for four years, recalled that he never lost a day in that time. "Sacco was a genius at his work," said his friend Joseph Moro, "that machine running so fast, sharp like a razor; you miss a thousandth of an inch and you ruin the shoe. He was quick, precise, a wonderful worker." According to his employer, he was the swiftest edge-trimmer of some three thousand who had passed through his factory doors.[8]

Sacco was nineteen when he returned to Milford, a sturdy and well-knit young man. Five feet five inches tall, he weighed about 145 pounds and had dark hair and brown eyes. He had "eyes that looked at you straight," said Mary Heaton Vorse, and "a friendly way with him almost like that of a child who had never known anything but affection." Lithe, vigorous, and good-looking, as acquaintances describe him, he was "clean-cut as a Roman coin," a "vital, radiant little bundle of energy," "very active, like a cat, a figure all of steel springs."[9] At the same time, however, he was quiet and self-effacing, modest in both manner and speech. "He didn't say much," a friend recalls. "He didn't drink. He was a very clean young man, in his language as well as in his person. You never heard any vulgarity from him." Henry Iacovelli's daughter remembers him as "a good-natured, easy-going person, with a friendly disposition." He was always courteous and polite, recalled Gemma DePasquale, and he "never spoke out of turn."[10]

Three evenings a week Sacco attended English classes, then compulsory for foreign workingmen. His teacher was Mary DePasquale, Gemma's older sister, a graduate of Framingham State Teachers College, the first Italian schoolteacher in Milford. The daughter of Foggian immigrants, among the earliest to settle in the town, she taught second grade at the Plains School, in addition to the classes at night. Her memories of Sacco were vivid. Where most of the other pupils showed up in their work clothes, dirty and sweaty, Ferdinando always arrived washed and showered and wearing a clean shirt. She remembered his courteous manner, his eagerness to learn. She liked him, as did everyone else in the community. "She thought the world of Sacco," her sister recalls. "He was cute and bright, an intelligent person in his own way."[11]

Sacco was, in short, a young man of exemplary character, besides being an excellent worker. In his leisure hours he enjoyed the outdoors, mingling and relaxing with his friends. One evening, in 1911, at a dance for the benefit of a paralyzed accordion player, he met Rosa Zambelli, who won a box of candy in the raffle. Sixteen years old, she had been born in the Lombardy region of northern Italy. Her father, a prosperous farmer who had fallen on hard times, emigrated to the United States with his wife and three older children, leaving Rosa to be educated in a convent. A few years later she rejoined her family, who had meanwhile settled in Milford, renting an apartment in the Plains section of town.[12]

Rosina, as she was called, was a girl of character, intelligence, and good looks. Small and slender, she had dark brown eyes, a fair complexion, and "fine copper-colored hair," in Katherine Anne Porter's description. Gemma DePasquale, who lived next door, remembers her as "small and pretty, with a little round face, rather quiet and shy. She was a doll."[13] Sacco, then twenty, courted Rosina for several months. At last, on May 1, 1912, "our love day," as Sacco calls it, he obtained her father's permission to buy her a wedding outfit. Ferdinando and Rosina went downtown to a clothing store and picked out a suit, a hat, shoes, stockings, and a slip. That accomplished, says Sacco, Rosina was "all dress up." "Mrs. Jack," he wrote to a friend from prison in 1923, "I wish you could see Rosina how nise she was look, while now the sufferance of today had make her look like a old woman." Sacco added: "I was never ambitious to buy her a diomonds and so-so but I always bouth everything could be natural and useful."[14]

Ferdinando was twenty-one and Rosina seventeen when they married. Taking leave of the Iacovellis, Sacco found an apartment at 11 East Main Street, next door to the Italian Catholic church. It was here, on May 10, 1913, that their first child, a son, was born. They named him Dante, "because you know Dante was a great man in my country," Sacco explained.[15] Needing more space, they moved to a larger apartment a few blocks away, at 76 Hayward Street. There they remained until 1917, when Sacco departed for Mexico. By then he was a fervent anarchist.

· · ·

Sacco's nine years in Milford were among the happiest and most fulfilling of his life. During this time he grew to manhood, learned a trade, married, and fathered a child. Everything that we know about the Saccos points to an untroubled and harmonious family: affectionate parents, a healthy, loving son, and a happy life in which parents and child shared alike. Sacco was devoted to his wife and son, Rosina with her "joyful smile," Dante "always my dear and lovely boy." Their greatest pleasure was to go on outings in the surrounding countryside or to the seashore to dig for clams.[16]

A solid workman of regular habits, Sacco had many friends in Milford, who remained loyal to him for the rest of his life. There was also a cousin, Nicola Sacco, who arrived from Torremaggiore in 1913. A year older than Ferdinando, he opened a bakery on East Main Street and began, like Nando, to raise a family.[17] To this day, Sacco is remembered with affection by the older residents of the town, for whom he was a hardworking young man and a credit to the community, incapable of committing the crimes with which he was charged. "I don't know anybody who said anything against Sacco," Gemma DePasquale observed. "He was a wonderful fellow, a gentleman in every sense of the word."[18]

On one level, then, Sacco appears as a model of the successful immigrant. Arriving as an impecunious youth, he quickly rose from the ranks of unskilled labor to become a moderately prosperous worker. The common picture of Sacco as a "good shoemaker," suggesting the small neighborhood cobbler, is misleading. Nor was he an impoverished proletarian, struggling to make ends meet. He was, rather, a highly skilled operative in a factory employing six hundred workers, on excellent terms with his employer, with whom he remained for seven years. His wages, moreover, normally between forty and fifty dollars a week, were substantially higher than those of most of his workmates. As Joseph Macone, an Italian-born banker in Milford, attested, he was able to send regular remittances to his parents in Torremaggiore, a fact confirmed by Sacco's father. "He used to send money every now and then," the elder Sacco told Eugene Lyons in 1921, "a little bit taken out of his earnings. It looked like big money to us."[19]

Given his relative prosperity, it may be asked, why did Sacco become an anarchist? He had not come to America as a radical. Ater all, he was not yet seventeen when he left Italy, and his political ideas, to the extent that he had any, were republican like his father's, tinged perhaps with the socialism of his brother. Puglia, to be sure, had its revolutionary tradition, being the birthplace of the noted Italian anarchist Carlo Cafiero (Barletta), the site of a failed revolt led by Errico Malatesta in 1874 (Castel del Monte), and the birthplace of Michele Angiolillo (Foggia), the assassin of the Spanish prime minister in 1897. But Sacco knew nothing of this. The conditions he saw in America turned him towards anarchism. Comparatively well off though he was, he was not blind to the sufferings of others, the poverty and squalor in the midst of plenty, the "injustice and cruel persecution in this free society of today, and specially for the poor people."[20]

For Sacco the appeal of anarchism was both ethical and emotional. His temperament was such that he could not ignore those less fortunate than himself. In a letter to his daughter, written shortly before his death, he writes that "the nightmare of the lower classes saddened very badly your father's soul." Of an ardent and compassionate nature, he grieved for the plight of the "weak ones that cry for help," the "prosecuted and the victim," and "all the legion of the human oppressed." For all his good fortune, as he saw it, he too was a worker, a victim of capitalist injustice, a "free soul that loved and lived amongst the workers class all his life."[21]

In conversations with his fellow workers, in the radical publications that came his way, Sacco began to find answers to the questions that were troubling him. At first he was drawn to the socialists and the Industrial Workers of the World, reading the I.W.W. weekly Il Proletario, edited by the poet Arturo Giovannitti. But events rather than newspapers turned him in the direction of anarchism. His conversion received a powerful impetus from the Lawrence strike of 1912, during which a group of Italian anarchists from Boston unfurled a banner proclaiming "No God! No Master!"[22] The fight of the textile workers in Lawrence became Sacco's fight. He was among those who collected money to feed the strikers and their families, and he contributed to the defense fund for Giovannitti and Joseph Ettor, arrested on trumped-up charges of murder. Interestingly, Fred H. Moore, who helped to secure their acquittal, was later to serve as chief defense attorney for Sacco and Vanzetti.[23]

It was during this period that Sacco developed an interest in libertarian ideas. In 1913 he began to attend the Circolo di Studi Sociali of Milford, an anarchist group with some twenty-five members, among them Saverio Piesco, Luigi Paradiso, and Riccardo Orciani, who was to figure in the Sacco-Vanzetti case. Both Piesco, a shoe worker, and Paradiso, a barber, had emigrated from Foggia province and lived in the same neighborhood as Sacco, with whom they became good friends. Orciani, an iron molder by trade, hailed from the town of Fano in the Marche, a region from which more than a few Milford Italians came.[24]

Sacco found these men, all of them about his own age, more sympathetic than other radicals he had met: more militant, more eager to learn, more willing to dedicate their energies to the cause of their fellow workers. He came to love them as his own family, the "noble legion of our friends and comrades." A few years later, wrote Sacco, describing this feeling of fellowship, he encountered a comrade on a street in Boston, and "just as soon as we saw each other we ran one into the embrace of the other and we kissed each other on both sides of the cheeks." It was only a short while since they had last met, "but this spontaneous affection it shows at all times in the heart of one who has reciprocal love and sublime faith and such a remembrance it will never disappear in the heart of the proletarian."[25]

Sacco threw himself body and soul into the anarchist cause. In anarchism, which he considered a "noble faith,"[26] he found an ideal, a philosophy, and a way of life that he embraced with all the passion of a convert. For all his satisfaction in his work, for all his devotion to his wife and son, anarchism became the chief object of his energies and emotions. It gave his life a new purpose and direction that it would otherwise have lacked. As a fraternity, a conception of society, a moral code all rolled into one, it became the motivating force of his existence.

Soon after joining the Circolo di Studi Sociali, Sacco began to subscribe to the *Cronaca Sovversiva* (Subversive Chronicle), an "Anarchist Weekly of Revolutionary Propaganda," as it described itself, published in Lynn by Luigi Galleani. Sacco's name appeared in the paper for the first time on August 2, 1913, appended to an appeal for funds to aid arrested strikers in Hopedale.[27] By then the main lines of his political creed were firmly established; indeed, his commitment to "the Idea," as the anarchists called their cherished doctrine, was so absolute that his life had no meaning apart from it.

Unlike Galleani, about whom more will be said later, Sacco was not a subtle thinker. He was, on the contrary, a man of few and relatively simple beliefs—capitalism is evil, government is slavery, war is a crime against humanity, freedom is essential for human development—to which he clung with passionate feeling. Anarchism, as he defined it, meant "no government, no police, no judges, no bosses, no authority; autonomous groups of people—the people own everything—work in cooperation—distribute by needs—equality, justice, comradeship— love each other." Humanity, to Sacco, was divided into two opposing classes, the oppressors and the oppressed, and "there will be always collision between one and the other." For Sacco the workers were invariably filled with a spirit of brotherhood and cooperation, while the bosses were ruled by ambition and greed. "Oppressed humanity," "victims of capitalism," were phrases often repeated in his letters. The state, he believed, existed to protect the interests of private property, and the history of all government had been "the martyrdom of the proletariat."[28]

Uncomplicated though these ideas may appear, Sacco's faith in them should not be underrated. He had "so complete a belief in his rightness and in the evil of corporate institutions," noted Gardner Jackson, "that he just had no doubts."[29] In the end, he was sure, truth, justice, and freedom would triumph over falsehood, tyranny, and oppression. To accomplish this, however, would require a social revolution, for only the complete overthrow of the existing order, the abolition of property and the destruction of the state, could bring the final emancipation of the workers.

Sacco saw himself as a "good soldier" in the revolution, in the battle against capitalism and government. He was deeply moved by the anarchist martyrs of the past, "the comrades that fight and fall yesterday for the conquest of the joy and freedom for all the poor workers." Enamored of the anarchist idea, he too was willing to fight and die for it; indeed, he would have deemed it an honor to sacrifice his life for the principles on which he had fastened his hopes. In prison, a decade later, he had a dream to this effect, a dream both terrible and beautiful, as he described it. In the dream Sacco found himself in the midst of a strike in a Pennsylvania mining camp. Suddenly soldiers came in, armed with rifles and bayonets, to break up a meeting of the workers. Sacco jumped up and urged the strikers to stand fast, while appealing to the soldiers to desist. "Remember that everyone of us we have mother and child," he declared, "and you know that we fight for freedom which is your fight." As he pronounced the word "freedom," a soldier took aim and fired. The bullet pierced Sacco's heart. He fell to the ground, and "with my right hand close to my heart I awake up with sweet dream!"[30]

Sacco's dream, for all its two-dimensional melodrama, attests to his devotion to his cause. Neither an organizer nor a speaker, he was rather a rank-and-file militant, a man of a type without which no radical movement can flourish. Single-minded in the pursuit of his ideals, he helped arrange meetings, distributed anarchist literature, and raised money for *Cronaca Sovversiva*. "In whatever concerns the *Cronaca*, I am with you," he wrote to the paper. "Yours for the revolution."[31] As in Lawrence, moreover, he contributed to defense funds for arrested radicals and workers. He also took part in strikes and demonstrations, distinguishing himself both by his perseverance and by his readiness to assume positions of danger.

The first such incident took place in the spring of 1913, when the workers of the Draper Company in neighboring Hopedale, where Sacco had been employed in 1908 and 1909, went out on strike over a wage dispute. A number of Sacco's friends worked at the plant, most notably Antonio Calzone. Sacco, though now a shoe worker, joined them in sympathy, along with Saverio Piesco, Luigi Paradiso, Riccardo Orciani, and other anarchists from Milford and nearby towns. It was his first taste of direct action, and he gave all his spare time to the task.

Sacco never did anything by half measures. Every morning he would travel to Hopedale and join the picket line, remaining until it was time to go to work in Milford. In the evening he would return to Hopedale and take part in the picketing again. Beyond this, he took on other tasks, such as collecting money to assist jailed strikers, so that he won "full confidence in his honesty and intelligence," said Joseph Coldwell, one of the leaders of the strike, which continued for three months before a settlement was reached. "He was not an orator," recalled Coldwell, "or even a fluent speaker, but he was a mighty good worker in detail matters and never hesitated to do his share of the appointed work." Sacco was "never in the limelight during the strike," added Coldwell. "He was one of the silent, active, sincere workers, giving of his time and money to help his fellow men."[32]

In August 1916 a similar episode occurred when the anarchists of Milford, among them Sacco, Piesco, and Paradiso, arranged a series of weekly meetings to raise money for the iron workers of the Mesabi range in Minnesota, then engaged in a prolonged and bitter strike. Active in the strike were Joseph Ettor, Carlo Tresca, and Elizabeth Gurley Flynn, all veterans of the Lawrence imbroglio of 1912; and Tresca, jailed on a fabricated murder charge, narrowly escaped being lynched.

The strike touched off demonstrations in Boston and other cities. The anarchists of Milford followed suit, holding open-air meetings near the center of town. These meetings brought them into conflict with the authorities, and tensions mounted on both sides. A climax was reached in December 1916, when Police Chief T. J. Murphy issued a ban on further meetings. The anarchists refused to comply. During their next meeting, on December 3, the police moved in and arrested

Sacco, Paradiso, and Piesco on charges of disturbing the peace. Convicted in Milford, they were sentenced to three months in prison, but the charges were dismissed by a Superior Court judge in Worcester, so that the men emerged without a criminal record.[33] This was Sacco's only brush with the law until his arrest on May 5, 1920, in connection with the South Braintree holdup.

In the wake of his arrest a greater misfortune occurred for Sacco when his infant daughter Alba, born less than a month earlier, died. "It was as if," said *Cronaca Sovversiva* in a message of condolence, "she did not care for this wretched world, dripping in blood and degradation."[34] The death of little Alba cast a pall over the Sacco household, which failed to lift in the months ahead. The winter of 1916–1917 proved to be Sacco's last in Milford. Once a respected workman, known for his industry and reliability, he was now viewed by local officials as "a rabid Anarchist."[35] On April 6, 1917, the United States entered the war in Europe. Less than two months later Sacco was on his way to Mexico. By then he had met Bartolomeo Vanzetti.

CHAPTER THREE

Vanzetti

VANZETTI, as we have seen, left Italy only two months after Sacco. Unlike Sacco, however, he traveled alone and, traveling from the extreme north of Italy, took a different route to the United States. His destination, moreover, was not Boston but New York. Leaving Villafalletto on June 9, 1908, two days before his twentieth birthday, he spent two days in Turin before proceeding to the border town of Modane. A two-day train ride across France brought him to the port of Le Havre, from which he sailed on June 13, in the hold of the liner *La Provence*, landing at Ellis Island on June 20.[1]

Millions of immigrants, as Vanzetti was aware, could duplicate the story of his voyage: the sickening steerage, the overbearing officials, the bustle and confusion of the city. Vanzetti later remembered standing at the Battery, a stranger with few possessions and little money, as the automobiles and trolleys rattled by. He had arrived at a time of economic crisis, when employment was hard to obtain. Fortunately, however, he was not without assistance. Giacomo Caldera, a cousin from Villafalletto, who had emigrated some years earlier and lived at Twenty-Fifth Street and Seventh Avenue, offered Vanzetti temporary shelter. Caldera, moreover, served as head cook in a men's club on West Eighty-Sixth Street, overlooking the Hudson River, and got Vanzetti a job as a dishwasher. Vanzetti worked there for three months, amid the purgatory of a New York summer, sleeping in a vermin-infested attic. Almost every night, he tells us, he sought escape in adjacent Riverside Park.[2]

Leaving the club in September 1908, Vanzetti found similar work at the exclusive Mouquin restaurant on Sixth Avenue and Twenty-Eighth Street. Though he learned a little French, conditions here were even worse than in his previous place of employment. The kitchen had no windows, the heat was unbearable, moisture fell from the ceiling on the workers, and overflow from the greasy sinks spread about the floor. Vanzetti worked alternately twelve hours one day and fourteen the next, with five hours off every Sunday. For this he earned a salary of five to six dollars a week. After eight horrible months he quit. He did so, as he wrote to his sister Luigia, partly because "my character cannot tolerate injustice" and partly out of fear of contracting lung disease, from which he had suffered in his youth.[3] Thereafter he preferred outdoor work when he could get it, eventually adopting the trade of a fish peddler.

For the next three months, alone and destitute, Vanzetti tramped the streets in search of a job. Then, at an employment agency, he met another desperate Italian, a fellow Piedmontese, who had not eaten for two days. Vanzetti bought him a meal. At the suggestion of his new acquaintance, they decided to seek work outside the city. With the last of Vanzetti's savings they bought tickets on a steamboat that sailed from New York up the Connecticut River to Hartford. Once there, they struck out into the countryside, knocking on doors and asking for work. But there was none to be found. One farmer, touched by their poverty, fed them and let them stay for two weeks, giving them odd jobs although he had no real need for their labor. Vanzetti never forgot the man's kindness. "I shall always treasure the memory of that American family," he wrote, "the first Americans who treated us as human despite the fact that we came from the land of Dante and Garibaldi."[4]

Resuming their search, they went from town to town and factory to factory, only to be sent away. "Nothing doing" was the standard reply. Other immigrants, here and there, gave them something to eat. In South Glastonbury, near Hartford, a countryman from Piedmont treated them to breakfast, and in Middletown two Sicilian women, a mother and daughter, gave them bread and apples and suggested that they might find work in Springfield, an industrial center up the Connecticut River in Massachusetts.[5]

This proved helpful advice. Arriving in Springfield, they at once got work in a brick factory, "one of the most exacting jobs I know," Vanzetti remarked. Vanzetti's companion did not stand the test, leaving after two weeks. Vanzetti, however, stayed on for ten months, living among a colony of northern Italians, natives of Tuscany, Piedmont, and Venetia, whose gaiety and warmth counterbalanced the arduous labor of the brickyards. In the evenings after work, someone would strike up a tune on an accordion or violin, and some would dance. "I, unfortunately," writes Vanzetti, "was never inclined towards this art and sat aside watching. I have always watched and joyed in other folk's happiness."[6]

From Springfield Vanzetti moved on to Meriden, Connecticut, an industrial town of thirty thousand inhabitants. There, for more than a year, he worked in a stone quarry, doing the "hardest unskilled labor."[7] After this, while still in Meriden, he performed a variety of jobs: cutting wood, digging ditches, installing telephones, and working in a food store selling fruit, candy, and ice cream. The town, surrounded by hills and lakes, boasted a good public library as well as a high school that offered evening classes, and Vanzetti took advantage of both to improve his English. An additional pleasure he found in learning the Tuscan dialect from an old Italian couple with whom he was living. For the most part, however, he led a solitary existence. "I have confidence only in myself," he wrote to his sister, "in my will, my honesty and firmness, and in my health if fate continues to preserve it. I hope to prevail."[8]

Wherever Vanzetti went, both in Connecticut and Massachusetts, friends counseled him to go back to his trade as a pastry cook, the skill that he had learned in Italy. The unskilled laborer, they insisted, was "the lowest animal there was in the social system."[9] Vanzetti at length heeded their advice. In the summer of 1911, after an absence of two and a half years, he returned to New York. Almost immediately he found employment as assistant pastry chef in the Savarin restaurant on Broadway. After eight months, however, he was unexpectedly dismissed. He found a similar position in a restaurant in the theater district, on Seventh Avenue between Forty-Seventh and Forty-Eighth Streets, only to be discharged again after four months. Vanzetti was puzzled. Apparently his work had been acceptable; there had been no complaints, and he had had no difficulty in getting his second job. Finally he learned the reason. The employment agencies were splitting their fees with the master chefs, and the greater the turnover, the more fees there were to split. Vanzetti's acquaintances, including Caldera, begged him not to despair. Stick to your trade, they urged, and so long as we have a bed and food to offer, you need not worry.[10]

There followed a period of privations and uncertainties. For five months Vanzetti walked the streets of New York, unable to find a job at his trade or even as a dishwasher. His savings exhausted, he sometimes slept in doorways, lining his clothes with newspapers to keep out the cold.[11] At length he found an employment agency on Mulberry Street in Little Italy that was hiring pick-and-shovel workers for a construction job near Springfield. Abandoning New York for good, he returned to Massachusetts.

Springfield was familiar territory to Vanzetti, who had labored there in a brickyard three years before. This time he was employed on a railroad section gang, living in a barracks settlement outside of town. The work was hard, but at least it was out of doors, better than the kitchens of New York. After swinging a pick for seven months—his pen name in later years was "Il Picconiere," the pick-axe man—Vanzetti had earned enough money to pay off his debts and to save a little besides. Then, with a friend, he drifted eastward to Worcester, the "heart of the Commonwealth," as it was called.

Vanzetti, now twenty-four, remained in Worcester for more than a year. His first job was for the municipality, carrying stones in the construction of a reservoir. He then went to work for the American Steel and Wire Company, one of the largest employers in town, ladling molten metal in the foundry. For a few months, in the spring of 1913, he worked as a laborer for a building contractor. Then, in the summer, he moved to Plymouth, which remained his home until 1917.[12]

.   .   .

Vanzetti, during these early years in America, had had a more difficult time than Sacco. Sacco, when he abandoned Italy, had had the company of an older brother; on arrival he had found a comfortable place to stay, in a congenial town, among *paesani* who offered support should trouble arise. He had learned a trade, earned good wages, married, and had a child. In spite of occasional setbacks, not least the death of his baby daughter, he had led a stable and happy existence in a community that he could call his home.

Vanzetti did not adjust so readily to the hardships of immigrant life. Thus far his experience in America had been one of hard, unrelenting toil, with periods of unemployment and near starvation. In contrast to Sacco, the skilled worker and settled family man, he belonged to the class of common laborers who washed dishes, dug ditches, pushed wheelbarrows, and wielded shovels, the most overworked and underpaid workers in America. Though far from being idle or lazy ("I was always working hard as a man could work," he declared at his trial in Dedham, "and I have always lived humbly"),[13] he never tried to develop a new skill or, except for a brief interval, to practice the trade of pastry chef which he had learned as a youth. Instead, he was one of the numberless itinerants of the period who, unlike Sacco, could not or would not adhere to the discipline of the new industrial order.[14]

As a result, he had to endure not only contempt for his menial status but also ethnic prejudice and abuse, from which Sacco, in his Milford sanctuary, was largely sheltered. (None, at any rate, is mentioned in his letters or other writings.) Not only was Vanzetti's name routinely mangled by Americans, but his accent and mannerisms were derided and his native traditions and points of view ignored, disdained, or treated as a kind of disloyalty. He had become a "foreigner," an intruder, the object of jibes and insults from men whom, he wrote to his sister, "I would have left in the dust had my English been a tenth as good as my Italian."[15]

A prey to employment agents, master chefs, and labor contractors, Vanzetti had learned the lot of many Italian-born workers in America: the crowded rooming houses, the loneliness, the back-breaking toil, the scornful epithets of "guinea" and "wop." To the bosses "I was a 'Dago,' to be worked to death," he told the labor reporter Art Shields. At his trial, when asked for an account of his employment, he mentioned having worked on the railroad and living in a shanty near Springfield. "In a shanty near Springfield?" asked the district attorney. "Yes, in a shanty," he bitterly replied, "you know, the little house where the Italian work and live like a beast, the Italian workingman in this country."[16]

These years, so full of privation, nevertheless offered compensations. Vanzetti took more than a little pleasure in his peripatetic life and the footloose adventure which it afforded. "Do you know," he later wrote, "that I never lose the joy of that vagabond freedom of working and living in the open. There was a guitar too, and many pipes, and when I was tired of disperated effort to sing as a tenor, I used to indulge in those minor echoes which, in case of waltzes, run as follows—um pa pa, um pa pa, and so on. Well, fulishness apart, that was life, and then I learned something that cannot be learned in the school."[17]

Wherever he went, moreover, Vanzetti spent his free time reading, as he had previously done in Italy. His appetite for knowledge was insatiable. "Ah," he recalls, "how many nights I sat over some volume by a flickering gas jet, far into the morning hours. Barely had I laid my head to the pillow when the whistle sounded and back I went to the factory or the stone pits."[18] He read omnivorously: history, philosophy, literature, science, religion. He studied the history of Greece and Rome, of the United States, of the French Revolution, of the Italian Risorgimento. He read Darwin, Spencer, and Laplace; the novels of Hugo, Tolstoy, and Zola; the poetry of Guerrini, Rapisardi, and Carducci. He reread Leopardi ("and wept with him") and returned to Dante's *Divine Comedy*, a favorite of his youth, much of which he knew by heart. But his main reading was social and political, ranging from Marx's *Capital*, Pisacane's *Political Testament*, and Mazzini's *Duties of Man* to the revolutionary syndicalism of Arturo Labriola and Enrico Leone. With particular interest he studied the works of the anarchists: Kropotkin, Reclus, Merlino, Malatesta, and others; and his most thumbed book, apart from *The Divine Comedy*, was Ernest Renan's *The Life of Jesus*, which proclaimed that "in one view Jesus was an anarchist, for he had no notion of civil government, which seemed to him an abuse, pure and simple."[19]

What he learned from his reading, combined with his experiences of daily life, determined Vanzetti's social philosophy. "I became," he remarks, "a cosmopolite perambulating phylosopher of the main road—crushing, burning a world within me and creating a new—better one."[20] Of all political groups, he became convinced, only the anarchists, through "incessant mental work," had made a clean sweep of the false and oppressive teachings "that were inculcated in us from our infancy." Only the anarchists, in contrast to other radicals, favored the abolition of government, the chief source of tyranny and subjugation. (Of the socialists he declared: "They are authoritarian, while we are libertarian; they believe in a State or Government of their own; we believe in no State or Government.") Only the anarchists, moreover, envisioned a completely new social order, shorn of inequities and injustice. "The anarchist go ahead and says: All what is help to me without hurt the others is good; all what help the others without hurting me is good also, all the rest is evil. He look for liberty in the liberty of all, for his happiness in the happiness of all, for his welfare in the universal welfare. I am with him."[21]

It was in Worcester, in 1912, that Vanzetti found his first anarchist comrades, "whom I remember with the strongest emotion," he later wrote, "with a love unaltered and unalterable."[22] In November of that year he sent his first twenty-five cent contribution to Galleani's *Cronaca Sovversiva*. From now on the overthrow of the existing social and political order became an avowed object of his life. Like Sacco, he had come to regard the capitalist system as the enemy of the workers, siding with "the poor and against the exploitation and oppression of the man by the man." "I preached," he declared, "I worked. I wished with all my faculties that the social wealth would belong to every umane creature, so well as it was the fruit of the work of all." As for governments, he maintained, they differ only in name; in substance they are all the same. "Power and abuse of power are synonims. The working class shall smash all the powers against it, not create a power for itself, except for self defense." In place of capitalism and government, Vanzetti called for a communal society "of free towns administered by their citozins" and sustained by a network of "workers' cooperatives" founded on "free initiative, both individual and collective. Mutual aid and co-operation shall be the very base of a completely new social system, or else, nothing is accomplished."[23]

As these quotations show, Vanzetti's attitude was essentially moral. To him the present system was the source of injustice, oppression, domination, falsity in human relations, cruelty, humiliation. He sought to bring about the opposite of all this—a reign of truth, love, honesty, justice, dignity, freedom. History he viewed as a struggle of the forces of good against the forces of evil—of the anarchists against the state—in which the former were destined to prevail. For "we are liberty and right, which means equality and justice; they are authority and privilege, which means tyranny and injustice. Such is the truth in its complete nakedness. Is not there an eternal war to the last blood against the two?"[24] Convinced that right and history were on his side, Vanzetti foresaw the possibility of a sudden overthrow of the existing order and the building of a new society on libertarian lines. He dreamed, as he put it, a "realizable, possible dream," namely "to have touch with mankind, to vivify the innate voice of brotherhood, and menace the lords, the tyrants of the land—as [did] the prophets of the oldest days."[25]

In this dream there was no place for organized religion. The church, Vanzetti wrote, "may sooth and console the anguish of this poor life of ours," but "I cannot believe any of the many religious beliefs which came under my mind's eyes." Yet his atheism betrayed a quasi-religious passion, his radicalism a messianic zeal. "I see with the eyes of my soul," he wrote, "how the sky is suffused with the rays of a new millennium." Anarchism, founded on an apocalyptic belief in a just and equitable society, had replaced the lapsed Catholicism of Vanzetti's youth. As Upton Sinclair observed: "He was an idealist if I ever knew one—a gentle, quiet, simple man, with a wonderful dream of justice for the working class and peace on earth; a dreamer and a religious man in the true sense of that word."[26]

This was an accurate perception. Vanzetti poured the whole strength of his idealistic nature into his anarchist cause. He attended meetings, delivered speeches, collected money, distributed literature, and contributed articles and notes to *Cronaca Sovversiva* and other publications. From anarchism, in return, he derived powerful moral and emotional sustenance. Anarchism, he said, was his "beloved," his "supremely beautiful" ideal. In some degree, no doubt, it filled the void left by the death of his mother as well as by his abandonment of the church. Furthermore, to the perambulatory worker that he was, it provided a mooring, a sense of belonging, which he had lost when he left his native soil. "Oh, friend," he later wrote, "the anarchism is as beauty as a woman for me, perhaps even more since it include all the rest and me and her. Calm, serene, honest, natural, viril, muddy and celestial at once, austere, heroic, fearless, fatal, generous and implacable—all these and more it is."[27]

During these early years, there was little to distinguish Vanzetti from other adherents of the *Cronaca Sovversiva* school. Like Sacco, he did not emerge into the limelight until their arrest in 1920. Before then he was just another rank-and-file militant, "unmarked, unknown," as he put it, "talking at street corners to scorning men." "Nameless in the crowd of nameless ones," he wrote, "I have merely caught a little light from that dynamic thought or ideal which is drawing humanity towards better destinies."[28]

· · ·

Vanzetti had left Worcester for Plymouth in the summer of 1913. What had prompted him to move is not known—probably, as in the past, the quest for work. What is remarkable, however, is that he remained in

Plymouth until 1917. After five years of wandering, he had finally found a place to settle down.

On arriving at Plymouth, landing place of the Pilgrims, Vanzetti found temporary quarters and began to look for a home. After searching for a month and a half, he rented a room in the house of Vincenzo Brini, a fellow anarchist and supporter of *Cronaca Sovversiva*. A man in his early forties, Brini and his wife Alfonsina, a warm-hearted woman who remained a devout Catholic despite her husband's anarchist beliefs, had come from a town near Bologna and spoke in the dialect of that region, as did many of the residents of North Plymouth, the predominantly Italian quarter of the town, where they lived with their three small children: Lefevre, age seven; Beltrando, six; and Zora, three. A few blocks away stood the Plymouth Cordage factory, where Brini had been employed for the past nine years, feeding bales of hemp into a machine. "It was very dusty work," Lefevre recalls, "no good for him. His overalls were so oily. I hated that job, and I think that it shortened his life."[29]

Brini, a steady wage earner, had saved enough over the years to purchase a two-story house on Suosso's Lane, one of the unpaved streets of North Plymouth, renting out rooms to make ends meet. "Our house was open to wayfarers," recalls his son Beltrando, "and there was a continuous flow of Italian immigrants in and out. When somebody needed a room people would say, 'Go to the Brinis.' That's how Vanzetti came to us—not because father was an anarchist but because we were known to take in transients. He came for a day, but he stayed for two, he stayed for three, and he stayed for four years."[30]

Lefevre (known as Faye) still remembers the day that he arrived. Vanzetti had stopped at the Amerigo Vespucci Club on Suosso's Lane, the social center of the local Italian community, and asked about lodgings. "Somebody told him to come to our house, diagonally across the street. He arrived with two suitcases, one black, one brown. We kids saw the suitcases and thought he might have some goodies! He had a mustache and a Vandyke beard. He wore a high collar and looked different from other people in our neighborhood. But he was neat in appearance and seemed kind. Mama showed him the room and he was pleased with it." "In no time he had captured our hearts," Lefevre wrote, "for he was kind, unselfish, a lover of nature, music, humanity, books, and all things good."[31]

Vanzetti's first job in Plymouth was as a gardener and handyman at the estate of a Mr. Stone on the seashore below the town. He worked there for nearly a year before finding employment—presumably with the aid of Vincenzo Brini—at the Plymouth Cordage Company. "The Cordage," as it was known, was the largest mill of its kind in the world and furnished the major place of employment for the town's growing immigrant population. Its two thousand workers, many of them Italians, labored more than fifty hours a week, transforming the sisal brought from Yucatan into binder-twine and rope. "At six o'clock in the evening," Lefevre Brini recalled, "the whistle blew and people filled the road. Peanut venders would be there to meet them with hot peanuts on Wednesday payday."[32]

Vanzetti began his job in the spring of 1914, loading coils of rope onto freight cars. It was outdoor work, and he did not mind it. In August, however, war erupted in Europe, and the company put on extra shifts to fill the rapidly increasing orders. Before the end of the year, Vanzetti was transferred to the indoor shops, where labor was desperately needed. This disconcerted him, reawakening old fears about his health; besides, he did not earn as much as he had done on his outdoor job. In January 1915, therefore, he quit the Cordage and returned to construction work of the kind that he had performed in Springfield and Worcester. In this he continued for the next two years, until he departed for Mexico.

In January 1916 a strike broke out at the Cordage. The first in the company's history, it was a sudden and unexpected walkout of workers from every part of the factory, completely shutting it down. The strike occurred at the peak of the busy season, when orders for binder-twine for next summer's harvest were pouring in, augmented by heavy orders from the warring nations of Europe. While profits were piling up, wages remained at nine dollars a week for the men and six for the women, who worked beside the men at the spinning machines. At the same time, the cost of living was also rising, especially for items like lentils, olive oil, and pasta, on which the Italian workers depended.[33] The demand was for increases to twelve and eight dollars in the basic pay.

As soon as the troubles began, Italian anarchists descended on Plymouth from nearby Massachusetts towns to lend the strikers a hand. Galleani himself, always eager to fan the flames of industrial conflict, came to agitate among the workers. Vanzetti, though he had left the mill a year before, took an active part in the strike, making speeches, collecting money, and taking his turn on the picket line. According to one source, he organized a parade in which the workers carried clams on the ends of sticks and held aloft a banner that read, "Do you expect us to live on this all our lives?"[34] In addition, he sent reports on the strike to *Cronaca Sovversiva* and traveled as far as Worcester and Springfield, where he had previously lived and worked, to speak at meetings and gather funds. "Worked from 6 A.M. to 10 or 11 P.M. during all the strike," he later wrote to William G. Thompson. "Been present every were and at every meeting; paid of my pocket the paper and stamps I used for it (some $20.); collected found; and lost 18 lbs. of my flash; fighting with every fool and kroock hanging around, and assuming all my responsablities proving myself untamiable, untimidable, and uncorructible; a man to be eliminated."[35]

The strike had erupted spontaneously, and the workers, though without a union, refused to let themselves be organized by the American Federation of Labor or the Industrial Workers of the World, who were ready and eager to do so. Representatives of both unions, moreover, ran into stiff opposition from the anarchists, among whom Vanzetti was a spokesman. Writing in *Cronaca Sovversiva*, he argued that the strike was an elemental expression of labor discontent, not an affair of organizations or theories. Disdaining socialism and syndicalism alike, he applauded the strikers' refusal to submit themselves to the authority of union officials. Meaningful change, he insisted, could be achieved only by the workers themselves, through their own cooperative efforts.[36]

After the plant had been shut down for a month, a general increase of one dollar was offered, neither a signal triumph for the workers nor a humiliating defeat. Vanzetti opposed the settlement as grossly inadequate, a mere sop to pacify the strikers. The Cordage, he later declared, "is one of the greatest money powers of this Nation. The town of Plymouth is its feudal tenure." The strikers, however, were anxious for a settlement, and more than once Vanzetti was pushed off the speakers' platform by indignant men. Finally, to his chagrin, the offer was accepted and the strikers returned to work. Vanzetti never regretted his stand. Of all the activists in the conflict, he maintained, "I was the only one who did not yield or betray the workers."[37]

Years later, in prison, Vanzetti laid part of the blame for his misfortunes at the door of the Cordage, which "would never forget or forgive me for the little that I had done in behalf of its exploited workers." His role in the strike, he maintained, had marked him as a dangerous radical. He had been blacklisted by the company and subjected to police surveillance, he said. As a result, it was difficult for him to get work anywhere in Plymouth, although all of his employers would concede that he was an industrious and dependable workman whose only fault lay "in trying so hard to bring a little light of understanding into the dark lives of my fellow-workers."[38]

Vanzetti's allegations, however, were later disputed. According to Samuel Eliot Morison, the distinguished Harvard historian, nobody was discharged from the Cordage for taking part in the strike, and all strikers who wished to return to work were taken back, no questions asked. Nor is there evidence of blacklisting—of Vanzetti or anyone else. Indeed, Vanzetti himself told Art Shields that he did not in fact know whether he had been blacklisted or not.[39]

Furthermore, as has been noted, Vanzetti had not worked at the plant for a year preceding the strike, nor is there any indication that he sought reemployment after it was over. When he quit his job, in January 1915, he had gone to work in the construction of a breakwater near Plymouth Rock, employed by the state of Massachusetts. That job done, he worked on another breakwater for several months, and then in the construction of a school opposite the railroad depot. "I worked to dig out the cellar," he testified at Dedham, "and I worked to help the bricklayers to carry the bricks, and so on. I do everything there as a laborer."[40] He also continued his anarchist activities, collecting money and distributing literature as in the past. Then, in 1917, he did a surprising thing for a militant anarchist: on May 5, three years to the day before his arrest, he took out his first papers for American citizenship.[41] By then the United States had entered the war, and Vanzetti was soon to leave for Mexico.

· · ·

What then are we to make of Vanzetti? Studious by nature, he was a man of lively intellect, acute sensibility, wide curiosity, and affable disposition. During the four years in which he boarded with the Brinis, he found a contentment and stability that his life in America had previously lacked. It was the closest thing to a home that he had had since leaving Villafalletto, and he took delight in the small intimacies of family life, helping in the garden, preparing breakfast on Sunday mornings, and lavishing affection on the children, whom he came to regard almost as his own. He took them for walks in the woods and along the shore, identifying the different flowers, animals, and birds, a passion of his own childhood in Italy. He helped them with their school work, accompanied them to the library, and taught them Italian (at home they spoke the Bolognese dialect), and they taught him English in return. By the time he left for Mexico, he could boast a respectable command of the language, reinforced by reading, conversation with fellow workers, and evening lessons given by a Protestant minister in Plymouth.[42]

Vanzetti was fond of Lefevre and Zora, but Beltrando became his "spiritual son." He encouraged the boy's interest in music and listened while he practiced the violin, criticizing in a helpful way. "He had a good ear for music," Beltrando recalls, "and would tell me when the notes were wrong—in 'Old Black Joe,' for instance, one of his favorite songs." Once Vanzettti came upon the boy when he was playing conductor to the victrola; instead of laughing, he told him that he took the performance as a promise.[43]

Beltrando, in turn, came to love Vanzetti and to idolize him as a model human being. "Vanzetti was like a father to me," he later remarked. "He was around more than my own father, as he didn't keep factory hours. He took an interest in everything I did and treated me with love and respect. And he treated animals the same way. Once he found a little kitten on the street with an infection all over its face. He brought it home, kept it in a box on the porch, washed its eyes with boric acid, and nursed it back to health. He loved nature, flowers, the sea with the same unadulterated love. As we walked in the woods or on the beach, he established in my mind, with his conversation and actions, values and virtues that have remained with me ever since. They have lasted my entire life, and my memory of him is still fresh sixty years after his execution."[44] Encouraged by Vanzetti, who always regretted his own lack of formal education, Beltrando later attended Boston University and went on to become the principal of the Willard School in Quincy, a member of several chamber music groups, and conductor of the Brockton Symphony Orchestra, a position he held for ten years. In part at least, he attributed these achievements to Vanzetti's inspiration.

In physical appearance Vanzetti was of medium height and build, standing five feet seven inches tall and weighing about one hundred fifty pounds. He had a melancholy face with prominent cheekbones, a long, straight nose, and deep-set liquid brown eyes—eyes, remarked Eugene Lyons, "of a tenderness that haunted one." His hair was cut short, and he wore a mustache and beard, which earned him the nickname "Barbetta" (Little Beard). He spoke in a melodious baritone voice, "charged with the passionate appeal of the dreamer and social rebel."[45]

He was a man of simple tastes and needs. He smoked a pipe and an occasional cigar and drank coffee but nothing stronger. "He didn't go to the club with Dad much," Lefevre Brini recalls. "He was not a drinking man and didn't play cards. He was a studious man. At home he liked to sit and read."[46] Nor did he go out with women. The Brinis, with whom he lived from the age of twenty-five to twenty-nine, could recall no female visitors, no girl friends, no flirtations or love affairs. Notwithstanding his obvious love of children, he showed no interest in marriage. "The thought of getting married has never crossed my mind," he wrote an aunt in December 1914. "I have never had a girl friend, and if I have ever been in love, it has been an impossible love, the kind that had to be stifled in my breast."[47]

This void, it would seem, stemmed from Vanzetti's intense, not to say abnormal, devotion to his mother, whose death had precipitated his emigration. For the rest of his life, including his years of incarceration, he could scarcely bring himself to write about her, feeling emotions too deep and having recollections too painful to set down on paper. Very likely, Vanzetti's memory of his mother affected his relations with the opposite sex, although when he does refer to women it is in wholly conventional terms, with no indication that he was "unhealthily introverted" or otherwise incapacitated. By 1913, at any rate, anarchism had become his greatest passion, supplanting all others, and he had renounced "the joys of love" for his ideal.[48]

In the large body of material surrounding Vanzetti, there is no further clue to his sexual nature. He led a simple, ascetic existence and liked it that way. "Epicurean joys," as he put it, did not appeal to him. He preferred the examples of Cincinnatus returning to the plough and of Garibaldi retiring to Caprera to grow vegetables in his garden. "A little roof, a field, a few books and food is all what I need," he said. "I do not care for money, for leisure, for mondane ambition." He had had ample opportunity to achieve prosperity, he adds, "to live what the world conceives to be a higher life than to gain our bread with the sweat of our brow." His father, in comfortable circumstances, had repeatedly begged him to come home to Villafalletto and oversee the family business. But Vanzetti had refused. He had denied himself "what are considered the commodity and glories of life, the prides of a life of good position, because in my consideration it is not right to exploit man. I have refused to go in business because I understand that business is a speculation on profit upon certain people that must depend upon the business man, and I do not consider that that is right and therefore I refuse to do that."[49]

Vanzetti's modesty of tastes and sweetness of nature must not, however, obscure the fact that he was a dedicated revolutionary militant. The state, as he viewed it, was an evil, tyrannical power of enslavement, oppression, and destructiveness. He favored a complete and radical change in the existing social order and was ready to use violence to achieve it. "We did not come to be vanquished," he declared, "but to win, to destroy a world of crimes and miseries and to re-build with its freed atoms a new world."[50] For all his faith in science and education, for all his determination to dispel the cobwebs of religion and superstition, his own Idea, the future anarchist society, resembled the kingdom of God on earth, a stateless order from which all evil, injustice, and inequality had been eliminated. "Vanzetti was anarchism personified," Beltrando Brini remarked. "He didn't want to be restricted or to acknowledge any boss. He believed in the perfectibility of human nature, something that does not exist. That was his blind spot."[51]

Nor must Vanzetti's intellectual gifts, substantial though they were, be exaggerated. He had a meditative mind, to be sure, always questioning, always reflecting; and through his reading he acquired an impressive store of knowledge. But his education was limited and unsystematic, as he himself was painfully aware. "My fundamental instruction," he confessed, "was too incomplete, my mental powers insufficient, to assimilate all this vast material."[52] Like many an autodidact, moreover, his mind was too rigid, his horizons too narrow, his confidence in the wisdom of his own judgments often misplaced. Although a self-styled man of reason, he was at times too violent in his language, too impassioned in his denunciations, too eager to impute base motives to his opponents.

Be that as it may, Vanzetti's years with the Brinis formed a happy and relatively tranquil interlude in his life. Plymouth, in their affectionate company, became his American hometown, the equivalent of Sacco's Milford. As time went on, he afterwards said, "it held more and more of the people dear to my heart, the folks I boarded with, the men who worked by my side."[53] In the spring of 1917 this came to an end. On April 6, for all President Wilson's assurances to the contrary, the United States declared war on Austria and Germany. Seven weeks later Vanzetti departed for Mexico, and a new phase of his life began.

CHAPTER FOUR

Anarchists

ANARCHISM, as we have seen, was Sacco and Vanzetti's strongest passion, the guiding beacon of their lives, the focus of their daily interests and activities. To ignore it, as some writers have done, is to forfeit any apprehension of their motives and aspirations, so crucial to an understanding of the case. "Both Nick and I are anarchists," Vanzetti himself declared, "the radical of the radical—the black cats, the terrors of many, of all the bigots, exploitators, charlatans, fakers and oppressors." "I am," he asserted, "and will be until the last instant (unless I should discover that I am in error) an anarchist-communist, because I believe that communism is the most humane form of social contract, because I know that only with liberty can man rise, become noble, and complete."[1]

Further statements of this kind, by Sacco as well as by Vanzetti, could be cited. What was the nature of the movement to which these men were so unswervingly devoted? Who were the Italian anarchists? Where did they come from? What did they want? And what did they achieve?

The first Italian anarchist groups in the United States sprang up during the 1880s, rooted in the large-scale immigration of the period. Most of the immigrants were of peasant and artisan stock, the anarchists not excepted. The initial group, formed in 1885 in New York City, which became a leading center of Italian anarchism in America, was called the Gruppo Socialista Anarchico Rivoluzionario Carlo Cafiero, Cafiero being one of the most famous anarchists in Italy during the late nineteenth century, an "idealist of the highest and purest type," in Peter Kropotkin's description.[2] Another group of the same name was founded two years later in Chicago, the focus of Italian anarchism in the midwest. The first newspaper published by Italian anarchists in the United States appeared in 1888, the year of Vanzetti's birth. Entitled *L'Anarchico* (The Anarchist), it was issued by the Cafiero Group in New York.

From New York the movement spread rapidly as the immigrants increased in number. At first, it was concentrated in the large port cities on the eastern seaboard, where the newcomers tended to settle. By the early 1890s, accordingly, we find Italian anarchist groups in such places as Boston, Philadelphia, and Baltimore, in addition to New

York. From the east, the movement gradually filtered westward, with circles appearing in Pittsburgh, Cleveland, and Detroit, as well as in Chicago. Finally, by the mid-1890s, groups were established on the Pacific Coast, the first, in San Francisco, being founded in 1894.

Among the factors that spurred the formation of these groups was the Haymarket affair of 1886–1887. It is often said that the explosion in Chicago, which caused the death and injury of several policemen and led to the hanging of four anarchists and the suicide of a fifth in his cell, precipitated the downfall of the anarchist movement in the United States. Yet precisely the opposite was the case. The trial of the Chicago anarchists, prominently reported in the press, kindled widespread interest in anarchist personalities and ideas. The unfairness of the proceedings, the savagery of the sentences, the character and bearing of the defendants—all this foreshadowing the trial of Sacco and Vanzetti a generation later—fired the imagination of young idealists, Italian and non-Italian alike, and won numerous converts to the cause. By giving the anarchists their first martyrs, the Haymarket executions stimulated the growth of the movement among both immigrants and native-born Americans, so that after 1887 the number of Italian groups rose swiftly.

Another important stimulus was the arrival from Italy of a succession of distinguished anarchist writers and speakers. Beginning in the 1890s, virtually every famous Italian anarchist visited the New World. Some stayed for only a few weeks, some for several years, and a few, like Luigi Galleani and Carlo Tresca, for much longer. The first major figure to arrive was Francesco Saverio Merlino, perhaps the most scholarly of the Italian anarchists, who landed in New York in 1892, during an early phase of the movement's development. Having lived in London for several years, Merlino, unlike other Italian anarchist leaders and many of the rank and file, was fluent in English. As a result, he was able to found not only one of the earliest Italian anarchist journals in this country, *Il Grido degli Oppressi* (The Cry of the Oppressed), but also the English-language *Solidarity*, directed towards native Americans as well as Italians who had acquired the language of their adopted land. Apart from launching these papers, a milestone in the history of the movement, Merlino conducted a speaking tour through the United States, remaining for some months in Chicago. His propaganda, both written and oral, gave anarchism a strong impetus, and it was unfortunate for the movement that he returned to Europe in 1893.[3]

But Merlino was only the first of a series of eloquent spokesmen. The second, Pietro Gori, who arrived in New York in 1895, had an even greater impact on the movement. Gori spent a year in the United States. Like Merlino, he was trained in the law, as Galleani was also.

(The rank and file, as has been noted, were virtually all working people.) These leaders, coming from middle-class and upper-class families, were akin to the Russian populists, those conscience-stricken noblemen, Bakunin and Kropotkin among them, who acknowledged a debt to the people and taught them the gospel of revolt. Gori, like them, came from a prosperous household; a university graduate, a lawyer by profession, he too had cast his lot with the poor. A magnetic and persuasive speaker, he was also a playwright and poet, whose works were read and performed at radical gatherings in America and Europe.

During his stay in the United States, Gori held between two hundred and four hundred meetings—estimates vary—in the space of a single year.[4] Accompanying himself on a guitar, he would begin to sing and thus to attract a crowd, which would stay to hear him lecture on anarchism. In this way he won many converts and started a number of anarchist groups. Gori resembled a Christian evangelist, wandering from town to town between Boston and San Francisco, preaching the gospel of anarchism. Tragically for the movement, he fell ill after his return to Europe and died in 1911, at the age of forty-five, depriving anarchism of one of its most beloved apostles.

After Merlino and Gori came Giuseppe Ciancabilla, among the most articulate if least well known of the Italian anarchist visitors. Ciancabilla, who had been born in Rome (Gori hailed from Messina, Merlino from Naples, Galleani from Piedmont, Tresca from the Abruzzi), arrived in 1898 and settled in Paterson, New Jersey, a stronghold of Italian anarchism in the east. He soon became the editor of *La Questione Sociale*, a paper which Gori had helped to establish in 1895 and which was already the leading organ of Italian anarchism in the United States. Ciancabilla eventually drifted westward, settling among the miners of Spring Valley, Illinois. After the assassination of President McKinley in 1901, when anarchist groups became targets of police repression, Ciancabilla was expelled from Spring Valley, and then from Chicago, where he had taken refuge. Driven from pillar to post, arrested, manhandled, evicted, he ended up in San Francisco, where Gori had lectured in 1895. He was editing a journal there called *La Protesta Umana* when he suddenly took ill and died in 1904, at the early age of thirty-two, one of the most capable of the Italian anarchists in America.[5]

On the heels of Ciancabilla came Errico Malatesta, who, although the most celebrated and widely admired of all the Italian anarchist leaders—the word "leaders" must be placed in quotes, as the anarchists at most recognized only mentors or guides—need be mentioned only briefly, since his stay lasted but a few months. Disembarking in 1899, he took up the editorship of *La Questione Sociale*. He also addressed numerous meetings, in Spanish as well as in Italian, throughout the east. During one of his lectures, in West Hoboken, New Jersey, the representative of a rival faction, or an individual with some private grudge—the motives of this man, Domenico Pazzaglia, remain obscure—drew a pistol and fired at Malatesta, wounding him in the leg. Malatesta, though seriously injured, refused to press charges against his assailant. (Interestingly, the man who subdued Pazzaglia was none other than Gaetano Bresci, the anarchist from Paterson who went to Italy in 1900 and assassinated King Umberto at Monza.) On leaving America, Malatesta stopped briefly in Cuba before proceeding to London. A few years later he returned to his native country where, until the advent of Mussolini, he carried on his anarchist activities. He died, while under house arrest, in 1932.[6]

. . .

We must linger somewhat longer over Luigi Galleani, who, during the first two decades of the twentieth century, was the leading Italian anarchist in America. One of the greatest radical orators of his time, a man of magnetic personality and bearing, Galleani inspired a far-flung movement that included Sacco and Vanzetti among its adherents. He also edited the foremost Italian-American anarchist periodical, *Cronaca Sovversiva*, which ran for fifteen years before its suppression by the American government.

Yet Galleani has fallen into oblivion. Today he is virtually unknown in the United States outside a small circle of scholars and a number of personal associates and disciples, whose ranks are rapidly dwindling. No biography in English has been devoted to him, nor is he so much as mentioned in most general histories of anarchism. His writings, moreover, remain for the most part untranslated, despite their impact on Italian radicals. What follows is merely a sketch, designed to acquaint the reader with an important figure in our story. The man whom Vanzetti acknowledged as "our master," he is yet to be accorded his proper historical place.

Galleani was born on August 12, 1861, in the Piedmont town of Vercelli, not far from the city of Turin, where Vanzetti had been apprenticed as a youth. The son of middle-class parents (his father was a teacher), he was drawn to anarchism in his late teens and, while studying law at the University of Turin, became an outspoken militant whose hatred of capitalism and government would burn with undiminished intensity for the rest of his life. Galleani refused to practice law, which he had come to regard with contempt, transferring his energies and talents to radical propaganda. Under threat of prosecution, he took refuge in France, but was soon expelled for taking part in a May Day demonstration. Moving to Switzerland, he visited the exiled French anarchist Elisée Reclus, whom he assisted in the preparation of his *Nouvelle géographie universelle* by compiling statistics on Central America. He also worked with students at the University of Geneva to arrange a celebration in honor of the Haymarket martyrs, for which he was expelled as a dangerous agitator. He returned to Italy and continued his agitation, which once more got him into trouble with the police. Arrested on charges of conspiracy, he spent more than five years in prison and exile before escaping from the island of Pantelleria, off the coast of Sicily, in 1900.[7]

Galleani, in his fortieth year, now began another odyssey, one that brought him to North America. Aided by Reclus and other comrades, he made his way first to Egypt, where he lived for the better part of a year among a colony of Italian expatriates. Threatened with extradition, he moved to London, but soon embarked for the United States, arriving in October 1901, barely a month after the assassination of McKinley. Settling in Paterson, Galleani assumed the editorship of *La Questione Sociale*, the leading Italian anarchist periodical in America. Scarcely had he installed himself in this position when, in June 1902, a strike erupted among the Paterson silk workers. Galleani, braving the antiradical hysteria that followed the shooting of McKinley, threw all his energies into their cause. In eloquent and fiery speeches he called on the workers to launch a general strike and free themselves from capitalist oppression. His powerful rhetoric and vision of total freedom raised his listeners to a high pitch of enthusiasm. Paul Ghio, a visitor from France, was present at one such oration. "I have never heard an orator more powerful than Luigi Galleani," he wrote. "He has a marvelous facility with words, accompanied by the faculty—rare among popular tribunes—of precison and clarity of ideas. His voice is full of warmth, his glance alive and penetrating, his gestures of exceptional vigor and flawless distinction."[8]

In the midst of the strike, during a clash between the workers and the police, shots were fired and Galleani was wounded in the face. He was indicted for inciting to riot but managed to escape to Canada. A short time after, having recovered from his wounds, he secretly recrossed the border and took refuge in Barre, Vermont, living under an assumed name among his anarchist comrades, who regarded him with intense devotion.

The Barre anarchist group, one of the earliest in New England, had been established in 1894. Its members were stone and marble cutters from Carrara and other northern Italian towns, who had virtually transplanted their way of life to the United States, following the same occupations, customs, and beliefs as they had in the old country. It was among these dedicated rebels that Galleani, on June 6, 1903, launched *Cronaca Sovversiva*, the mouthpiece for his incendiary doctrines and one of the most important and ably edited periodicals in the history of the anarchist movement. Though its circulation never exceeded four or five thousand, its influence, reaching far beyond the confines of the United States, could be felt wherever Italian radicals congregated, from Europe and North Africa to South America and Australia. To Vanzetti, among many others, Galleani was by far the ablest of the Italian anarchist editors, beside whom the others were mere "gnomes."[9]

In 1906, during a polemical exchange with Giacinto Menotti Serrati, the socialist editor of *Il Proletario* in New York, the latter revealed Galleani's whereabouts. Galleani was taken into custody. Extradited to New Jersey, he was tried in Paterson in April 1907 for his role in the 1902 strike. The trial, however, ended in a hung jury (seven for conviction, five for acquittal), and Galleani was set free.

Galleani returned to Barre and resumed his propaganda activities. Now in his late forties, he had reached the summit of his intellectual powers. Over the next few years his fiery oratory and brilliant pen carried him to a position of undisputed leadership within the Italian-American anarchist movement. Intense, learned, patriarchal, Galleani had a resonant, lilting voice with a tremolo that captivated his audience. He spoke easily, powerfully, spontaneously, and his bearing was of a kind that made his followers, Sacco and Vanzetti among them, revere him as a kind of high priest of the movement, to which he won more converts than any other single individual.

Galleani was also a prolific writer, pouring forth hundreds of articles, essays, and pamphlets that reached tens, perhaps hundreds of thousands of readers on several continents. He never produced a full-length book: the volumes appearing over his signature, such as *Faccia a faccia col nemico*, *Aneliti e singulti*, and *Figure e figuri*, are collections of pieces previously published in *Cronaca Sovversiva*. *La Fine dell'anarchismo?*, Galleani's most fully realized work, itself began as a series of articles defending his creed from an assault by a former comrade. In June 1907, shortly after Galleani's acquittal at Paterson, the Turin daily *La Stampa* published an interview with Saverio Merlino, who had meanwhile recanted his anarchism and become a socialist. Merlino, whose interview was titled "The End of Anarchism," pronounced anarchism an obsolete doctrine, torn by internal disputes, bereft of first-rate theorists, and doomed to early extinction. Galleani was incensed. "The end of anarchism?" he asked in *Cronaca Sovversiva*, adding a question mark to the title of Merlino's interview. Just the opposite was true. In an age of growing political and economic centralization, anarchism was more relevant than ever. Far from being moribund, "it lives, it develops, it goes forward."[10]

Such was Galleani's reply to Merlino, elaborated in *Cronaca Sovversiva* between August 1907 and January 1908. Combining the spirit of unrestrained insurgency with Kropotkin's principle of mutual aid, Galleani put forward a vigorous defense of communist anarchism against socialism and piecemeal reform, extolling the virtues of spontaneity and variety, of autonomy and independence, of self-determination and direct action, in a world of increasing standardization and uniformity. A revolutionary zealot, he preached a militant form of anarchism which advocated the overthrow of capitalism and government by violent means, dynamite and assassination not excluded. The depth of his hatred of capitalism moved him to denounce all partial reforms as corruptions and betrayals. He would brook no compromise with the elimination of economic and political oppression. Nothing less than a clean sweep of the established order would satisfy his thirst for the millennium. "We do not argue about whether property is greedy or not, if masters are good or bad, if the State is paternal or despotic, if laws are just or unjust, if courts are fair or unfair, if police are merciful or brutal," he said. "When we talk about property, State, masters, government, laws, courts, and police, we say only that *we don't want any of them*."[11] To his disciples, Galleani seemed the embodiment of the spirit of revolt.

Galleani produced ten articles in response to Merlino. He had intended to write still more, but day-to-day work for the movement—editing *Cronaca Sovversiva*, arranging meetings, issuing pamphlets, conducting lecture tours—prevented him from doing so. In 1912 he moved *Cronaca Sovversiva*—which he described as "a rag of a paper that lives on crusts and bits of bread, with the support and pennies of five thousand beggars"[12]—from Barre to Lynn, Massachusetts, where he had won a devoted following. As before, he engaged in uninhibited polemics, denounced government repressions, glorified acts of reprisal, and called for the destruction of existing political, economic, and religious institutions. What he expressed was not a social philosophy as much as a cry of indignation, a call for militants to resist, by force if necessary, the regimentation and bureaucratization, the brutality and corruption, of the prevailing system.

·   ·   ·

Such was the figure who, more than any other, breathed life into the Italian anarchist movement in America. His followers, nearly all of them manual laborers, numbered in the thousands. They came from every corner of Italy, north and south, east and west, and had settled in all parts of the United States. In New York they included garment and construction workers, in Paterson operatives in the great silk factories. We find them among the quarry workers of Barre, the shoe workers of Lynn, the construction workers of Boston, the cigar workers of Philadelphia and Tampa. They were numerous among the miners of Pennsylvania, Ohio, and Illinois; and in Chicago and Detroit, in San Francisco and Los Angeles they were represented in a variety of trades, from barber and tailor to bricklayer and machinist.

The names with which they adorned their groups and circles—"Autonomy," "Demolition," "The Insurgents," "The Eleventh of November" (date of the Haymarket executions), "The Twenty-Ninth of July" (date of Bresci's assassination of King Umberto)—proclaimed their adherence to the school of Galleani. But by no means were they his slavish disciples. Rivalries and disputes were commonplace, erupting not only on matters of doctrine and tactics but also on the most trivial questions of personality. Ancient quarrels, bred in Italy, flared anew on American soil. Galleani himself, for all his vaunted allegiance to freedom and diversity, set an example of righteous intolerance that few of his coadjutors could match. So certain was he of the correctness of his pronouncements that all who dared challenge them stood condemned as corrupt allies of government and capital, if not as outright traitors and spies. Thus arose the spirit of the sect, that bitter, narrow orthodoxy which is the bane of every ultra-radical movement.

Ideologically, the Italian anarchists fell into four categories: anarchist-communist, anarcho-syndicalist, anarchist-individualist, and just plain anarchist, without the hyphen. These categories overlapped; there were no hard-and-fast divisions between them. As followers of Galleani, Sacco and Vanzetti considered themselves anarchist-communists, rejecting not only the state but also the private ownership of property. The anarcho-syndicalists, among whom Carlo Tresca was a powerful influence, placed their faith in the trade-union movement, shunned by and large by the anarchist-communists, who feared the emergence of a boss, a *padrone*, endowed with special privileges and authority.

The third group, the anarchist-individualists, distrusted both the communal arrangements of the anarchist-communists and the labor organizations of the anarcho-syndicalists, relying instead on the actions of autonomous individuals. Some of the more interesting, not to say exotic, Italian anarchist periodicals were published by individualists, such as *Nihil* and *Cogito, Ergo Sum* ("I think, therefore I am," with emphasis always on the "I"), both appearing in San Francisco early in the century, and *Eresia* (Heresy) in New York some twenty years later. Their chief prophet was the nineteenth-century German philosopher Max Stirner, whose book *The Ego and His Own* served as their testament.

The fourth group, which deserves mention if only because it is so often neglected, consisted of anarchists who refused to attach any prefix or suffix to their label, calling themselves "anarchists without adjectives," not communist anarchists, syndicalist anarchists, or individualist anarchists; and the figure they most admired was Malatesta, who preached an undogmatic brand of anarchism that encompassed a range of elements. All four groups, of course, shared the fundamental beliefs of all anarchists, above all the total rejection of authority and the need to "make the propaganda," to publicize their "beautiful Idea."

It has been noted that almost all Italian anarchists, and especially the Galleanists, disdained conciliatory measures and piecemeal economic and social change. Achieving limited improvements, they argued, would only blunt the revolutionary ardor of the workers, weaken their will to resist, and delay the final overthrow of capitalism. Impatient with the reformist methods of socialists and liberals, they espoused more militant tactics, the tactics of direct action. Because of this, the Italian anarchists did not play a conspicuous role in the organized American labor movement, differing in this respect from their Russian and especially their Jewish counterparts, who were prominent in the textile unions, above all the International Ladies' Garment Workers' Union and the Amalgamated Clothing Workers of America. Not that the Italian anarchists were completely estranged from these unions, but their role was not a significant one, in part because of their suspicion of formal organizatons that might harden into hierarchical and authoritarian shape, with their own bureaucrats, bosses, and officials.

Unlike the Russian anarchists, who organized a Union of Russian Workers in the United States and Canada boasting nearly ten thousand members, the Italians contented themselves with participating in strikes and demonstrations. The strike, as they saw it, made clear the fundamental conflict between labor and capital, slaves and masters, increasing the sense of workers' solidarity, deepening the chasm between them and their exploiters, and spurring them to further action. Thus did the Italian anarchists view the strikes in which they were active, Galleani at Paterson in 1902, Sacco at Hopedale in 1913, Vanzetti at Plymouth in 1916. These confrontations, in their eyes, were manifestations of permanent revolt, episodes in the social war, steps towards the total emancipation of the workers.

In forming groups, participating in strikes, and mounting protests and demonstrations, the Italian anarchists were creating a kind of alternative society, one which differed sharply from the capitalist and statist regime that they condemned. They had their own circles, their own beliefs, their own culture; they were building their own world in the midst of a system they opposed and detested. Rather than await the millennium, they tried to live the anarchist life on a day-to-day basis within the interstices of American capitalism. They formed, in effect, tiny enclaves, little nuclei of freedom, as they saw it, which they hoped would spread and multiply throughout the world.

After ten or twelve hours in the factory or mine, the anarchists would come home, eat supper, then go to their clubs and begin to churn out their journals and leaflets on makeshift presses. Aldino Felicani, founder of the Sacco-Vanzetti Defense Committee, is an example of such an anarchist, and the literature which he collected over the years, extensive as it was, constituted a mere fragment of the output of these self-educated workers, a token of their idealism and dedication. Approximately five hundred anarchist newspapers were published in the United States between 1870 and 1940, in a dozen or more different languages. Of these, the number of Italian papers—including the *numeri unici* issued on special occasions—approached a hundred, an astonishing figure considering that they were produced by ordinary workers in their spare time, mainly on Sunday and in the evening. And in addition to the newspapers and journals, of which more were issued by the Italians than by any other immigrant group, a flood of books and pamphlets rolled off the presses, including anticlerical as well as anarchist works, such as Sébastien Faure's *Dio non esiste* and Johann Most's *La peste religiosa*, which were sold at gatherings and through *Cronaca Sovversiva* and other papers.

Beyond their publishing ventures, the Italian anarchists engaged in a range of social and cultural activities that enhanced their feeling of solidarity while enriching their daily existence. Life was hard for these working-class immigrants, but there were moments of happiness and laughter. They had their orchestras and theater groups, their picnics and outings, their lectures and concerts; they organized dances, recitals, and similar entertainments, imparting a new revolutionary content to customary social activities. Every fall, for instance, the traditional harvest festival (*la festa della frutta*) served as an occasion to raise money for "the propaganda." Raffles were held for the same purpose—at one raffle, in Springfield, Massachusetts, the prizes offered were an eighteen-jewel watch, a two-volume illustrated encyclopedia, a barrel of flour, three gallons of olive oil, and a Savage revolver.[13]

Hardly a week went by without some social activity, usually with a radical twist. Leafing through the old newspapers, one encounters a picnic at the restaurant of Mrs. Bresci, widow of the assassin of King Umberto, in Cliffside Park, New Jersey. (The police afterwards drove her out of town, along with her two small daughters.) Such picnics were important occasions, not merely to eat and dance, but also to raise money for the movement. New York and New Jersey anarchists made excursions up the Hudson in rented steamboats, and when they reached Bear Mountain, or some other bucolic setting, out came the bread and wine, the accordions and mandolins, followed invariably by the collection.

Attending lectures was another popular activity, and especially the lectures of Galleani, who was prized above all other speakers. You could be sure of an exciting evening if *il maestro* was on the platform. His eloquence, combined with a personal magnetism that few could resist, always ensured him a large audience, for whom a lecture (in those days the longer the better) was both inspiration and entertainment. The lectures were held in rented halls and in anarchist clubhouses—that of the Gruppo Autonomo of East Boston, for example, or of the Gruppo Diritto all'Esistenza of Paterson, or of the Gruppo Gaetano Bresci of East Harlem, or perhaps of a Circolo di Studi Sociali, dozens of which flourished throughout the country. Open *Cronaca Sovversiva* and you will see them listed, with the weekly or monthly contributions of their members, usually only twenty-five or fifty cents. And yet it was such contributions that would keep the Sacco-Vanzetti Defense Committee in operation through seven years of struggle in behalf of the accused men.

The Italian anarchists also had their dramatic societies, a particularly interesting feature of the radical counterculture. Amateur theater groups sprang up in large cities and small towns, among them one in Milford, in which Sacco and Rosina took part. "My wife is a fine actress," said Sacco to Eugene Lyons, "and the two of us used to arrange for dramatic performances and to raise money for all sorts of causes."[14] These groups—the Filodrammatica Sovversiva of Providence, the Filodrammatica "I Liberi" of New Britain, the Filodrammatica "Arte e Libertà" of Lynn are examples—put on hundreds of plays, complete with prompter's box and homemade scenery, with such titles as *The Ideal, Without a Country, Social Tempests, The Assassination of Francisco Ferrer*, and *The Martyrs of Chicago*. The last, of course, dealt with the Haymarket tragedy, a landmark in the history of anarchism, which, as Sacco put it, "will never be forgot." A special favorite, also linked with the Chicago martyrs, was Pietro Gori's *First of May*, which opened with Verdi's chorus "Va, pensiero," rededicated, in Gori's words, to "the great flowing Ideal with which the shining future trembles," the ideal of anarchism.[15]

Anarchist schools—often named after the Spanish educator Francisco Ferrer, executed in Barcelona in 1909—formed another part of this alternative culture. There were Italian and non-Italian Ferrer

Schools, also called Modern Schools, a name that better conveys their main objective—an education to suit the modern, scientific age, in contrast to that of the parochial schools, drenched in the spirit of religious dogma and superstition, or of the public schools, in which generals and presidents, conquest and war, were habitually glorified and exalted. The Modern Schools were schools in which the children, educated in an atmosphere of freedom and spontaneity, would learn about working-class movements and revolutions, as well as how to think and live according to their own lights and in harmony with their neighbors. By the time of the First World War at least three such schools conducted in Italian had been founded: in Boston, in Paterson, and in Philadelphia. All were Sunday and evening schools and attended by adults as well as children.

The anarchists, finally, substituted their own commemorative dates and rituals for traditional religious and national celebrations. In place of Christmas and Easter and Thanksgiving, their principal holidays were the anniversary of the Paris Commune on March 18, the day of working-class solidarity on May 1, and the anniversary of the Haymarket executions on November 11. Every year, in every part of the country, hundreds of meetings were held to commemorate these occasions, for which Galleani was the most sought-after speaker. In a similar vein, one reads of Emma Goldman on a lecture tour in 1899, stopping in Spring Valley, Illinois, among a fervent crowd of Italian miners, who had brought her their babies to be baptized—with the names not of religious saints but of rebels and popular heroes (Spartaco, Rivolta, Comunardo, Cafiero)—and then stayed to listen to her speak on the emancipation of women and the "necessity of the unhampered development of the child."[16]

Such, then, was the character of the movement to which Sacco and Vanzetti adhered. They subscribed to its newspapers (their dues are recorded in the columns of *Cronaca Sovversiva*, to which they also contributed articles and notes); they attended the lectures of Galleani and other speakers; they distributed the announcements of these lectures and circulated the literature of their movement; they frequented the concerts and picnics and acted in anarchist plays; they took part in demonstrations (Sacco, when arrested in 1920, had in his pocket the notice of a protest meeting at which Vanzetti was scheduled to speak) and agitated during strikes. Afterwards Vanzetti, from his cell at Charlestown, continued to write articles for the anarchist press, above all for *L'Adunata dei Refrattari*, a successor to *Cronaca Sovversiva*.

Both men, it must be emphasized, were social militants, advocates of relentless warfare against government and capital. Far from being the innocent dreamers so often depicted by their supporters, they belonged to a branch of the anarchist movement which preached insurrectionary violence and armed retaliation, including the use of dynamite and assassination. Such activities, they believed, were replies to the monstrous violence of the state. The greatest bomb throwers and murderers were not the isolated rebels driven to desperation but the military resources of every government—the army, militia, police, firing squad, hangman. Such was the position of Sacco and Vanzetti, as it was of their mentor Galleani, who showered praise on every rebellious deed and glorified the perpetrators as heroes and martyrs, sacrificing their lives for the oppressed.

To the very end, Sacco and Vanzetti remained dedicated anarchists, continuing their work even in prison. Through their articles and letters, through their speeches in court, they were propagating the ideas of their creed. In doing so, they were at one with Malatesta, for whom the conquest of liberty demanded an unrelenting struggle. What mattered, Malatesta declared, was "not whether we accomplish anarchism today, tomorrow, or within ten centuries, but that we walk towards anarchism today, tomorrow, and always."[17]

CHAPTER FIVE

Mexico

ON APRIL 6, 1917, the United States declared war on the Central Powers and entered the European conflict. To Galleani and his associates, who had opposed the war since its outbreak in 1914, this came as unwelcome news. True to their antimilitarist convictions, they rejected all wars except the "social war," which would overthrow capitalism and the state. When Kropotkin declared his support for the Entente, fearing that German authoritarianism and regimentation might prove fatal to social progress in Europe, his stand was vigorously challenged by Galleani, for whom the war was an imperialist struggle for power and profit, with the workers serving as cannon fodder, so that it was absurd to favor either side against the other.[1]

For the duration of hostilities Galleani carried on an incessant campaign of antimilitarist and antipatriotic propaganda. Opposing the war with all the eloquence at his command, he denounced it both in *Cronaca Sovversiva* and in speeches in Boston and other cities. A slogan which he used on such occasions, "Contro la Guerra, contro la Pace, per la Rivoluzione!" (Against the War, Against the Peace, For the Revolution!), became a rallying cry among his disciples. Vanzetti, for one, wrote his aunt in Italy that it was the poor, not the rich, who were compelled to do the fighting, which cost them "their blood, tears, misery, lives."[2] For Sacco, similarly, it was a "war for the great millionaire," from which only the Morgans and Rockefellers stood to gain. "What right we have to kill each other?" he asked. "I been work for the Irish, I have been working with the German fellow, with the French, many other peoples. . . . Why should I go kill them men? What he done to me? He never done anything, so I don't believe in no war. I want to destroy those guns."[3]

With America's involvement in the conflict, the anarchist movement entered a critical period. On May 18, 1917, six weeks after hostilities began, Congress passed a military conscription act, requiring every male between the ages of twenty-one and thirty, whether or not an American citizen, to register with his draft board on June 5. Although aliens of draft age were compelled to register, they were not liable to military service unless they had—as in the case of Vanzetti—begun the process of naturalization. Failure to register carried a penalty of up to one year in prison.

The passage of the conscription act placed the anarchists in a quandary. The vast majority, including Sacco, had not applied for American citizenship and had no intention of doing so. Nor, being aliens, were they susceptible to the draft. Why then must they be forced to register? It all seemed senseless and confusing. Besides, the very act of registration was anathema to the anarchists, who disdained any concession to the state. What then were they to do?

Galleani provided an answer. In an article entitled "Matricolati!" (Registrants), published in *Cronaca Sovversiva* on May 26, he alerted his followers to the dangers of registration. Today, he wrote, aliens are not liable to conscription, but what about tomorrow? Suppose that noncitizens are mobilized to labor in factories and on farms. What will you do then? Once you register, the authorities will have you on their rolls; they will know where to find you should they want you. Compulsory registration, he argued, violated the Thirteenth Amendment to the Constitution, which prohibits "involuntary servitude." You need not collaborate with the warmongers, he declared. If you refuse to register in the thousands, the authorities will be hard put to arrest you. Nor will they send you into the army, as they know that such men would take every opportunity to sabotage the war effort. At worst you may be sent to prison for a year. Consider the alternatives, for you yourselves must decide. The storm is swiftly approaching, and the powers that be are afraid. The old world is crumbling. It teeters on the brink of collapse.[4]

Galleani stopped short of advocating outright resistance to the draft. To his followers, however, his message was clear: Get out! Do not register! Go where the authorities cannot find you! Many responded to his call. Some assumed false identities, took shelter among friends, or moved to new locations. Others, like Joseph Moro, left their jobs to seek work where they were not known. "I didn't register for the draft," he later recalled, "so I couldn't remain in Stoneham where people knew me. I went to Taunton and got a job in a stove factory, working in the stock room. Galleani lived not far away, on a farm in Wrentham. A number of comrades, refusing to register and out of work, stayed there with him and killed time by fixing up the barn."[5] A small group from Roxbury took refuge in Canada, crossing the border on foot, while others, Sacco and Vanzetti among them, headed for Mexico.

· · ·

Towards the end of May, immediately after the publication of "Matricolati!," Sacco quit his job at the Milford Shoe Company, where he had worked for the past seven years. Though devoted to his wife and son, he remained foremost an anarchist; Galleani had given the order and he obeyed. Going to Boston, he attended a meeting of Galleanists who were planning to leave for Mexico. It was here that he met Vanzetti for the first time, though he had known of him through the pages of *Cronaca Sovversiva*.[6] During the ensuing months the two became intimate friends.

Sacco was now twenty-six years old, Vanzetti just short of twenty-nine. Sacco, as an Italian citizen, was not liable to military duty. In addition, he had a dependent wife and child. Vanzetti, a bachelor, had taken out his first papers and was therefore eligible to serve. This he refused to do. "I go away for not to be a soldier," he later declared, "not to make a soldier, not to go to the war."[7] Nor, as a staunch antimilitarist, would he register, in compliance with the law. On this he and Sacco were agreed. Better, as Galleani had commanded, to get out.

To avoid registration, however, was not their only motive for leaving. Less than three months before, revolution had erupted in Russia, toppling the tsarist regime. This, for the Galleanists, was the harbinger of a general conflagration, from which all Europe, including Italy, would emerge transformed. Ardent rebels, they yearned to go back to their homeland and take part in the coming upheaval. Revolution, they felt, was in the offing. Any day, any week, it would spread across the continent, ushering in a new era of freedom in which government, classes, and exploitation would cease to exist. They were concerned, however, lest the United States, having joined the war as Italy's ally, might block their efforts to return. Hence their urgent desire to depart for Mexico, from which, when the moment arrived, they could embark for Europe.[8]

Barely a week after their initial meeting, Sacco and Vanzetti left Boston for Mexico. With a group of fellow Italian anarchists they traveled by train via New York, Cleveland, Detroit, St. Louis, and San Antonio. Then, assisted by Mexican comrades, they crossed the Rio Grande at Laredo and proceeded to the city of Monterrey.[9] There, over the next few weeks, other Italian anarchists joined them, part of the growing exodus of Galleanists who had heeded the master's call.

All told, some sixty *Cronaca Sovversiva* anarchists took refuge in Mexico between the spring and fall of 1917.[10] A handful were caught while attempting to cross the river and held in Texas jails for several months,[11] though the majority managed to get through. They came from many parts of the United States, from Massachusetts to California, particularly from cities with substantial Italian populations, such as New York, Philadelphia, and Chicago. The largest contingent came from Boston, the hub of the Galleani movement.

The anarchists who arrived in Mexico included some of the most militant of Galleani's followers. From Chicago came Umberto Postiglione (nicknamed "Hobo"), who had edited *Cronaca Sovversiva* during the second half of 1916, while Galleani conducted an extended lecture tour. On Galleani's return, Postiglione himself embarked on a tour of the east and midwest. At length he returned to Chicago, where his own journal, *L'Allarme*, had been suppressed. Soon afterwards he left for Mexico.

Notable among the other exiles was Emilio Coda, a coal miner from eastern Ohio, whose violent temperament mirrored his commitment to direct action, which he had been preaching for several years.[12] Coda, like Vanzetti and Galleani, was a native of Piedmont, hailing from the province of Novara, where he had been born into a peasant family in 1881. At thirty-six, older than most of his fellow exiles, he was not obliged to register for the draft. He went to Mexico, rather, to prepare for the revolution in his homeland, which he expected to break out at any moment. Five feet four inches tall and weighing 140 pounds, Coda was compact and strongly built, with blue eyes, reddish hair, and a ruddy complexion to match. Eugene Lyons described him as a "little red-haired anarchist who liked to talk violence."[13]

And talk violence he did, whenever the opportunity arose. In August 1915 he was arrested at Dillonvale, Ohio, accused of instigating a riot. At nearby Piney Fork he had already been detained on a similar charge but released for lack of evidence. Coda, moreover, practiced what he preached. During a wildcat strike at Dillonvale in the winter of 1916–1917, two coal tipples and a company store were burned and Coda fell under suspicion. "His reputation in the coal fields was such," noted an agent of the Justice Department's Bureau of Investigation, "that when these fires were heard of everyone first thought of Coda."[14]

Coda, at the same time, had become a thorn in the flesh of the United Mine Workers hierarchy. As secretary of the local at the mine in Rayland, Ohio, where he worked, he refused to take orders from higher echelons. Indeed, he threatened union leaders with physical harm. As one of them put it, "Coda has always been against the officials of the United Mine Workers of America." He was, according to the Ohio president of the union, "the most dangerous character in the Ohio coal fields."[15]

Coda, throughout this period, remained a faithful disciple of Galleani. He sent articles and money to *Cronaca Sovversiva*, along with donations for Galleani's private use, and kept his mentor informed of the situation among the miners. It was Coda who arranged the meeting when Galleani spoke at Dillonvale in November 1916, and was Galleani's host for the night. Coda, in turn, spent a week at Galleani's farm at Wrentham in June 1917, before his departure for Mexico.

Of comparable militancy but quieter temper was Giovanni Scussel of Philadelphia, a man "of great heart, lively intelligence, and profound conviction."[16] A northerner like Coda, with sandy hair and fair complexion, he had emigrated in 1905 from Agordo in Belluno province, at the foot of the Dolomite mountains. At thirty-five, a year younger than Coda, he was likewise ineligible for the draft. He too went to Mexico not to avoid registration, for which he was overage, but to prepare for the revolution in Italy. In Philadelphia, where he had worked as a brick mason, he had already been in trouble with the police. "A man of courage," as a comrade remarked, "he was always in the front line of the struggle."[17]

Of the Massachusetts contingent, in addition to Sacco and Vanzetti, a few merit special attention. Amleto Fabbri, afterwards a secretary of the Sacco-Vanzetti Defense Committee, was a shoe worker from the town of Beverly. A native of the Romagna, a region noted for its radical tradition, he was "an anarchist of the old school," as acquaintances describe him, "beloved for his nobility of character."[18] Another shoe worker was Adelfo Sanchioni of Revere, later active with Fabbri on the Sacco-Vanzetti Defense Committee. Umberto Colarossi, a bookkeeper from East Boston, was a Galleanist of an ultra-militant stamp. Young, dark, intense, he rivaled Coda and Scussel in his devotion to insurrectionary methods, including the use of dynamite. Along with propaganda by the deed, he championed propaganda by the word, writing and speaking for *Cronaca Sovversiva*. His cousin, Vincenzo Colarossi, a tailor in Boston's North End, was to serve on the Sacco-Vanzetti Defense Committee.[19]

Two other Massachusetts activists warrant attention, as they will figure very prominently in our story. The first, Mario Buda, would be present with Sacco and Vanzetti on the night of their arrest, and the authorities would seek to link him with the South Braintree holdup. A small, balding man with a little mustache, deep-set hazel eyes, and a large nose that earned him the nickname "Nasone" (Big Nose), Buda had been associated with *Cronaca Sovversiva* for several years, as a subscriber and contributor of money. Cool, self-possessed, serious, he seldom gave evidence of his emotions. His manner, rather, was quiet and thoughtful. At the same time he exhibited "a certain kind of stubborn pride, so far as his opinions and principles are concerned," noted Edward Holton James of Boston, who interviewed him in 1928.[20]

A Romagnolo like Amleto Fabbri, Buda had been born in Savignano, a town on the Rubicon River, where his father was employed as a gardener, planting trees and vines for the local landowners. In 1907, a year before Sacco and Vanzetti, Buda emigrated to the United States and settled in Massachusetts. A bachelor like Vanzetti, he too led a peripatetic life. He worked at a series of jobs in the area around Boston: gardening, laying pipe for the telephone company, doing construction work on a power plant, building freight cars for the New Haven & Hartford Railroad. Hearing that wages were higher in the west, he traveled to Colorado but could not find work. Drifting eastward again, he landed a job in Washington, Illinois, sleeping in a box car to conserve his earnings. After this he worked in Wisconsin on the construction of a bridge.[21]

In 1911 Buda went back to Italy and worked for his father in Savignano. But wanderlust again overcame him. In 1913 he returned to the United States, to the Roxbury district of Boston, a haven for Italians from the Romagna, many of them disciples of Galleani. This time Buda stayed put, dividing his time between earning a living and participating in anarchist activities. His first job on his return was in a hat factory in Framingham, to which he commuted from Roxbury. With his savings, he sent for his younger brother Carlo and found him a job in a tailor shop. Soon afterwards the two went to work for the Daloz Cleaning Company in Boston. On learning the trade, they opened a cleaning store of their own in Wellesley, catering to the students at the women's college.

From his return to America to his departure for Mexico four years later, Buda was a conspicuous figure in the Galleani movement. He not only took part in the picnics and theater recitals; as a member of the Circolo Educativo Mazziniano of Roxbury, he helped to organize an anarchist school. A believer in direct action, moreover, he could be counted on during strikes and demonstrations. It was during the Hopedale strike of 1913, where he came to join the agitation, that he first met Sacco; and he met Vanzetti in Plymouth during the Cordage strike of 1916.

On September 25, 1916, Buda was arrested during an antiwar demonstration in Boston's North Square, in which protestors clashed with the police. Charged with inciting to riot, he was tried together with two comrades, Federico Cari and Raffaele Schiavina, the manager of *Cronaca Sovversiva*. Cari was sentenced to three months in prison, and Schiavina was acquitted for lack of evidence. Buda, whose refusal to take the oath infuriated the judge, received the maximum sentence of five months. His conviction, however, was reversed on appeal.[22]

An uncompromising militant, who rejected docile submission to the state, Buda was thirty-three years old when America entered the war, hence past the age required for registration. Yet he chose, like Coda and Scussel, to go to Mexico, eager to join the coming revolution in Europe.

Like Buda, the other activist who commands our attention was a native of the Romagna region. Carlo Valdinoci, a twenty-two-year-old carpenter, came from the town of Gambettola in Forlì province, a short distance from Buda's Savignano. Known as "Carluccio" (Charlie), he was cheerful and outgoing, in contrast to the taciturn Buda. Unlike Buda, moreover, he was blessed with striking good looks. Tall, broad shouldered, and powerfully built, with handsome features and clean-shaven face, he cut a glamorous figure. Everyone noticed his hair: thick, dark, wavy, and combed in the pompadour style. A stylish dresser, his tastes ran to striped suits, colorful ties, and a variety of caps and hats. Around his neck he often wore a red bandana, which heightened his romantic appeal. Women, whom he invariably treated with respect, found him irresistible.

Yet Valdinoci and Buda had much in common. Both, for all their differences of temperament and appearance, were anarchists of an intransigent stripe. Both were determined to answer force with force, not only as a matter of self-defense but of principle and honor. Both were capable, intelligent, and possessed of strong character. Both, finally, were unwavering in their devotion to Galleani and his mouthpiece *Cronaca Sovversiva*.

Valdinoci, a bachelor, had been an anarchist since 1913, when he emigrated to the United States. He lived then at 170 Norfolk Avenue in Roxbury with his older brother Ercole and with Domenico Ricci, a *paesano* who arrived on the same boat. All three were fervent Galleanists, as was the Valdinocis' younger sister Assunta, who joined them from Italy soon afterwards. Assunta, known as "Susie," found a job in a bleaching mill, while Ercole and Carlo worked at the A. H. Hess Company, a pottery factory in Cambridge, where Ercole was regarded as "an agitator."[23] A reliable worker, however, he managed to hold on to his job. Carlo, on the other hand, quit Hess in 1914 to work as a free-lance carpenter. The following year the Valdinocis, together with Ricci, left Roxbury for Somerville, where they rented an apartment at 680 Somerville Avenue.

By then Valdinoci, not yet twenty-one years old, was devoting all his spare time to *Cronaca Sovversiva*. Apart from contributing articles and notes, he collected money for the paper, raised funds to defend arrested anarchists, distributed literature, and filled orders for pamphlets and books. From April 1916 until his departure for Mexico he served as the paper's publisher. In addition, he organized a range of social events, including a dance to commemorate the Paris Commune.[24]

Valdinoci's manner was friendly and affectionate, and he made a strong impression on all who knew him. He was "one of the best in the bunch," declared a fellow exile in Mexico, "jovial and always ready to help the comrades in any way possible."[25] In some respects, it has been suggested, he was a *mafioso* in the old sense of the word, that is, of possessing the qualities of manhood, courage, and good looks (he was always carefully groomed and dressed), comporting himself with assurance, strength, and self-reliance, and having faith in his ability to handle any situation, however challenging or precarious, that might arise. To the extent that this is true, Valdinoci played the "soldier" to Galleani's "godfather." The parallel, however, must not be pressed too far. For, in contrast to the criminal mafia, Galleani was the leader of a movement suspicious of leaders, a movement, moreover, which preached the loftiest ideals of freedom, equality, and self-sacrifice as opposed to authority, hierarchy, and personal aggrandizement. As one Italian anarchist expressed it: "The anarchists are guided by ethical principles. They are concerned about oppression and exploitation. They care deeply about the workers and their conditions. You cannot be an anarchist without loving people. And I never heard of a *mafioso* who loved people."[26]

. . .

Such were the companions of Sacco and Vanzetti in Mexico. Of the sixty or so who had made the journey, perhaps half, including Buda and Valdinoci as well as Sacco and Vanzetti, occupied a group of adobe houses on the outskirts of Monterrey, among the foothills of the Sierra Madre Oriental. There they lived communally, in so far as this was possible, practicing the creed of cooperation and brotherhood that they preached. Those who were able to got jobs. Buda found work cleaning hats and clothes, a skill he had acquired in Massachusetts. Vanzetti, by the same token, found a place in a bakery, and engaged in the trade that he had learned as a youth in Italy. Sometimes he took his wages in bread, which he brought home to share with his friends.[27]

In his free time, as was his habit, Vanzetti read a good deal and wrote letters to the Brinis and to his family. By now he had shaved off his beard, which he was never again to grow back. He adopted a pseudonym, calling himself Bartolomeo Negrini. Sacco followed suit, taking the first name of his recently deceased brother Nicola and the maiden name of his mother, Mosmacotelli. Valdinoci, in the same way, became Paco Carlucci, from "Carluccio," his longtime nickname.[28]

Living communally in Monterrey forged a special relationship among these *sovversivi*, binding them together into a tightly knit underground fraternity. Young, energetic, determined, they formed an inner circle of ultra-militants within the larger Galleanist movement. Rebels to the core, they prepared for their return to Italy where, they had convinced themselves, the social revolution was about to begin.

But their hopes were doomed to disappointment. Although the war continued unabated, the revolution failed to spread. Week after week they waited, but no conflagration took place. Life in Mexico, in the meantime, proved more difficult than they had anticipated. Jobs were scarce, and most of them could not find work. As their savings dwindled, letters came from the United States telling of high wages in the wartime boom and how easy it was to avoid registration. The anarchists soon wearied of their exile. Nerves became frayed, tempers short, and quarrels occasionally broke out. By early September, as Valdinoci wrote to Schiavina, the group was already breaking up, "the reason for remaining together having failed."[29]

One by one the anarchists slipped back across the border. Sacco was among the first to go. He could not get work in Monterrey and suffered much from being separated from his family. As he later explained at his trial: "I leave my wife here and my boy. I could not stay no more far away from them."[30] At the beginning of September he left.

Vanzetti went a week or two later. As early as July 16 he had written his family in Italy that he was planning to leave. By then he had spent nearly two months in Monterrey, months of "prospects, hopes, uncertainties, and anxieties." He would stay a while longer, he said, to see how the draft law was being enforced. "It seems that the threat of conscription and deportation by the United States is merely a bluff; if that is so, so much the better for me."[31] About six weeks later Vanzetti crossed the border and made his way to St. Louis. After a brief stay, he went on to Youngstown, Ohio. There he remained for the better part of a year, before returning to Massachusetts.

By the end of November 1917 the rest of the group had also departed. Salvatore De Filippis, a future member of the Sacco-Vanzetti Defense Committee, was stopped at the border and jailed for six months at Corpus Christi, Texas, for lacking a draft registration card.[32] The others reentered the country without difficulty. Buda traveled to Chicago, where he stayed for several months before moving to Iron River, Michigan, and adopting the name of "Mike Boda," while Valdinoci and Scussel went to Youngstown to join Vanzetti. (Scussel had meanwhile Americanized his first name to John, by which he was thereafter known.) Of the remainder, one traveled to Cuba and a few to Central and South America, among them Umberto Postiglione. Renato Sanchioni, Adelfo's younger brother, married a Mexican woman and brought her back to Massachusetts.[33]

. . .

Sacco, still calling himself Nicola Mosmacotelli, stopped briefly in Ohio to visit his brother-in-law Joseph Zambelli and then proceeded to Cambridge, Massachusetts, where Rosina and Dante had moved after his departure for Mexico.[34] They never returned to Milford, where Sacco, being well known, might have been arrested for failing to register for the draft.

In Cambridge Sacco found work at the New England Candy Company, where he remained for three weeks. Every morning he scanned the want ads in the *Boston Globe* for an opening in his own trade. At last he was hired as an edge-trimmer by the Victoria Shoe Company in East Boston, a manufacturer of women's footwear. Sacco, who had never trimmed women's shoes before, found the work awkward and slow, so that he was earning only two dollars a day and quit after only a week. He then went to work for Rice & Hutchins in South Braintree, the site of the 1920 holdup. Here, however, he could not be placed as an edge-trimmer and was given unskilled work which paid only thirteen dollars a week. After eight or nine days he left for a position in Haverhill, which proved to be scarcely better. Between these shoe jobs he worked as a laborer on construction jobs in and around Boston, wielding a pick and shovel and carrying iron. Eventually he landed a well-paying job with the Taylor Shoe Company in Brockton, but he quit after a few months when he was required to purchase a Liberty Bond. "I don't believe in war," he asserted, "and don't allow anyone to tell me how I spend my wages."[35]

This was a difficult period for the Saccos, moving from town to town in search of work. At one point, in Brockton, Rosina was compelled to find a job in order to make ends meet. It was hard on Dante, too, five years old and about to be enrolled in school. And Sacco, still using his alias, faced arrest at any time.

Suddenly, in the fall of 1918, matters took a brighter turn. Through a friend in Milford (probably Henry Iacovelli) Sacco learned that Michael Kelley, the superintendent of the Milford Shoe Company who had taught him edge-trimming, had since started his own business in Stoughton, a few miles from Brockton, where the Saccos were then living. It was called the Three-K Shoe Company, the three K's being Michael Kelley, the owner, and his sons George and Leon, whose faces adorned the boxes in which the shoes were shipped to retailers. At the beginning of November, shortly before the Armistice, Sacco appeared at the factory and asked Mr. Kelley for work. (He was again using his own surname, while keeping his new first name, Nicola.) At first Kelley did not remember him. Then he recalled the deft young Italian he had trained nine years before. Calling his son George, superintendent of factory operations, he said: "George, if you need an edge-trimmer give this fellow some consideration because I think he is a good man; if I remember him right in Milford he was a good edge-trimmer."[36]

Sacco remained with the Kelleys for the next eighteen months, working there from November 2, 1918, to May 1, 1920, four days before his arrest. As in Milford, he was a model employee, neat, reliable, and efficient. "Now, he was a very steady worker," George Kelley recalled. "He worked steady from seven in the morning until quitting time at night and was on the job every day that you could expect any healthy man to work."[37] The elder Kelley agreed. Himself the son of Irish immigrants, he showed none of the anti-Italian prejudice so common in Massachusetts at the time. On the contrary, he liked his Italian workmen, whom he considered dependable and hardworking. An old-style family proprietor of conservative bent, he scorned trade unions with "their unreasonable methods," encouraging his hands to get along on their own initiative. Kelley was especially partial to Sacco: "He was very sociable and seemed to be all right in every way. A good worker. Very steady. He never lost a day. It is my recollection he was right on the job all the time. He was in early and stayed late. He was a great fellow to clean up everything. He was wonderful about that."[38]

Skillful and industrious, Sacco was soon earning excellent wages, at times as much as eighty dollars a week. "He was a hard worker," said Michael Kelley. "The ordinary fellow would not make as much as that because he would not have the ambition to." During the winter of 1919–1920, Sacco earned extra money by going to the factory at ten o'clock at night to bank the boiler and arriving at five in the morning to get the building heated before the men arrived for work. Mr. Kelley trusted him completely. He gave him the keys to the factory, "and the whole thing was in his hands there in the evening after everybody had gone home." For this Sacco received an extra twenty-six dollars a month. By the time he left Kelley's employment he had accumulated more than $1,500 in a savings account.[39]

During their year and a half in Stoughton, the Saccos rented a house owned by Michael Kelley situated directly behind his own home at Park and Third Streets. It was a pleasant little bungalow, with a wood-burning stove, at the edge of a grove of oaks beside a stream. The Saccos and the Kelleys were on friendly terms. Michael Kelley described Sacco as an "attentive family man" and a quiet neighbor, who did not receive noisy company. During his free hours Sacco liked nothing better than to work in his garden. He would be there in the morning before going to work and in the evening until it was too dark to see. It was "a beautiful garden," Michael Kelley recalled, "with plenty of vegetables, and Mrs. Kelley was very nice to the family, and he would say, 'Mrs. Kelley, if you know anybody that wants any tomatoes, I have got plenty of them in my garden.'" Sacco was very attentive to his vegetables, Kelley added. "In the dry season he would bring water out by the pail and water things thoroughly. He was right on the job."[40]

Sacco's life in Stoughton was full and happy. He loved his pretty wife and handsome son. (A daughter, Ines, was born after his arrest and never knew her father as a free man.) After seven years of marriage, he and Rosina were still "like sweethearts," recalled Joseph Moro, who visited them during this period. On free afternoons they took walks in the adjacent woods, "gathering wildflowers here and there and resting under the shade of trees, between the harmony of the vivid stream and the gentle tranquility of mother nature," as Sacco later wrote to his son. Often, during the evening, they would visit friends, sometimes taking Dante along. On the way home Dante would fall asleep in his father's arms, and "Rosina she youst halp me to carry him and in that same time she youst get Dante in her arm both us we youst give him a warm kisses on his rosy face." "Those day," added Sacco, "they was a some happy day."[41]

Dante, now a schoolboy, was Sacco's constant companion, both at home "and wherever I used to go." After school he would go to the factory and stand by his father's bench, piling up soles that fell from Sacco's hands. "That boy was my comrade, my friend," said Sacco. "He would say—'let me help, papa, I like to help.'" When Sacco was through with his work, he and Dante raced each other home. In the evening there was work in the garden and about the house. And there were "meetings, always meetings!"[42]

The "meetings," of course, refer to Sacco's continued involvement in the anarchist movement. Not long after settling in Stoughton, he affiliated himself with the Gruppo Autonomo of East Boston, which met regularly on Sunday afternoons and whose members included several of his fellow exiles in Mexico. At Three-K, moreover, Sacco would talk to his workmates about anarchism, trying to arouse their interest. "Sacco was a skillful and reliable worker," a grandson of Michael Kelley remarked. "One time, however, he distributed radical literature in the factory, and Grandfather and Uncle George cautioned him against it. Not only as the owners did they want peace in the factory, but there was an element of concern for Sacco as well. He was like part of the family."[43]

The conservative Irish family could not understand Sacco's radicalism. There was no money in it, they told him. Besides, it was dangerous nowadays, during the months of political repression following the war. Sacco was an able young fellow and could soon become a prosperous citizen, maybe even open a factory of his own some day, just as Michael Kelley had done. "Stop talking, Nick, till this time of antiradical excitement is past," warned George Kelley. "You can't reform the world in a day. You will surely get into trouble." But Sacco would not be restrained by prudence. "Oh, George," he replied, "it is my heart that talks."[44]

The Kelleys never lost their affection for Sacco, despite all the troubles ahead. "Grandmother was extremely fond of him," her grandson recalled. "She always stood up for him and couldn't believe that he could do those nefarious things. She was taken with the whole family and assisted at Ines's birth. They were aware of his radicalism but didn't know what to make of it. They saw him as a good worker, a family man, a kind person. Grandmother asked him to kill a chicken now and then, and he was very squeamish about it. He didn't like killing chickens. It was an odd relationship between an Irish business family and an Italian worker. 'Give up the radical stuff! Be an American!' Grandfather would tell him."[45] For the rest of his life Michael Kelley retained his faith in Sacco's good character. He said: "A man who is in his garden at 4 o'clock in the morning and at the factory at 7 o'clock, and in his garden again after supper and until nine and ten at night, carrying water and raising vegetables beyond his own needs which he would bring to me to give to the poor—that man is not a 'holdup man.' "[46]

· · ·

Vanzetti, as we have seen, left Mexico in September 1917, a week or two after Sacco. He no longer had his beard, but he had let his mustache grow long and droopy, giving him the appearance of an "amiable walrus."[47] After stopping for a while in St. Louis, he went on to Youngstown, "the city of smoke," as he called it, where, still under his alias Negrini, he found a job in a steel mill. There he remained for the next ten months, before moving to Farrell, Pennsylvania, across the state line, where he worked as a pick-and-shovel man. In the fall of 1918, he returned to the Brinis in Plymouth, reassuming his real name.[48]

A year and a half had passed since Vanzetti's departure for Mexico. The Brini children had missed him, especially Beltrando. "I remember the day of his return," the boy later recalled. "I was on my way home and from the distance caught a glimpse of his head through the window. I was overjoyed to see him. He gave me confidence and self-esteem. He made me feel like something."[49] The Brinis, however, did not have a place for Vanzetti. The children were growing up and needed what room was available. Besides, Alfonsina, the mother, had taken a job at Puritan Mills—she worked as a "specker," picking threads out of the cloth—and could no longer take in boarders. Her husband found a room for him with Frank and Mary Fortini at 35 Cherry Street, only a few blocks away, so that Vanzetti was able to visit them two or three times a week.[50]

To earn a living, Vanzetti went back to construction jobs of the type he had performed in the past. This sustained him for the next few months, but it "robbed me of much of my original vitality," he complained. So he began to cast about for something else. In the spring of

1919 a friend of his, a fish peddler who had decided to return to Italy, offered to sell him his cart, knives, and scales, along with a bell to summon customers. Vanzetti grasped the opportunity and so became a fish vendor.[51]

Although he did not earn much, Vanzetti enjoyed his new occupation. It was outdoor work, which he had always preferred, and it gave him the independence that he craved. It also brought him into contact with the people of North Plymouth, mostly Italian and Portuguese immigrants. Among them Vanzetti, with his long mustache, sad smile, and gentle humor, became a familiar figure. Twice a week he got a barrel or two of fish, either from local dealers in Plymouth or by express from Boston; on occasion he traveled to Boston himself and bought fish at the docks. In the morning he pushed his cart, loaded with eels, haddock, cod, halibut, and swordfish, making change, weighing out the fish, and chatting with the customers in Italian, Bolognese, and English. Between the houses he could see the gleaming stretch of Plymouth bay, the sandy islands beyond, the white dories at anchor. It was better than construction work.[52]

Vanzetti peddled his fish fairly steadily between the spring and fall of 1919, until the weather became bitter. December 24, he tells us, was the last time he made his rounds that year. "A brisk day of business I had, since all Italians buy eels that day for the Christmas Eve feasts."[53] After Christmas he returned to his odd jobs: cutting ice, shoveling snow, digging ditches, wheeling coal, pouring concrete, and laying a water main at Puritan Mills, where Alfonsina Brini was employed. "I can almost say," he later wrote, "that I have participated in all the principal public works in Plymouth. Almost any Italian in the town or any of my foremen of my various jobs can attest to my industry and modesty of life during this period."[54]

Vanzetti's mode of life in Plymouth knew no calendar. He had no regular employment. He peddled fish in good weather, worked at odd jobs when he could find them, and continued to read a good deal, mostly on radical subjects. Like Sacco, he kept up his anarchist activities. He too now frequented the Gruppo Autonomo in East Boston, mingling with his comrades from Mexico. He also lectured on occasion in Brockton and other towns, invariably drawing a favorable response. "I knew Vanzetti pretty well," Joseph Moro recalls. "He came up to Haverhill two or three times to speak at meetings. That was in 1919. He was a good speaker, so attractive to listen to. One time he came to our house. He had hurt his forehead at work and wore his cap over the bruise. My mother asked, 'Who is he?' But once we sat down to eat and talk we all loved him. He was like a child. He wrote me beautiful letters. Talking to him you could fall in love with him. He talked like a poet—he was born to be a poet—and he knew what he was talking about."[55]

Thus Vanzetti lived and labored during his last year and a half of freedom. In March 1920, when the weather improved, he went back to peddling fish. When the supply was scarce he would dig for clams on the flats between the town pier and the Cordage.[56] By April he was planning to go into fishing himself, in partnership with Frank Jesse, a Plymouth man who owned some dories. But on May 5 he was arrested. A few days earlier, Beltrando Brini had encountered Vanzetti on Suosso's Lane. "I was playing ball," the boy recalled, "and it went into a neighbor's yard. I jumped the fence to retrieve it and trampled on the vegetables in the garden. The owner came out and scolded me, and I sassed the man back. Vanzetti was coming down the street and saw it all. He came up to me, got down on one knee, so that his face was close to mine. He told me in a quiet way that I had done the wrong thing. I felt sorry. I swore that I would never do it again. A few days later Vanzetti was arrested. I never saw him again as a free man."[57]

1. Sacco's parents, nephews, and nieces in Torremaggiore

2. Vanzetti with his parents and sister Luigia, Villafalletto, about 1897

3. Sacco in 1908, shortly after his arrival in America

4. Luigi Galleani in the United States, about 1912

all'aperto, in piccole proporzioni in strato sottilissimo ed interrotto e quindi accenderla con un cerino legato all'estremità di un bastone. In questo modo la nitroglicerina abbrucia lentamente e SENZA ALCUN PERICOLO.

Per esperimentare se la nitroglicerina ottenuta è buona, se ne fa assorbire un grammo da ¼ di grammo di tripolo, e s'impasta bene con un pezzo di legno. Poi si prende un pezzettino della pasta, come un grano di riso, si mette sopra un pezzo di ferro e con un martello a manico lungo si batte un colpetto secco. Si ottiene così, senza pericolo, una detonazione come una fucilata.

DINAMITE.

La dinamite è una pasta fatta con nitroglicerina ed una sostanza assorbente in polvere. Essa è molto facile ad adoperare, trasportare e conservare. Siccome ormai la dinamite è diventata molto comune, in generale riesce più comodo il procurarsela, senza mettersi a fabbricare la nitroglicerina che serve a far la dinamite. In tal caso c'è da studiare il modo di maneggiarla e adoperarla. Essa si adopera nelle cave di pietra e di zolfo (a Carrara, Belluno, Boratella, Sicilia, nel Bresciano, ecc.) nei lavori stradali e negli arsenali. Si può quindi avere per mezzo di minatori, soldati del genio, ecc. Una scusa valevole è quella della pesca di contrabbando, al quale uso è adoperata spesso nelle campagne, buttando la cartuccia con la capsula e la miccia (rivestita di catrame o di cera) accesa nell'acqua dove sono i pesci. Prima di adoperare la dinamite che si riceve bisogna sempre provarla.

— 20 —

La salute è in voi!

5. *La Salute è in voi!*, Galleani's bomb manual. The cover, based on an 1893 woodcut by the French artist Charles Maurin, depicts Ravachol before the guillotine. In the distance crops are ripening and the sun is rising, heralding a new dawn of liberty.

6. Aldino Felicani, about 1915

7. Raffaele Schiavina, about 1917

8. *Cronaca Sovversiva*, May 26, 1917, with Galleani's "Matricolati!"

9. Vanzetti in Mexico, 1917

10. Vanzetti after his return to Massachusetts, 1918

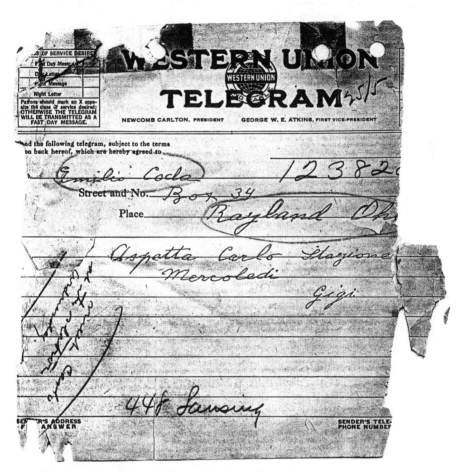

11. Telegram from Luigi Backet to Emilio Coda, January 14, 1918, instructing him to meet Carlo Valdinoci at the Steubenville station

12. Attorney General A. Mitchell Palmer

PLAIN WORDS.

The powers that be make no secret of their will to stop, here in America, the world-wide spread of revolution. The powers that must be reckon that they will have to accept the fight they have provoked.

A time has come when the social question's solution can be delayed no longer; class war is on and cannot cease but with a complete victory for the international proletariat.

The challenge is an old one, oh "democratic" lords of the autocratic republic. We have ben dreaming of freedom, we have talked of liberty, we have aspired to a better world, and you jailed us, you clubbed us, you deported us, you murdered us whenever you could.

Now that the great war, waged to replenish your purses and build a piedistal to yours saints, is over, nothing better can you do to protect your stolen millions, and your usurped fame, than to direct all the power of the murderous institutions you created for your exclusive defence, against the working multitudes resing to a more human conception of life.

The jails, the dungeons you reared to bury all protesting voices, are now replenished with languishing consciencious workers, and never satisfied, you increase' their number every day.

It is history of yesterday that your gunmen were shooting and murdering unarmed masses by the wholesale; it has been the history of every day in your regime; and now all prospects are even worse.

Do not expect us to sit down and pray and cry. We accept your challenge and mean to stick to our war duties. We know that all you do is for your defence as a class; we know also that the proletariat has the same right to protect it self, since their press has been suffocated, their mouths muzzled, we mean to speak for them the voice of dynamite, through the mouth of guns.

Do not say we are acting cowardly because we keep in hiding, do not say it is abominable; it is war, class war, and you were the first to wage it under cover of the powerful institutions you call order, in the darkness of your laws, behind the guns of your boneheaded slave.

No liberty to you accept but yours; the working people also have a right to freedom, and their rights, our own rights we have set our minds to protect at any price.

We are not many, perhaps more than you dream of, though but are all determined to fight to the last, till a man remains buried in your bastiles, till a hostage of the working class is left to the tortures of your police sy-tem, and will never rest till your fall is complete, and the laboring masses have taken possession of all that rightly belongs to them.

There will have to be bloodshed; we will not dodge; there will have to be murder: we will kill, because it is necessary; there will have to be destruction; we will destroy to rid the world of your tyrannical institutions.

We are ready to do anything and everything to suppres the capitalist class, just as you are doing anything and everything to suppress the proletarian revolution.

Our mutual position is pretty clear. What has been done by us so for is only a warning that there are friends of popular liberties still living. Only now we are getting into the fight; and you will have a change to see what liberty-loving people can do.

Do not seek to believe that we are the Germans' or the devil's paid agents: you know well we are class conscious men with strong determination, and no vulgar liability. And never hope that your cops, and yours hounds will ever succeed in ridding the country of the anarchistic germ that pulses in our veins.

We know how we stand with you stand with you and know how to take care of ourselves.

Besides, you will never get all of us... and we multiply nowadays.

Just wait and resign to your fate, since privilege and riches have turned your heads.

Long live social revolution! down with tyranny.

THE ANARCHIST FIGHTERS.

13. *Plain Words* leaflet, June 2, 1919

No.98733/80.

Port of **New York, N. Y.**

JUN 24 1919 , 191

WARRANT FOR DEPORTATION OF

RAFFAELE SCHIAVINA

EXECUTED

JUN 24 1919 , 191

S. S. "Duca degli Abruzzi" J.

(Name.) *Frank J. Carter*

(Title) *Watchman*

NOTE.—This warrant should be properly indorsed and returned to the Bureau of Immigration immediately after execution. 14—411

Ellis Island, N. Y. H.,
June 28, 1919.

To the Bureau:

Within warrant of deportation, No. 54390/181, is returned
to the Bureau, alien Raffaele
Schiavina having been deported
on s/s "Duca degli Abruzzi,"
June 24, 1919.

Assistant Commissioner.

14. Deportation warrant for Schiavina, June 24, 1919

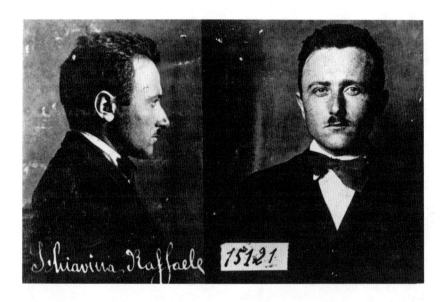

15. Schiavina (top) and Galleani in Italy following their deportation from the United States

16. Andrea Salsedo

17. *Are They Doomed?* by Art Shields, 1921. The cover, by Robert Minor, shows the death of Salsedo, May 3, 1920.

18. Sacco's passport, Boston, May 4, 1920, the day before his arrest. Note photograph of Sacco, Rosina, and Dante.

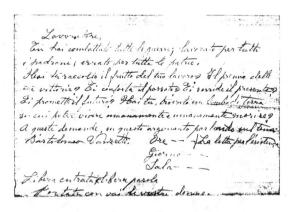

19. Announcement drafted by Vanzetti on the night of his and Sacco's arrest, May 5, 1920

20. Sacco (left) and Vanzetti after their arrest, May 1920

21. The Wall Street explosion, September 16, 1920

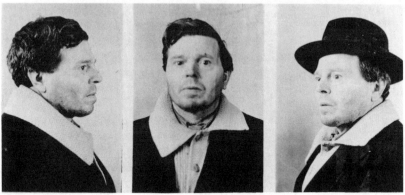

22. Mario Buda (top) and Nicola Recchi under arrest in Mussolini's Italy

23. Vanzetti (left) and Sacco, Dedham courthouse, 1923

24. Demonstration for Sacco and Vanzetti, Boston, March 1, 1925

25. Alien Registration Card of Ella Antolini, Boston, February 22, 1942

26. Nicola Recchi in Buenos Aires, 1971. Note stump of left hand.

PART TWO

Red Scare

Face to Face with the Enemy

AMERICA'S ENTRY into the war in April 1917 ushered in a period of repression of civil liberties unprecedented in the nation's history. A wave of xenophobia and superpatriotism swept the country. President Wilson himself set the tone. In his Flag Day address of June 14, 1917, he declared: "Woe to the man or group of men that seeks to stand in our way in this day of high resolution."[1]

Following the president's lead, the majority of Americans demanded unquestioning loyalty, subservient conformity, and "100 percent Americanism" for all residents, citizens and noncitizens alike. Fears of radicalism, heightened by the revolution in Russia, fanned a spirit of reaction that mounted as the war progressed, providing a foretaste of the Red Scare of 1919–1920. Throughout the country private individuals and groups—the National Security League, the American Defense Society, the American Protective League are examples—took it upon themselves to enforce patriotism, seeing subversives in every corner and making life miserable for anyone suspected of harboring antiwar views. The government, for its part, increased its surveillance of anarchists and other militants, viewing radical agitation of every kind as obstruction of the war. "May God have mercy on them," declared Attorney General Thomas W. Gregory, "for they need expect none from an outraged people or an avenging Government."[2]

On June 15, 1917, the day after his Flag Day speech, President Wilson signed the Espionage Act, which set penalties of up to twenty years imprisonment and fines of up to $10,000 for persons aiding the enemy, interfering with the draft, or encouraging disloyalty in the armed forces. The law also empowered the postmaster general to deny the mails to printed matter urging treason, insurrection, or forcible resistance to federal laws. The Sedition Act of May 16, 1918, extended these penalties to anyone who obstructed the sale of Liberty Bonds, discouraged recruitment, or uttered, printed, wrote, or published any "disloyal, profane, scurrilous, or abusive language" against the government, constitution, flag, or uniform of the United States, or advocated the curtailment of production of materials necessary to the prosecution of the war.

Under this Draconian legislation—unparalleled since the Alien and Sedition laws of 1798—the authorities instituted widespread censorship of the press and banned scores of radical newspapers from the mails. Mere criticism of the government and its war policies became cause for arrest and imprisonment. Altogether some fifteen hundred prosecutions were carried out under the Espionage and Sedition Acts, resulting in more than a thousand convictions. Among those imprisoned was the socialist leader Eugene Victor Debs, whom Sacco, although an anarchist, admired as "one of the most model and sincere faithfulness to the class workers of the American socialist movement."[3] In the fall of 1918, Debs, who had been four times a candidate for president of the United States, polling 900,000 votes in 1912, was sentenced to ten years in prison for making an antiwar speech in Ohio. The following March his conviction was upheld by the U.S. Supreme Court, Oliver Wendell Holmes delivering the unanimous opinion.

In a similar case, the socialist congressman Victor Berger received a twenty-year sentence from Judge Kenesaw Mountain Landis, the future baseball commissioner, for an editorial in the *Milwaukee Leader* branding the war a capitalist conspiracy. (Berger's conviction, however, was reversed by a higher court, which found Landis's conduct of the trial prejudiced.) Judge Landis, moreover, presided at the Chicago trial of 101 IWW activists, charged with conspiring to hinder the war effort. "Small on the huge bench," as John Reed described Landis, "sits a wasted man with untidy white hair, an emaciated face in which two burning eyes are set like jewels, parchment skin split by a crack for a mouth; the face of Andrew Jackson three years dead."[4] The trial lasted five months, from April to August 1918, and all the defendants were found guilty. As in the Berger case, Landis, detesting radicals of every stripe, imposed harsh sentences: fifteen defendants (Big Bill Haywood among them) received twenty years imprisonment plus heavy fines; thirty-three others were given ten years and the rest shorter terms. Pronouncing sentence, Landis praised the jury for doing its duty. "In times of peace," he declared, "you have a legal right to oppose, by free speech, preparations for war. But when once war is declared, that right ceases."[5]

Along with socialists and IWWs, anarchists, as might be expected, were prime targets of the antiradical crusade. Their uncompromising opposition to the war brought down on them the full panoply of government repression. Throughout the country anarchist clubhouses were raided, men and women beaten, equipment smashed, libraries and files seized and destroyed. Lectures and recitals were disrupted, newspapers and journals suppressed. On April 14, 1917, barely a week after America joined the war, federal agents invaded the offices of *L'Era Nuova* in Paterson, New Jersey, and arrested its editor Franz Widmer. Soon afterwards the paper was suppressed. Two months later, on

June 15, Emma Goldman and Alexander Berkman were arrested at the offices of *Mother Earth* in New York and charged with conspiracy to interfere with the draft. Tried in federal court, they were speedily convicted and sentenced to two years in prison, Berkman at Atlanta, Georgia, Goldman at Jefferson City, Missouri. Both Goldman's *Mother Earth* and Berkman's *The Blast* were shut down.

Cronaca Sovversiva was soon to follow. Since the appearance of "Matricolati!," with its criticism of draft registration, Galleani had been the object of scrutiny. The Department of Justice considered him "the leading anarchist in the United States" and described *Cronaca Sovversiva* as "the most rabid, seditious and anarchistic sheet ever published in this country."[6] In June 1917 *Cronaca* was banned from the mails by order of the postmaster of Lynn, where the paper was published. A new monthly journal, entitled *Pane e Libertà*, intended as a companion to *Cronaca*, never appeared.[7]

Nor was this all. On June 15, the same day on which Goldman and Berkman were detained in New York, federal agents raided *Cronaca*'s offices, temporarily halting publication. That morning Galleani was arrested at his home in Wrentham, where he lived with his wife and five children. Based on the publication of "Matricolati!" he was charged with conspiracy to obstruct the draft. Indicted on the same charge were the paper's printer, Giovanni Eramo, and its publisher, Carlo Valdinoci. Eramo, arrested in Lynn, was taken to Boston, where he and Galleani were arraigned and released under $10,000 bond. On June 13 the men appeared in federal court to answer the charges against them. Entering a plea of guilty, they were fined $100 and $300, respectively.[8]

Valdinoci, however, was nowhere to be found. He had been wanted since the latter part of May, following the appearance of "Matricolati!" Federal officials, combing through *Cronaca Sovversiva*, discovered a notice of a raffle to raise money for the paper in which the prizes were a set of books, a barrel of homemade wine, and a .38-caliber Colt revolver. This raffle was of a type long sponsored by the *Cronaca* without interference from the government. Yet the Bureau of Investigation now seized on it as a pretext to crack down on the paper. Valdinoci, as publisher, was a primary target. On May 29 agents of the Boston office of the Bureau, led by Harry M. Bowen, raided his apartment in Somerville. Valdinoci was not at home, but a search of the premises revealed that he had been mailing raffle tickets from a post office box in Cambridge. A federal warrant was thereupon issued for his arrest on charges of illegally conducting a lottery through the mails.[9]

Agents sent to the Cambridge post office waited for Valdinoci to call for his mail. He never appeared. Returning to his home in Somerville, they were unable to find him and were told by neighbors that he was "often away." "It is very evident from the investigation," complained Agent Fred J. Weyand, "that Valdinoci travels around considerably." Yet further efforts were made to apprehend him. Over the next few weeks agents continued to call at his home, search his rooms, and question neighbors and friends. All to no avail. Postal investigators who were called in to assist in the case fared no better. "I have cooperated with Special Agent Bowen in an effort to locate Valdinoci but without success," wrote Inspector R. E. Nelson, "and it is my opinion that he is not in Boston or vicinity and that in all probability we will never be able to locate him."[10] This proved an accurate prophecy. Valdinoci had disappeared, and all efforts to discover his whereabouts foundered.

Unbeknown to his pursuers, Valdinoci had taken refuge in New Britain, Connecticut, the site of a *Cronaca Sovversiva* group. Finding work as a carpenter, he received mail through the postal box of Giobbe and Irma Sanchini, a young anarchist couple with a baby daughter, by whom he was given shelter. There he remained for six weeks. During this time he was indicted with Galleani and Eramo for conspiracy to hinder the draft. The Bureau of Investigation redoubled its efforts to find him. On a tip from an informer named Frank Bellucci, the Boston office learned that he would be at the offices of *Cronaca Sovversiva* at 32 Oxford Street in Lynn on July 8. Entering the premises, agents found a group of Italians folding the paper for distribution. Valdinoci, however, was not among them. From Bellucci the agents then learned that he was expected at an anarchist club at 41 State Street, Lynn, the following day at 11 A.M. When they arrived, however, they found that Valdinoci and nine others had left for Boston on the 9 A.M. train, the first leg of a journey to Mexico. The Boston office was immediately notified. Agents rushed to South Station but failed to catch the noon train to New York, on which Valdinoci and his comrades were believed to be traveling. They learned, however, that the party would be stopping in Providence to pick up additional men before proceeding to New York by steamer. Two agents, accompanied by a federal marshal, drove posthaste to Providence. There they found the original group, now enlarged to fourteen, waiting at the Colonial Line pier. All were there but Valdinoci. Outmaneuvering his pursuers, he did not stop in Providence with the others but went straight through to New York and points south, arriving safely in Monterrey. Unlike Galleani and Eramo, he was never arrested and brought to trial.[11]

. . .

Though anarchists of all nationalities fell victim to the repressions (the Mexican rebel, Ricardo Flores Magón, received the maximum sentence of twenty years provided under the Espionage Act), Italians were among the hardest hit. During 1917 and 1918 *Cronaca Sovversiva* groups were raided in Boston, Providence, Paterson, New York, Philadelphia, Chicago, and other cities. In New Britain, Connecticut, Giobbe and Irma Sanchini, who had harbored Valdinoci before his flight to Mexico, were arrested and threatened with deportation for starting a defense fund for Galleani and Eramo. Scores of their comrades, from coast to coast, likewise found themselves behind bars, accused of such offenses as obstructing the war effort, insulting the flag, and failing to register for the draft.[12]

The Galleanists viewed these developments with mounting indignation. Persecution of anarchists and other "victims of reaction," as they called them—antiwar socialists like Debs, IWW militants like Haywood, labor activists like Tom Mooney and Warren Billings, falsely convicted of bombing a preparedness parade in San Francisco—was more than they were willing to tolerate. Their code of honor taught that revolutionaries should retaliate against the repressive use of force, that submission to the state was cowardly and unworthy of a true anarchist. To be a rebel, they insisted, was to refuse to cringe before the authorities. From propaganda by the word their mood swung towards propaganda by the deed, a euphemism for armed resistance.

Galleani himself was the first to call for action. The spirit of resistance lay at the root of his conception of anarchism, and in *Cronaca Sovversiva* he had from the start justified insurrectionary methods of struggle. In 1914, under the title of *Faccia a faccia col nemico* (Face to Face with the Enemy), the Gruppo Autonomo of East Boston had published a collection of Galleani's articles defending propaganda by the deed and exalting its practitioners—wielders of dagger, pistol, and bomb—as martyrs in a holy cause, avenging heroes moved by a spirit of self-sacrifice and a passion for retribution. In a report by the Department of Justice, *Faccia a faccia col nemico* was described as the "glorification of the most anarchistic assassins the world has ever seen."[13] Mere possession of the book, with its striking red cover and gilded lettering, branded one as a dangerous subversive.

High on Galleani's honor role of avengers were the French terrorist Ravachol, guillotined in 1892; the Italian Sante Caserio, who stabbed to death the president of France in 1894; another Italian, Michele Angiolillo, who shot and killed the Spanish prime minister in 1897; and, above all, Gaetano Bresci, an immigrant to America, who left Paterson in 1900 to assassinate King Umberto at Monza. Galleanists in East Harlem, New York, christened their group in Bresci's honor, while another group, in Pittsburgh, called themselves "The Twenty-Ninth of July," the date on which he carried out his deed.

Such were the saints and redeemers to whom the Galleanists turned for inspiration. In America they had their counterparts in Alexander Berkman, who shot and wounded Henry Clay Frick during the Homestead strike of 1892, and Leon Czolgosz, the assassin of President McKinley in 1901. Another example was that of Jean Crones, a chef at the University Club in Chicago. At a banquet in February 1916 to honor Archbishop Mundelein, newly elevated to cardinal, Crones laced the soup with arsenic. Two hundred guests became ill, though none of them fatally, since he had put in so much poison that the victims vomited it up. Crones, thought to be of German origin, managed to escape, issuing taunts and challenges to his pursuers. In fact, he was an Italian anarchist—his real name was Nestor Dondoglio—and a Galleanist. Sheltered by comrades, he was never apprehended. He died sixteen years later in Connecticut.[14]

Slayers of tyrants, wreakers of vengeance, fighters for freedom, as the Galleanists saw them—no praise was adequate for these hero-martyrs, ready to sacrifice themselves for the Cause. Yet another of this breed was Clément Duval, a Parisian anarchist and jewel thief who, captured in 1886, stabbed the arresting officer and defended his action with the words: "The policeman arrested me in the name of the law; I struck him in the name of liberty." Duval was led out of court shouting, "Long live anarchy! Long live the social revolution! Ah, if ever I am freed, I will blow you all up!"[15]

Galleani's admiration for Duval—for his audacity, his daring, his defiance of the authorities—was unbounded. When Duval escaped from Devil's Island in 1901 and found his way to the United States, he was hidden by Galleani's associates, with whom, like Crones, he remained for the rest of his life (he died in Brooklyn in 1935 in his eighty-sixth year). Galleani translated Duval's memoirs, which he serialized in *Cronaca Sovversiva*, and afterwards published them in book form, a token of his esteem for his French comrade.[16] Volume One of this material appeared in 1917, edited by Andrea Salsedo, who will later figure prominently in our story.

Galleani, however, did more than glorify the memory of terrorists and assassins. In 1905 he published a forty-six-page bomb manual entitled *La Salute è in voi!* (Health Is in You!) in the Library of Social Studies. The manual called for "vengeance" against tyrants and oppressors. "Redemption," it proclaimed, "springs from audacious revolt." Bound in red covers and priced at twenty-five cents, it was advertised in *Cronaca Sovversiva* as "an indispensable pamphlet for all comrades who love self-instruction." As Robert D'Attilio has shown, *La Salute è in voi!* was adapted from a guide to explosives compiled by Professor Ettore Molinari, a chemist at the Politecnico in Milan, himself an anarchist and friend of Galleani.[17] According to Inspector Thomas J. Tunney of the New York City bomb squad, Galleani's handbook was "accurate—and very practical." This, however, proved not to be the case, to the misfortune of several anarchists who tried to use it. At one point, indeed, *Cronaca Sovversiva* had to warn its readers to correct an error in the formula for making nitroglycerine.[18]

In any case, several years were to pass before the Galleanists put the manual to use. The first recorded instance occurred in 1914 and involved the Bresci Group of New York, the largest and most militant in the city, whose name conveys its ultra-radical character and readiness to commit acts of violence. A counterpart of the Gruppo Autonomo of East Boston, it met in the basement of 301 East 106 Street, in the Italian section of East Harlem, where its theatrical society, the Filodrammatica Sovversiva, performed antimilitarist plays and where Galleani and Emma Goldman came to lecture. Its members, mostly from Sicily and the Mezzogiorno, included Andrea Ciofalo, Alfredo Conti, Giuseppe Sberna (secretary of the group), and Frank Mandese, whose barber shop on Second Avenue served as a gathering place for comrades. (Other hangouts in the neighborhood were Albasi's grocery on East 106 Street and the Vesuvio restaurant on Third Avenue near 116 Street.) All were staunch supporters of *Cronaca Sovversiva*, and Ciofalo, Conti, and Sberna were among the group of ultra-militants who went to Mexico in 1917.

Trouble began for the Bresci Group during the spring of 1914, when America lay in the grip of a depression and hundreds of thousands of men were out of work. A young New York anarchist named Frank Tannenbaum (later a distinguished historian at Columbia University) led a group of unemployed men into the churches to demand food and shelter, an attempt to dramatize the plight of the jobless. On March 4 Tannenbaum and his followers were evicted from the Church of St. Alphonsus on West Broadway. He was charged with inciting to riot and convicted and sentenced by Magistrate John A. L. Campbell to the maximum penalty of one year in prison plus a $500 fine.

During this same period an incident occurred in Colorado which swiftly brought matters to a head. On April 20, during a coal miners' strike at Ludlow, a detachment of militia attacked a tent colony, killing five miners and a boy. The soldiers then poured oil on the tents and set them ablaze. Eleven children and two women were smothered to death. Afterwards, three prisoners, including a leader of the strike, were savagely beaten, then murdered. The Ludlow massacre, as the episode quickly became known, touched off protests throughout the nation. In New York on May 10, Reverend Bouck White, pastor of the Church of the Social Revolution, led a march to the Calvary Baptist Church, of which John D. Rockefeller, Jr., principal owner of the Ludlow mines, was a parishioner. Police were summoned and arrested Reverend White, along with an anarchist named Milo Woolman. Brought before Judge Campbell, they were sentenced to six months' imprisonment.[19]

In the ensuing weeks a plot took shape to blow up Rockefeller's home near Tarrytown, New York. Headed by Alexander Berkman, who had spent fourteen years in prison for his assassination attempt on Henry Clay Frick, the conspirators included anarchists from the Ferrer Center on East 107 Street along with members of the Bresci Group. On July 4, 1914, an explosion occurred in a tenement on Lexington Avenue between 103 and 104 Streets. Three anarchists—Arthur Caron, Carl Hanson, and Charles Berg, all associated with the Ferrer Center—were killed. A bomb, intended for Rockefeller, had gone off prematurely. Later the same day Frank Mandese was arrested in Tarrytown "in uncomfortable proximity" to Rockefeller's estate.[20] He was soon released for lack of evidence, but the police raided the Bresci Group and roughed up its members, whom they suspected of complicity in the plot.

Nor did matters end there. During the fall of 1914 a rash of bombings occurred in different parts of the city. On the afternoon of October 13, the anniversary of the execution of Ferrer, a bomb exploded in St. Patrick's Cathedral, causing minor damage. That same evening dynamite was found outside St. Alphonsus's Church, where Frank Tannenbaum had been arrested in March. A week later a bomb exploded in the rectory of the church, causing slight damage. A brief respite followed. Then, on November 11, the anniversary of the Haymarket executions, a bomb went off in the Bronx Court House, where once again damage was slight. On November 14, in the most audacious attempt of all, a bomb was placed in the Tombs police court beneath the seat of Magistrate Campbell, who had sentenced Tannenbaum and the others. He was just about to ascend the bench when the device was noticed and disarmed.

In none of these incidents were the perpetrators arrested. The police, however, suspecting anarchists, focused their investigation on the Bresci Group. In January 1915 Inspector Tunney, head of the bomb squad, ordered a bilingual officer, Detective Amedeo Polignani, to infiltrate the group. There Polignani met two young anarchists, Frank Abarno and Carmine Carbone, protégés of Frank Mandese. Carbone, a cobbler, had lost the fingers of his right hand in the act of preparing bombs, possibly linked with the incidents of the previous fall.

Winning their confidence, Polignani plotted with Abarno and Carbone to blow up St. Patrick's Cathedral. Following instructions in *La*

Salute è in voi!, the three made a number of bombs, and on March 2 Abarno and Polignani went to the cathedral. Abarno placed a bomb by a pillar. He was just about to light the fuse when he was seized by the police. Moments later Carbone was arrested at his home. Both men were charged with conspiracy to bomb the cathedral and brought before Judge Charles C. Nott, Jr., of the Court of General Sessions of New York. A copy of *La Salute è in voi!*, taken from Carbone's room, was introduced as evidence during the trial.[21]

The Bresci Group maintained that this was a blatant case of entrapment. According to Mandese and Sberna, who organized a defense fund for their comrades, Abarno and Carbone, inveigled into the scheme by Polignani, were "victims of a dark plot of the New York police."[22] Inspector Tunney rejected these charges, insisting that the anarchists had acted on their own initiative. The jury apparently agreed. Both men were convicted, and Judge Nott, "stubborn as a mule," in the description of *L'Era Nuova*, sentenced them to six to twelve years in prison.[23]

Galleani, in *Cronaca Sovversiva*, published a series of articles on the case. He too accused the police of framing Abarno and Carbone through the use of an *agent provocateur*. A photograph of Polignani accompanied each article. As to the earlier bombings, however, Galleani was surprisingly candid. Tracing the history of the 1914 explosions, from Lexington Avenue in July to the attempt on Judge Campbell in November, he as much as admitted that anarchists were responsible. Those bombings, he declared, in contrast to the St. Patrick's affair, had been "*attentats*, more or less serious, more or less successful, but so distinctive that they cannot be classified among the tricks of the police." Nor, for their part, could the police attribute them to the Black Hand but rather "must delve into the unexplored world of the 'rebels,' without church, without commandments, without priests, extending from the Battery to Harlem between the two rivers, impalpable, elusive, inexorable, like ether and like destiny."[24]

What then must be done? asked Galleani. "Continue the good war," he advised his disciples, "the war that knows neither fear nor scruples, neither pity nor truce," the war to exterminate "the vampires of capital." Such remained "the task of the hour."[25]

And the war indeed continued. But in 1916 the theater of battle shifted from New York to Boston, where atheist and antimilitarist demonstrations in the North End triggered clashes with the police. On September 25, as was earlier noted, a rally against military preparedness led to the arrest of Mario Buda, Federico Cari, and Raffaele Schiavina. In the ensuing weeks further demonstrations took place to show solidarity with the "political victims." On December 6, after a violent struggle with the police, three more militants were arrested. The youngest, Alfonso Fagotti, later to be deported with Galleani, received an eighteen-month prison sentence for stabbing an officer in the hand with a butcher knife.[26]

On December 17, in reprisal, a bomb was exploded at the Salutation Street station, headquarters of the harbor police. Though no one was injured, physical damage was considerable. Carlo Valdinoci, who himself may have had a hand in the explosion, started a fund for his arrested comrades.[27] All except Fagotti were released. A few months later, following America's entry into the war, Valdinoci was charged with hindering conscription. Avoiding arrest, as we have seen, he succeeded in escaping to Mexico.

. . .

In Mexico, as time slipped by, the Galleanists grew increasingly restive. They chafed at the mounting repressions north of the border. The more certain they were of the truth of their gospel, the more indignant they became when the authorities sought to suppress it. Men of energy and determination, they could not stand idly by while their comrades were being imprisoned, their presses silenced, their meetings disrupted and dispersed. Worst of all was the persecution of Galleani. To harass their mentor, to interfere with *Cronaca Sovversiva*, was an offense in which they refused to acquiesce. What was at stake was nothing less than their "right to exist," as they put it, their freedom to spread the Idea.[28]

The arrest of Galleani in June 1917 stirred his followers in Mexico into action. An overwhelming desire to retaliate, to strike back at the state that was stifling and crushing their movement, took possession of them. "On your feet, comrades!" exclaimed Emilio Coda. Refuse to turn the other cheek! The persecution of Galleani, of Mooney and Billings, of Emma Goldman and Alexander Berkman, must not go unanswered. As the vanguard in the social struggle, the struggle against war and reaction, we must combat the enemy with every means at our command. "Comrades," Coda exhorted, "to your posts!"[29]

Between June and September 1917 a conspiracy took shape among the Mexican exiles for the purpose of armed retaliation. Coda himself was a key participant, along with Buda and Valdinoci. Their confederates included Scussel of Philadelphia, Sacco and Vanzetti of Boston, Ciofalo, Sberna, and Conti of New York. It was a small group, a few dozen comrades at most. What they lacked in numbers, however, they made up in courage, resourcefulness, and self-discipline. These qualities they possessed in abundance, together with a range of manual skills (Valdinoci was a carpenter, Scussel a brick mason, and the others likewise were good with their hands). All were young men (Valdinoci, the youngest, was twenty-two; Coda, the oldest, thirty-six) who prided themselves on their toughness and daring and who, both by temperament and conviction, were committed to uncompromising direct action. All, moreover, were of peasant background, born and raised in villages and towns. They shared the peasant's tenacity of purpose, the peasant's deep-seated distrust of government ("the law works against the people," ran the proverb), the peasant's fierce loyalty to clan and group, the peasant's hatred of power and privilege, the peasant's yearning for vengeance against his oppressors.

Thus the Mexican interlude, brief as it was, forms a critical phase of our story. An awareness of this fact is essential to an understanding of what was to follow. For, during the summer of 1917, a group of anarchists came into being whose function was to carry out bombings. Determined, self-possessed young men, they would not yield meekly to repression. On the contrary, their tactics, their organization, their very mental attitude had been shaped for the purpose of retaliation. A Justice Department agent later speculated that they had gone to Mexico to receive instruction in the use of explosives.[30] While little evidence has come to light to sustain this hypothesis, the possibility cannot be ruled out. Their primary motive, as we have seen, was to prepare for the revolution in Italy, in which they hoped to play an important part. The revolution, however, failed to come. So they turned their energies back to the United States, where they resolved to combat political repression.

Valdinoci in particular was eager to do battle with the authorities. Always optimistic and self-assured, he was confident, as Buda wrote to Schiavina, that "everything is in our favor." Buda himself was less certain. His destiny, he said, might be "to break stones for ten years" in a federal prison. Yet he too was ready for action. Soon he would recross the border, he vowed, and then he would "plant the poof."[31]

CHAPTER SEVEN

Carlo and Ella

By October 1917 Valdinoci, Buda, and most of their comrades had returned to the United States. Arming themselves, often assuming new names, they plunged into an underground existence. For the next three years conspiracy became their way of life. They refused to acknowledge any authority save that of their own code of honor, the code of secrecy and self-reliance, which bound them together in their struggle against the state. They had no leaders; all worked together on terms of equality and mutual respect. Shunning large-scale organization, they operated in small, close-knit groups suitable for militant action that could be planned and executed without mobilizing large numbers and without direction from above. For support, they could rely on an extensive network of *sovversivi* who, raising them to the status of heroes, provided assistance as well as shelter from the police.

Before the year was out, a war had begun in which anarchists with bombs stood on one side and the authorities on the other—"face to face with the enemy," in the title of Galleani's book. The opening battle stemmed from an incident in Milwaukee, which occurred as the exiles were preparing to leave Mexico. On September 9, a Sunday, Reverend Augusto Giuliani, pastor of the Italian Evangelical Church, held an open-air "loyalty" rally in the city's predominantly Italian Bay View section, where the Francisco Ferrer Circle, a Galleanist group, had its clubhouse. Reverend Giuliani had completed his speech and the crowd had begun to sing "America" when members of the Ferrer Circle rushed the platform and tore down the American flag. Police moved in and opened fire. Antonio Fornasier, director of the Circle's theater group, was shot through the heart and killed instantly. His comrade Augusto Marinelli drew a pistol and fired back but was mortally wounded in the chest; he died in the hospital five days later. A third anarchist, Bartolo Testalin, was shot in the back but survived. Two detectives were also wounded, neither of them seriously. Eleven anarchists, including a woman, Mary Nardini, described by the police as the "instigator" of the riot, were placed under arrest. The police then raided the Ferrer club, roughed up its members, and seized a quantity of anarchist literature.[1]

The incident in Milwaukee propelled the Mexican exiles into action. Vowing to retaliate, Buda crossed the border and traveled to Chicago, the center of Italian anarchism in the midwest. Valdinoci and Scussel had meanwhile gone to Youngstown, Ohio, possibly in company with Vanzetti. Over the next few weeks, during October and November 1917, plans were laid to avenge the death of their comrades. To turn the other cheek was out of the question. The authorities, having sown the wind, would reap the whirlwind.

On November 24, just after dark, a bomb was placed in the basement of Reverend Giuliani's church. Before it could explode, however, it was discovered by the scrubwoman's eleven-year-old daughter, who sounded the alarm. The bomb, made of iron pipe about a foot in length and eight inches in diameter, was removed to police headquarters and placed on a table for inspection. Detectives were handling the device, joking about it, when suddenly it went off. The blast killed ten detectives—among them one of the two who had been wounded at the September 9 rally—and a woman who had come to file a robbery complaint. Five other detectives and a police lieutenant were seriously injured. The station was a total wreck.[2]

Someone had planted "the poof," as Buda had vowed to do before leaving Mexico. Possibly it was the work of local anarchists from the Ferrer Circle; more likely, however, Buda himself was responsible, together with Valdinoci, the latter coming from Youngstown to assist him. After the explosion, Chicago Police Chief Hermann Schuettler, still remembered after thirty years for arresting the Haymarket anarchists, sent two Italian-speaking detectives from his bomb squad to aid in the investigation, but the culprits were never identified.[3] The authorities and general public were outraged. A bomb had gone off; policemen had been killed; and anarchists would pay for the crime.

At the end of November, the anarchists seized at the open-air meeting—Mary Nardini, her husband Pasquale, the wounded Bartolo Testalin, and eight others—were put on trial for assault with intent to commit murder. The trial, denounced by Emma Goldman as a "frame-up,"[4] opened the day after the burial of the bomb victims, when feeling against the anarchists ran high. That Mary Nardini—dubbed "the queen of the anarchists" by the press—refused to salute the American flag further inflamed passions against the defendants. Though charged with shooting the two detectives on September 9, they were really, some observers believed, being tried for the explosion of November 24—there were eleven defendants, it was noted, one for each person killed in the police station—which occurred while they were all in prison. Testalin, for one, demanded to know exactly whom he was accused of having attempted to kill; after all, he himself had been shot in the back at the rally and kept in detention ever since. Why, furthermore, were eleven anarchists being tried when only one or two had actually participated in the shoot-out?[5]

The prosecuting attorney, Winfred C. Zabel, provided an explanation. Citing the Haymarket trial of 1886, in which eight anarchists were convicted of murdering policemen, Zabel fell back on a theory of conspiracy: even if some defendants had not fired at the detectives, all, as at the Haymarket, had been party to a preconcerted plan. To demonstrate their intentions, Zabel read extracts from anarchist publications confiscated at the defendants' clubhouse. In these extracts, according to the *Milwaukee Journal*, "President Wilson was pictured as worse than Villa, the Red Cross was referred to as a fraud, the Liberty Bond as a slavery bond; the Italians were urged to resist selective service, soldiers were called upon to desert, matrimony was mocked, free love exalted and the church and state condemned."[6]

The jury deliberated only seventeen minutes before bringing in a verdict. Despite the flimsy evidence against them, all of the defendants were found guilty. Judge A. C. Backus, pronouncing sentence, lashed out at their anarchistic views: "You have said that the American flag is a rag, the president ready to be killed, America a jail, the church to be destroyed and the ministers and priests killed." Then he added: "All of you are aliens, in this country but a few years. You have cast aside all of the American institutions which have offered you advancement. This is the greatest country in the world. By your anarchistic teachings and doings you sought to destroy by violence. You are not a creative or constructive force. Your purposes are destructive and ruinous, and the court must measure out such punishment as commensurate with the crime which all of you have committed." This said, he sentenced all eleven to twenty-five years in Waupun State Penitentiary. The authorities, in addition, took custody of the Nardinis' five-year-old daughter, though relatives had offered to take care of her.[7]

The militants, as can be imagined, were not prepared to let matters rest there. Outraged by the treatment of their comrades, they were determined to strike back, the harder and swifter the better. The farcical trial, the savage sentences, merely intensified their desire for revenge. At the end of December, after sentence was passed, Buda, Valdinoci, and their associates hatched a new scheme of retaliation.

By now Valdinoci was back in Youngstown, where he and Scussel had been living since October. Valdinoci was using two new aliases, Carlo Lodi and Carlo Rossini, Lodi being his mother's maiden name and Rossini the married name of an older sister in Italy. Both men were heavily armed. For support, moreover, they could rely on the Gruppo Anarchico of Youngstown, consisting of fellow Galleani militants, one of whom, Arduino Tremonti, had found them jobs at the Youngstown

Sheet & Tube Company where he worked. Although they boarded with another family, they received their mail at Tremonti's home at 448 Lansing Avenue.

Together with Buda in Chicago, with whom they maintained continuous communication, Valdinoci and Scussel worked out a plan of reprisal against the prosecutors of the Milwaukee defendants. Whether Sacco and Vanzetti were involved is not known. Vanzetti, as we have seen, was living in Youngstown at this time, having gone there from Mexico by way of St. Louis. (Valdinoci and Scussel had taken the same route—indeed, the three may have traveled together.) Under the alias of Negrini, he too was employed in a steel mill, quite possibly Youngstown Sheet & Tube.

Was all this merely coincidence? Probably not. More than likely he was in league with the others, though no hard evidence for this has come to light. Sacco, too, as has been noted, stopped in Ohio after leaving Mexico, apparently to visit his brother-in-law. In January 1918, moreover, he corresponded with the Youngstown Anarchist Group.[8] Beyond this, however, there is nothing to link him with the conspiracy.

· · ·

At this point a young woman enters our story whose complicity in the Youngstown affair is beyond question. Only eighteen when the plot unfolded, Gabriella Antolini (known as Ella to her comrades) had been born in 1899 of an indigent peasant couple in Ferrara province. In 1907, when not yet eight, Ella, along with her family (parents, three older brothers, and a younger sister), was recruited as a contract laborer to harvest cotton and sugar cane in Louisiana. The work proved grueling and life was hard, even harder perhaps than in Italy. After five miserable years, moving from town to town, living in shacks, scraping out a bare existence, Ella, together with her parents and sister, went back to Ferrara, leaving her brothers behind. All three—Luigi, Alberto, and Renato—went north to seek a better life. Renato, the youngest, took up farming in Vineland, New Jersey, while Luigi and Alberto found work as bricklayers in New Britain, Connecticut, a mill town southwest of Hartford. The following year, 1913, their parents and sisters left Italy to join them.[9]

By then Ella was thirteen years old. After a year in elementary school, her only formal education in America, she went to work in a factory to contribute to the family's support. In her free time, however, she was an avid reader, in English as well as in Italian. Intelligent, alert, she hungered for knowledge, devouring books on a wide range of subjects. Her favorites were literature and art, but, influenced by her brothers, who had meanwhile converted to anarchism (Alberto now subscribed to *Cronaca Sovversiva*), she turned her attention increasingly to social issues.

One day, in 1915, Alberto invited a friend, an anarchist named August Segata, to the Antolini home at 129 Lawlor Street. Segata, a twenty-three-year-old factory hand, was an Italian with Austrian citizenship who hailed from the Trentino region.[10] An opponent of the war, he would later refuse to register for conscription; neighbors described him as "a rank socialist and anarchist." Introduced to Ella, he was taken with her at once. Not yet sixteen, she was slim, petite, and well-proportioned, with a fair complexion, light brown hair, and blue-green eyes, as well as being lively and affectionate. A year later, on May 1, 1916, Ella and "Gugu," as she called him, were married and moved into an apartment at 236 Oak Street, not far from the home of her parents.[11]

By now Ella was an avowed anarchist. That her husband and brothers were devout Galleanists had undoubtedly hastened her conversion. By the time she was seventeen, at any rate, she had joined the Gruppo I Liberi of New Britain, a circle of *sovversivi*, Giobbe and Irma Sanchini among them, who had opened a club at 85 Mill Street in the industrial section of town. Before long Ella was taking part in the whole range of the group's activities, from picnics and dances to lectures and theatrical performances, including *Primo Maggio* by Pietro Gori. At the factory where she worked, the Fafner Bearing Company, she "often talked socialism and was also very much in favor of anarchy," her foreman would later recall.[12] In the anarchists, and especially in the Sanchinis, she found a close-knit, affectionate family, a whole new way of life. "Your parents were dear to me," she wrote to the Sanchinis' daughter many years later. "From the first moment that I met them they were like my brother and sister (*come fratelli*)."[13]

Over the next year and a half Ella became acquainted with many other Galleanists scattered through the towns of New England, to which I Liberi's dramatic recitals took her. Young as she was, her strong character, vivacious personality, and striking good looks made her a much adored figure in the movement, trusted and respected by her comrades. With her passionate and rebellious nature, she felt herself increasingly drawn to the activist element, above all to Valdinoci and Schiavina, the publisher and the manager of *Cronaca Sovversiva*. Both men hailed from Emilia-Romagna, Ella's own native region. Sharing their faith in the power of individual example, she became one of a small company of women direct-actionists, ready to fight for her Ideal.

Ella first encountered Valdinoci in June 1917, when the crackdown following the publication of "Matricolati!" drove him to seek refuge in New Britain. They met at a dance, sponsored by the Gruppo I Liberi, and later on other occasions, "always with my husband, nothing wrong," she afterwards felt obliged to explain.[14] They had sensed a strong mutual attraction, however, and when Valdinoci fled to Mexico they kept up a correspondence until his return to the United States.[15]

For several months communication was interrupted. Then, in early January 1918, a letter arrived from Valdinoci urgently summoning Ella to Youngstown. The call came in the wake of the sentencing of the Milwaukee defendants. For Valdinoci and his confederates the time had come to act, and Ella could play a useful part.

Ella responded without delay. On Saturday, January 12, she and her husband packed their bags and left New Britain for Hartford. From there they traveled by train to Youngstown, arriving at midnight the following day. At the station they took a taxi to 910 West Woodland Avenue, where Valdinoci and Scussel were boarding with an Italian family named Coda (no relation, apparently, to Emilio). They were greeted by Valdinoci, and the three sat up all night by the stove, engaged in intense conversation. Finally, exhausted, they went to bed and slept until 3 P.M.

Later that day, January 14, Ella and Segata left the Coda house and registered at the York Hotel as "Mr. and Mrs. Albert Bianchi" of Hartford, Connecticut. The following morning they met with Valdinoci and two other men. One of them was Luigi Backet (originally Bacchetti), a Galleanist from Detroit, where he had been a distributor of *Cronaca Sovversiva*. For several weeks, however, he had been living in Youngstown, raising money for the Milwaukee defendants. Such funds as he could collect he forwarded to Sebastiano Secchi in Chicago, treasurer of a defense committee which, for a fee of $5,000, had retained the celebrated Clarence Darrow to undertake an appeal. Like Valdinoci and Scussel, it might be noted, Backet worked at the Youngstown Sheet & Tube Company and got his mail at the Tremonti address.

The other man, calling himself "Mario Rusca," had come to Youngstown from Chicago. He showed Ella a black leather grip. The grip, he said, contained dynamite, and her mission was to take it to Chicago, from where it would be used to carry out reprisals in Milwaukee. Ella agreed to the task. Warning her to be careful, Rusca wrote his address on a piece of paper and said that he would meet her at the station.[16] Rusca, it would appear, was Mario Buda.

The next day, leaving her husband in Youngstown, Ella, accompanied by Valdinoci, boarded a train for Steubenville, some sixty miles to the south. Under their seat they stored the bag of dynamite. Why they should have gone to Steubenville, seventy-five miles off the direct route to Chicago, remains a mystery. As a Bureau of Investigation agent later noted, "It is quite a roundabout trip from Youngstown to Steubenville, and the mission must have been an important one."[17]

One thing is known, however. Emilio Coda was in the Steubenville area, having returned to the coal fields where he had worked before going to Mexico. Boarding with a comrade in Tiltonsville, he was employed in the town of Rayland, a few miles below Steubenville, as a cutter in a mine operated by the Crawford Coal Company. It is also known that, on October 17, 1917, he had shipped a twenty-pound box to a comrade in West Hoboken, New Jersey. The box, according to the Bureau of Investigation, contained dynamite.[18]

That Coda had access to dynamite may explain Valdinoci and Ella's detour. It may be that additonal explosives were needed, beyond what the black grip contained. From Youngstown, in any event, Backet sent Coda a telegram instructing him to meet Valdinoci at the station ("Aspetta Carlo stazione mercoledi").[19] When the train arrived, however, Coda was nowhere in sight. He had not received the telegram, having left two days earlier for a United Mine Workers convention in Indianapolis. He would not return until the 26th.

After a fruitless search for Coda, Carlo and Ella found a room in Steubenville. That night the two became lovers. Carlo was twenty-three, Ella eighteen, and they made an attractive pair. The affair, however, was short-lived. The following day, January 17, Ella departed for Chicago. Carlo accompanied her to the station and put her on the afternoon train. Nattily dressed, he had on a dark green coat with an astrakhan collar and a fur cap. Ella, her hair in bangs, wore a close-fitting hat with a gilt rose ornament and a dark coat over a plaid blouse and brown skirt. On Carlo's instructions, she had checked her suitcase through to Chicago, but not the black grip, which Carlo carried on board and placed in her pullman compartment. Then he kissed her goodbye. They never saw each other again.

As Carlo and Ella entered the train, the porter, T. W. Johnson, took notice. Something about them—their manner, their gestures, the expression in their eyes, the way they handled the black bag—aroused his suspicion. He studied Valdinoci and was afterwards able to provide a good description. This done, he went about his duties.

Once the train had pulled out of the station, Ella looked into the bag. Her curiosity had gotten the better of her. What she saw was thirty-six sticks of dynamite, neatly wrapped in paper. Nervously she closed the bag and tried to read, opening a *Young Folks' History of Rome*, which she had brought along for the journey. After reading for several hours she had something to eat. She went to sleep about 11 P.M.

Meanwhile the porter had devised a plan. During the night he turned off the heat in Ella's compartment. She awoke early the next morning, half frozen in the bitter January cold. She summoned the porter, then followed him to another car, leaving the black grip behind. The heating, he assured her, would soon be fixed. As she waited, he entered her compartment, opened the black bag, and discovered the contents. Sealing the compartment, he alerted the conductor, who telegraphed ahead to Chicago.[20]

Ella had meanwhile been waiting. By noon the train was approaching Chicago. Worried, she returned to her compartment to retrieve the black bag. She found herself locked out. Despite her insistent demands, the porter would not let her enter. At 12:30 P.M. the train drew into Union Station. When she was not allowed leave the train, Ella knew that she was going to be arrested.[21]

In moments the train was swarming with police. Captain William Briggs of the Pennsylvania Railroad police, Union Station Officer C. W. Carey, Lieutenant John Loftus, Patrolman William McDonald, and Detective Sergeants Frank Folsom and Timothy O'Brien all came aboard. Allowing the other passengers to dismount, they placed Ella under arrest. The suitcase she had checked through was already in their possession. It contained nothing unusual. Apart from her clothing and personal effects, there was a photograph of her father and mother and a lock of black hair given to her in Steubenville by Valdinoci. In the leather grip, however, the police found the thirty-six sticks of dynamite along with a loaded .32-caliber Colt automatic.[22] As they began to search her compartment, Ella tried to destroy the piece of paper on which Rusca had written his address by slipping it into her mouth and chewing it. She was noticed, however, by a detective, who pried it loose. Ella put up a struggle, biting the officer on the hand, but was quickly subdued. The address, though still legible, turned out to be a vacant lot.

The search completed, Ella was removed from the train and questioned inside the station. The story she told was a mixture of half-truths and outright lies, designed to confuse her questioners. She gave her name as "Linda José," a character in a play put on by her theater group.[23] (She thought of it, she later testified, when she realized that she was going to be arrested). She gave her age as sixteen and her place of residence as Youngstown. The man who put her on the train was "Carlo," but she refused to give his last name. Yes, she knew that the black grip contained dynamite but had no idea of its intended use. Her "uncle" had asked her to bring it to Chicago, and she was doing so.

Following this initial interrogation, Ella was taken to the offices of the Department of Justice in Chicago's Federal Building. Here she was turned over to Clinton G. Clabaugh, midwest division superintendent of the Bureau of Investigation. To Clabaugh, who thought her well educated and fluent in English, she repeated the story she had told at Union Station, adding only minor details. Late that afternoon, she was arraigned before a United States Commissioner on charges of illegal possession of dynamite. After a brief hearing, she was remanded to the Lake County Jail at Waukegan in default of $20,000 bail.[24]

Over the next few months Ella was subjected to intensive questioning. Faithful to the anarchist code of silence, she refused to provide further information. She would not give her own real name, much less that of Valdinoci or the others, flatly denying the existence of any conspiracy. According to a fellow prisoner at Waukegan, who reported their conversations to the police, Ella said that "if they are waiting for her to make a confession they may keep her until she is grey, because she has no confession to make."[25] Questioned by U.S. Attorney Borrelli in Chicago, she again claimed ignorance of any plot:

BORRELLI: Did you know what dynamite is used for?

ELLA: I knew it was used in mines.

BORRELLI: The question is do you know what dynamite was used for?

ELLA: Why certainly, I knew it was an explosive.

BORRELLI: And you knew it was used in mines, for blasting purposes?

ELLA: Yes.

BORRELLI: You knew it was used in blowing up buildings too?

ELLA: I knew it was an explosive.[26]

To reporters who interviewed her at Waukegan, Ella proclaimed her own anarchist faith. "I do not believe in God, government, or laws," she said. "I do not believe in war. I do not care what they do with me." But she admitted nothing and named no names. To her comrades this made her a hero ("She never talked," they exulted).[27] While the newspapers dubbed her the "dynamite girl," to the authorities she remained "Linda José." It was weeks before they learned her true identity. "She's the cleverest girl I have met in all my experience in investigation," said Superintendent Clabaugh. "She is saturated with anarchy; seems to have been raised in its atmosphere."[28]

Ella's mission had ended in failure. Valdinoci and the others, however, remained at large, determined as ever to carry out their plan. On the night of April 15, 1918, while Ella remained a prisoner at Waukegan, two bombs were planted at the home of District Attorney Zabel, the prosecutor of the Milwaukee case. Neither went off, however. The fuse on one had been dampened by a rain which had fallen during the night. The other, which was to have been ignited by a bottle of acid dripping onto a cylinder within, also malfunctioned.

Because the bombs did not explode, experts were able to examine them. Each, weighing about twenty pounds and wrapped in black cloth bound with rope, contained enough dynamite and metal slugs to destroy Zabel's house and kill anyone inside. The bomb with the acid, it should be noted, was a duplicate of the one that had exploded in the police station the previous November. "This is nothing more than an attempt at retaliation for being instrumental in sending the twelve [sic] Italians implicated in the Bay View riot to Waupun for twenty-five years," said Zabel.[29] His analysis was surely correct. The perpetrators, however, were never identified, and the case remained unsolved.

· · ·

In the meantime Ella's fate was being decided. In February 1918, after the authorities learned her true identity, a mail cover was placed at the Antolini residence in New Britain. The object, of course, was to identify her accomplices, above all the mysterious "Carlo." But no further information emerged, not even in letters between Ella and her family, who were much distressed by her arrest. Writing to her brother Luigi, Ella repeated (with minor variations) the story that she had told the police. In May Luigi traveled to Waukegan to visit Ella in jail, bringing some family snapshots and a supply of books. Renting a room in South Chicago, he found work as a bricklayer at the Illinois Steel Company.[30] He never returned to New Britain, remaining in Chicago for the rest of his life.

On June 3, 1918, Ella was indicted by a federal grand jury, charged with unlawful transportation of explosives. On October 21 she appeared for trial at the U.S. District Court in Chicago's Federal Building. The judge was none other than Kenesaw Mountain Landis, fresh from imposing severe sentences upon the IWW defendants. Ella's fate was no different. Though she pleaded guilty and had no previous criminal record, she was sentenced to eighteen months imprisonment plus a $2,000 fine, the maximum sentence allowed under the law.[31]

At that time women convicted of federal crimes were incarcerated in state prisons, and Ella, in November 1918, was sent to the Missouri State Penitentiary at Jefferson City. Her comrade Giobbe Sanchini dedicated a poem in her honor, which he sent as a token of encouragement. The following year, together with Galleani, he and his wife were deported. They would never see Ella again. "The adversities of life separated us too early," wrote Ella long afterwards to their daughter.[32]

When Ella arrived at Jefferson City, the prison contained some twenty-six hundred inmates, of whom approximately eighty were women. Twenty of these were federal prisoners from all parts of the country.[33] The most celebrated was Emma Goldman, then forty-eight years old and serving a two-year sentence for hindering conscription. Goldman welcomed her young comrade with open arms. Ella, she wrote, was "like a beam of sunshine, bringing cheer to her fellow prisoners and great joy to me." "She was a proletarian child," said Emma, "familiar with poverty and hardship, strong, and socially conscious." Working together in the sewing room, making overalls, jackets, and suspenders, the two became intimate friends ("Little Ella, grown into my heart as my own child"). For all her youth and inexperience, noted Emma, Ella "shared my conception of life and values" and provided "intellectual comradeship with a kindred spirit."[34]

In April 1919, six months after Ella began serving her sentence, a third female radical, Kate Richards O'Hare, arrived at Jefferson City. Forty-three years old, a friend and political associate of Eugene Debs, O'Hare was the most prominent woman socialist in America, occupying a position comparable to Goldman's among the anarchists. Like Debs, she had been convicted under the Espionage Act for delivering an antiwar speech. Under a five-year sentence, she joined Emma and Ella (a "dear little Italian girl," she called her) in the sewing shop, working nine hours a day, six days a week. Emma, wrote O'Hare to her family, "mothered and babied" both Ella and herself. "It is certainly a great thing to have two women like the two 'politicals' with me here. Emma is very fine and sweet, and intellectually companiable, while the little girl is a darling. We have really interesting times."[35]

Although their views diverged on many points, the three had a good deal in common, above all their hatred of capitalism and their opposition to the war. Soon they were inseparable. They ate together in the dining room and occupied adjacent cells—"the American Revolutionary Soviet," O'Hare called it. "Emma is on one side of me and Ella on the other, and the executive committee hold nightly conclaves to direct by wireless the affairs of the universe. Just imagine what interesting stories the historian of the future can write of this strange trio and our doings."[36]

Ella, in O'Hare's description, was "small, dainty, sweet, and naturally clean and refined." She had been "framed" by the Department of Justice "in the hope of forcing some damaging confessions from her concerning a group of radically inclined Italians." Such was O'Hare's version of the story, her source being Ella herself. When the group fell under suspicion, O'Hare continues, "Ella started to Chicago to find a better job, and on the way the brave, vigilant, sleuths discovered some dynamite in her grip in the usual·manner in which sleuths find bombs. She was taken to Chicago and there for many weeks she stood firm through all the brutalities that could be forced upon her. It chills me with horror to hear her tell in her simple girlish way of these hellish weeks she lived there alone and supported only by her sublime courage. But she was game to the last and never betrayed even the names of her comrades. She stood her trial, took her sentence, and is serving her time. Her loyalty, courage, poise and sweet cheerfulness makes me ashamed. If I deserve any credit, she deserves a hundred times more. Some day I can write the story of little Ella, and it will be one that can thrill the girlhood of the coming ages."[37]

Throughout their confinement, Ella, Emma, and Kate remained true to their radical ideals. On May 1, 1919, for example, they held a little celebration in the workshop. "It was a strange May Day for me," wrote O'Hare. "Emma Goldman was ill, but little Ella, the Italian girl, and myself wore our colors. It was all that we could do. Emma gave us a bit of red ribbon, and we wore it above our hearts while we bent to the task at the roaring machines. It was a strange sight—yet how typical of our capitalist system. The dirty, grimy shop, whose windows are so high that no sunbeams can ever fall upon its inmates."[38]

There were happier moments, however, including a "scrumptuous supper" of roast chicken with stuffing, cranberry jelly, hot chocolate, and an Italian cake that Ella's mother sent. On June 5, moreover, the female inmates were treated to a picnic. "It was really a very enjoyable affair," wrote O'Hare. "They loaded all the women in two huge auto trucks, the band in another, and took us out to McClung Park for the afternoon. It is a beautiful park, has one of the most artistic dancing pavilions I have ever seen and wonderfully well equipped. The band played for the dancing and the girls made the most of the semi-freedom after the long months of severe repression. The whole thing was a strange and wonderful experience and will make an interesting chapter in the book of my prison memoirs."[39]

Another such occasion fell on September 10, Ella's twentieth birthday. "I must not fail to tell you what a nice birthday Ella Antolini had," wrote Kate O'Hare to her family. "I am sure that it will go down in her memory as a happy birthday, even tho spent in prison. She received a lot of lovely letters and many nice little gifts which meant more to her than any of the senders can imagine. She is such a child and yet so brave and sweet and courageous. Life has been so frightfully hard and bitter and yet she is like a beam of sunshine. In all the months I have been here I have never seen her face clouded or heard from her any but words of love and kindness. We had the strangest party you can imagine. Emma, Ella, and I, each locked in our monkey cage, unable to see each other, but able to converse and pass things back and forth. We had an extra nice supper, read all the birthday letters and viewed the presents. Just as we were finishing, Mrs. Schulenburg's box of cookies came and Elijah Backus' box of lovely Chinese candy. These just finished our party and when the lights went out we knew that even steel walls and iron bars cannot shut out love and happiness."[40]

That same month, however, the "American Revolutionary Soviet" was dissolved when Emma Goldman completed her sentence and returned to New York. Three months later, at the height of the Red Scare, she was deported to her native Russia. For Ella, Emma's departure left a void not easily filled. Yet Kate O'Hare rose to the occasion. Following Goldman's example, she undertook to supervise Ella's education. "Ella and I are unusually good companions for women of so great difference in age," she observed. "She is a strange mixture of very mature woman and naive child, and I never tire of her company, which is more than I can say of most women. She is so eager for education and absorbs all sorts of things like a sponge. She reads all the books I get and tells me all about them while we walk up and down the courtyard during recreation. She says they 'taste' better if she thinks them over and makes sure that she understands. She is reading that book on Theosophy now and I have been explaining the theory of reincarnation steadily for two or three days and she does ask the most astounding questions, many that are too much for me."[41]

Through her reading and conversation with O'Hare and other prisoners, Ella's English improved steadily. "Her command of grammar is remarkable," noted O'Hare, "because she read English before she could speak it and hence has only the literary vocabulary. I have never heard her use a word of slang or say 'aint' or 'have saw' or any of the atrocities that our children pick up in the streets. She speaks quaintly because she says she thinks in Italian and translates it into English. She is very proud of the fact that she is beginning to think in English now. She reads with the dictionary in her lap and looks up every word she does not understand, and if it is not in her little dictionary she insists on my giving her the pronunciation and the meaning of the word." "All she knows of the English language," added O'Hare," she has learned from books, and she has seemingly read the best. I think her brothers must be unusual also, for she says they spend all their spare money on good books. Of course, since she has been here she has had Emma first and now me to direct her reading, and she does an astonishing amount of it. I got books on American history from the library for her, and she is wading right thru them. I have insisted on her reading a few good American novels, also a few English, but she will have none of the *Ladies Home Journal* stuff."[42]

Apart from her copious reading, O'Hare also encouraged her pupil to write, particularly about her own experiences, and found the results impressive. "I find that Ella has a remarkable faculty of drawing the most vivid word pictures of her life and experience," noted O'Hare, "and I am having her write her story in her own naive but vivid way. When she has finished I will type it for her, and I think it will be a wonderful story of emigrant disillusion and the creation of an anti-social attitude."[43] The more Ella wrote, the greater became her passion to continue. "Ella has been bitten by the writing bug," said O'Hare, "and she plunges away with all the abandon of the amateur writer." In a short time she had accumulated "a mass of stuff, enough to make a book of three hundred pages and every bit of it of the most thrilling interest."[44]

But Ella never completed her memoirs. On December 4, 1919, immigration officers appeared at Jefferson City with a warrant for her deportation to Italy. On January 3, 1920, having completed her prison sentence, she was removed to St. Louis and jailed in lieu of $10,000 bond. There, over the next few weeks, she awaited a hearing of her case. Though kindly treated, as she wrote to Kate O'Hare, she was bored and lonesome away from her friends. Also the food was barely edible; and if Ella complained, noted O'Hare, "it must be very bad indeed, for she is not the complaining sort." Kate, for her own part, sorely missed her young companion, on whom she had lavished so much affection. "I feel terribly alone now that Ella is gone," she lamented. "We have been such close friends thru so many soul trying experiences that there is a bond between us that seldom exists between two women of such disparity of years."[45]

At Kate's urging, her husband, Frank O'Hare, who lived in St. Louis, secured an attorney for Ella. Kate felt somewhat relieved. "She is very brave and philosophical," she wrote of Ella, "but naturally has a dread of being subjected to the horror of Ellis Island, the steerage passage, and being dumped alone and friendless in what is to her now a strange country. Of course, there may be some lingering bits of sanity and decency remaining here and there among the administration officials, and she may escape the fate that has overtaken so many helpless aliens, but I am very apprehensive."[46]

Between January and April 1920 Ella underwent a hearing before an immigration inspector to decide whether her offenses warranted expulsion. That she was guilty of transporting explosives was indisputable. The government, however, was unable to show that she was an anarchist and, as such, subject to deportation. As a result, Ella was allowed to go free. After a "farewell chop suey supper," arranged by Frank O'Hare, she returned to her family in New Britain. Kate rejoiced at the outcome. "In the nine months Ella and I spent together I grew to love her very sincerely," she wrote. "Poor child, her life has been so hard and barren and she is such a sunny, loving creature and so hungry for the sweet, fine things in life that I sincerely hope some of them may become possible for her." Seven weeks later O'Hare herself was set free, her sentence commuted by President Wilson.[47]

.   .   .

In the wake of Ella's arrest in Chicago, the Bureau of Investigation launched an investigation of the dynamite conspiracy. At first there was little to go on, as Ella refused to talk. Then she made a fatal error. On January 20, 1918, from the Waukegan jail, she addressed a letter to Carlo Rossini at 448 Lansing Avenue in Youngstown.[48] "Rossini," of course, was Valdinoci, and the address was that of Arduino Tremonti, where he received his mail. Jail officials intercepted the letter and turned it over to Superintendent Clabaugh.

Ella had blundered badly. Her purpose was to reassure Valdinoci that she had not given him away. Instead, she had given the Bureau of Investigation the lead that it needed. Clabaugh at once notified Charles F. DeWoody, Special Agent in Charge of the Cleveland office, who put his best man on the case. His name was Rayme W. Finch, a recent addition to the Bureau. Young, tall, heavy-set, with dark hair and mustache, Finch possessed both energy and brains. He was eager to get to work.

On January 22 Finch went to Youngstown, where, aided by city policemen, he searched the Tremonti premises. Nothing incriminating was found. From Mrs. Tremonti, however, Finch learned that another man, by the name of Scussel, whom her husband had known for several years, also picked up his mail at their house. Scussel, she added, worked as a bricklayer at the Youngstown Sheet & Tube Company, where her husband was employed.[49]

Finch went to Youngstown Sheet & Tube, where, identifying himself as a federal agent, he asked for Scussel. Scussel, summoned from his work, gave his address as 910 West Woodland Avenue and denied any knowledge of a dynamite plot. Finch, seeing that he could get nothing out of him, left. He went at once to the Woodland Avenue address, which turned out to be the residence of Luigi Coda, a middle-aged Italian with a wife and a twenty-one-year-old daughter. The daughter, Penn Coda, born in the United States, was at home when Finch arrived. She willingly answered his questions. Scussel, she said, together with another man named Carlo, had been boarding with her family for several months. Carlo's last name she gave as Lodi. Finch, however, correctly guessed that he and Rossini were the same person.[50]

By now it was 6:30 P.M. and Scussel returned from work. Much to his consternation, he was greeted at the door by Finch. Though lacking a warrant, Finch asked to see the room which Scussel shared with Lodi. Scussel consented. A quick search revealed a suitcase belonging to Lodi. Opening it, Finch discovered an envelope addressed to Paco Carlucci in Monterrey, Mexico, which, said Scussel, was Lodi's "real name." Finch also found "a red book in Italian, which, when interpreted, was shown to be a book on anarchy."[51] The book, it turned out, was *Faccia a faccia col nemico*, Galleani's glorification of dynamite and propaganda by the deed.

Most interesting to Finch, however, was a brand new blue-steel .38-caliber Smith & Wesson revolver, complete with holster and ammunition. This too he found in Lodi's suitcase. Moments later, among Scussel's belongings, Finch discovered a twin of this revolver, also brand new, with cartridge belt and identical holster. Both holsters, Finch noted, featured "home-made improvements," and neither gun had ever been fired. Their serial numbers (235595 and 235627) indicated that they had been acquired at the same time and place. According to Scussel, he had bought his the previous year in San Antonio.[52]

Confiscating the weapons, Finch brought Scussel to his room at the Ohio Hotel and questioned him for several hours. He then placed him under arrest. From Youngstown Scussel was removed to Cleveland and held in the Cuyahoga County Jail for further questioning. Soon afterwards a team of federal agents was sent to Youngstown. Scussel and Lodi's room was now thoroughly searched, yielding a quantity of correspondence and other materials. From the information obtained, agents in Chicago raided the home of Sebastiano Secchi, treasurer of the defense fund for the Milwaukee prisoners, with whom Scussel had been in correspondence. From Secchi additional documents were confiscated, after which a number of Chicago anarchists were taken in for questioning. No incriminating evidence was found, however, and all were shortly released.

Finch's work, however, had just begun. On January 23, the day after he arrested Scussel, he took Penn Coda to dinner at the Ohio Hotel in hopes of eliciting further information. Miss Coda talked freely. Identifying a photograph of "Linda José," she gave a remarkably full account of her visit to Youngstown. In addition, her detailed description of Carlo Lodi tallied with the one obtained from the pullman porter who had observed him at the station in Steubenville. In particular she focused on Lodi's hair, jet black, as Finch reported, and combed in a pompadour. It was "very curly and described by Miss Coda as 'beautiful hair.' "[53]

Finch now set out to locate this Lodi, or Rossini, whose real name, Valdinoci, was as yet unknown to him. Apart from Miss Coda's description, he had another important lead. During his search at West Woodland Avenue, he had found an unsigned postal card addressed to Scussel and postmarked Dillonvale, Ohio, near Steubenville. Dated January 19, 1918, the day after Ella's arrest, it reassured Scussel that the writer was safe and "in good health."[54]

Finch was convinced—correctly—that the card had been written by Lodi. He therefore left for Dillonvale to find him. Resourceful though he was, however, Finch was no match for Valdinoci. Valdinoci, the master escape artist, had a nose for impending danger. Continually on the move, he remained a step ahead of his pursuer. From Dillonvale, then Steubenville, Finch stalked his prey through the mining camps of eastern Ohio. He questioned postmasters, policemen, informers—all to no avail. "We have been for a week within a few hours of catching up with Carl," wrote DeWoody to Clabaugh, but so far without success.[55]

By now additional agents had been put on the case. To assist them, Clabaugh sent the lock of Carlo's hair which had been found among Ella's possessions and which, Clabaugh noted, "she was very reluctant to surrender."[56] A photostat of Carlo's handwriting was also sent. Neither produced any result. Meanwhile Finch continued to track him. Early in February the trail led him to Yorkville, a town on the Ohio River. There he questioned Mrs. Anna Tisca, an Italian woman who ran the local post office, but "felt it advisable not to go too far with her," he reported, "on the principle that there are very few honest Italians."[57] Valdinoci, in any case, had slipped away. He was last sighted in Fairmont, West Virginia, after which the trail became cold.

Yet Finch was not left empty-handed. While searching for Lodi, he learned that a comrade of his, Emilio Coda, had returned to the Steubenville area after attending a miners' convention in Indianapolis. Finch notified his superior, DeWoody, who in turn wrote to A. Bruce Bielaski, Director of the Bureau of Investigation in Washington, recommending that Coda be taken into custody.[58] Bielaski issued the necessary orders.

On February 11 Coda was arrested at Rayland, where he worked, and taken to the Cuyahoga County Jail in Cleveland, where Scussel had preceded him. After more than two months of interrogation by DeWoody and his assistants, both men were transferred to Chicago, where the Department of Justice sought to implicate them in the Ella Antolini case. Both denied any connection with the affair. Coda, observed a guard who had escorted him from Cleveland, had "an exceedingly sarcastic attitude in talking to the officers." Considered a "very dangerous anarchist" by the Bureau, he was indicted by a federal grand jury on charges of conspiring to transport dynamite across state lines. The charges, however, failed to stick, and after several months of further questioning both Coda and Scussel were released.[59]

For the time being at least, the investigation had reached a dead end. Ella, to be sure, had been captured before her dynamite-laden grip could be delivered, yet bombs had been planted at the Milwaukee prosecutor's house. Worse still, her confederates, far more dangerous than she, remained on the loose. Following their release, Coda and Scussel dropped out of sight, not to resurface for many months. Mario Buda, by the same token, slipped away after the arrest of his comrades. Living in the shadows, remaining inconspicuous, he never came under suspicion.

In Youngstown the situation was similar. After Scussel's arrest, Backet and Segata disappeared from the city. Backet, returning to Detroit, wrote to the Youngstown Sheet & Tube Company, asking for his tools. A Bureau of Investigation agent was at once sent to his address, but he was nowhere to be found. Searching the premises, the agent confiscated a shotgun, a revolver, and a supply of ammunition, along with anarchist literature and a photograph of Backet. Finch urged that further efforts be made to track him down. "It is my opinion," he wrote, "that the apprehension of Backet is most essential to the successful prosecution of the anarchist group or gang involved in the interstate shipment of this dynamite. I would recommend that the Detroit office use every means at its disposal to apprehend this man."[60] Backet, however, got away. As for Segata, he too had vanished from sight, the authorities suspecting that he had returned to Italy. At any rate, he was never heard from again.[61]

And what of Vanzetti, alias Negrini, who was probably involved in the conspiracy? Like Backet and Segata, he left Youngstown after the arrest of Scussel, finding shelter with a comrade outside of town.[62] A few weeks later he moved again, across the state line to Pennsylvania. There he lay low for two or three months before returning to Massachusetts. Like Buda, he was never a suspect in the case.

Of Valdinoci, meanwhile, no trace could be found. The most important of the conspirators to escape arrest, he had vanished into thin air. Before long, however, he would reappear and resume his vendetta against the authorities. The Youngstown conspiracy, for all its intense drama, was merely a foretaste of things to come.

CHAPTER EIGHT

Deportations Delirium

AN IMMEDIATE result of the Youngstown episode was to reawaken the government's interest in *Cronaca Sovversiva*. It will be recalled that, following the publication of "Matricolati!," federal agents had raided the paper's offices and arrested Galleani and Eramo, who were indicted on charges of conspiracy to obstruct the draft. Valdinoci, too, had been indicted but had managed to avoid arrest. Thereafter matters had quieted down. Valdinoci had fled to Mexico, while Galleani and Eramo, convicted and fined, had resumed publication of the paper.

With the uncovering of the Youngstown conspiracy, however, *Cronaca Sovversiva* once more attracted federal attention. Materials found in Valdinoci and Scussel's room—literature, photographs, correspondence—revealed that the conspirators had been in continuous communication with the paper, which seemed to have had a role in the affair. As one Bureau of Investigation agent put it: "This publication, and persons connected with same, and other persons mentioned as subscribers, have appeared as parties in the Linda José dynamite case."[1] This discovery led the Bureau back to Massachusetts.

It was Finch who first recognized the connection. By February 1918 it was already clear to him that the "primary actors" in the conspiracy were closely linked with *Cronaca Sovversiva*. Realizing this, he suggested to DeWoody, his superior in Cleveland, that a thorough investigation of the paper be inaugurated. DeWoody agreed, and on February 11 he and Finch traveled to New York to confer with Director Bielaski. Impressed with their findings, Bielaski instructed Finch to proceed to Massachusetts and conduct a preliminary inquiry.[2]

Finch went to Boston the next day. There, conferring with agents at the local Bureau office, he learned of the raid on *Cronaca Sovversiva* the previous June and of the arrest and prosecution of Galleani and Eramo. He learned, too, that *Cronaca Sovversiva*, although banned from the mails, was being distributed by American Express to locations around the country. All this interested Finch greatly. What interested him even more, however, was what he learned of the paper's publisher, Carlo Valdinoci. This was a name that he had not previously encountered, though he had been dogging its owner for weeks. Finch learned how Valdinoci had been indicted, how he had evaded his pursuers, how he had escaped from Massachusetts to Mexico. Valdinoci, he was told, was a carpenter, young, attractive, and strongly built. He had abundant curly dark hair. For Finch everything fell into place. In a flash he realized that Valdinoci was "no other than CARLO LODI, who was in Mexico under the name of PACO CARLUCCI."[3]

On February 16 Finch returned to New York and presented his findings to DeWoody. On the basis of what he had learned, he proposed a new raid on *Cronaca Sovversiva*. Its purpose would be threefold: to link the paper with the shipment of dynamite to Chicago; to obtain information that might lead to the apprehension of Valdinoci; and to secure evidence that would warrant the deportation of Galleani and his lieutenants. DeWoody was easily persuaded. On February 18 he and Finch traveled to Washington and put the proposal before Bielaski. Bielaski gave it his full support.[4]

On February 22, 1918, a team of Bureau of Investigation agents, federal marshals, and local police raided the *Cronaca Sovversiva* office at Lynn. Finch himself was in charge of the operation. Armed with a search warrant, he seized thousands of documents of various kinds, including a photograph of Vanzetti with Galleani and letters from Buda and Valdinoci. Furthermore, though unable to locate the paper's subscription list, he secured a more or less complete roster from the address labels on copies of the latest number, bundled and ready for shipping. More than three thousand names and addresses were thus obtained, including those of Sacco and Vanzetti.

The raid on *Cronaca Sovversiva* marked an important step in the government's efforts to suppress the Galleanist movement. Its chief result, according to Anthony Caminetti, the Commissioner General of Immigration in Washington, was "to secure a considerable quantity of original evidence indicating the activities and whereabouts of a large number of leading anarchists in the country whom it is desired to take into custody."[5]

The first to be detained was Raffaele Schiavina, the twenty-three-year-old manager of the paper. Schiavina was working in the office when the agents arrived. Fair, blond, and neatly dressed, with a quiet dignity that impressed all who met him, he looked more like a teacher or pharmacist than a peasant from Ferrara province, where he had been born, the son of a humble family, in 1894. In fact, he had been trained as a bookkeeper, earning a diploma at a technical high school. Emigrating to the United States in 1913, he settled in the shoe town of Brockton and supported himself by his trade, working as a bookkeeper for a bakery and an insurance company. At that time he considered himself a socialist. At a picnic, however, in the summer of 1914, he met a fellow Italian who gave him Kropotkin's *Memoirs of a Revolutionist*, which struck a deeply responsive chord. Inspired by the author's idealism and nobility of character, Schiavina became an anarchist. He read whatever anarchist literature he could get and subscribed to *Cronaca Sovversiva*. Attendance at lectures by Galleani confirmed him in his new creed.[6]

Galleani, for his own part, recognized the ability of his young disciple. In April 1916 he entrusted Schiavina, now twenty-two years old, with the administration of the paper, a position in which he continued until the raid. That same month Valdinoci was named as the paper's publisher, and the two young militants, both natives of Emilia-Romagna, soon became intimate friends.

As manager of *Cronaca Sovversiva*, Schiavina's duties were many. In charge of daily operations, he handled the entire range of administrative matters, from subscriptions and correspondence to finances and circulation. Galleani, who called Schiavina his "bank book,"[7] relied on him implicitly and, when correcting proofs or similarly engaged, would often spend the night in his room. (Schiavina then lived at 209 Summit Street in Lynn.) After Galleani's arrest in June 1917, Schiavina took the precaution of hiding the subscription list with Augusto Rossi, a trusted comrade in Newton, to whom he would go to prepare each new issue for distribution. Hence Finch was unable to find it during the February 1918 raid.

Beyond all this, Schiavina contributed articles to the paper, invariably written with clarity and grace. He also lectured widely in Massachusetts and neighboring states, holding forth on such topics as "The American Plutocracy," "The Struggle for Existence," and "Who Are the Anarchists and What Do They Want?" In October 1917 an agent from the Boston office of the Bureau of Investigation heard him speak at Milford, behind the bakery owned by Sacco's cousin Nicola, and found him "a clever, fluent speaker," if "somewhat vain." Schiavina, noted the agent, was "an incorrigible, self-confessed anarchist, who has no use for any country."[8]

In September 1916, as we have seen, Schiavina and Mario Buda were arrested during an antiwar rally in Boston. A year later, after delivering an antiwar speech in New York, Schiavina was detained again on charges of obstructing the draft, for which he himself had refused to register. Released on bail, he returned to Massachusetts and resumed his work on *Cronaca Sovversiva*. He did not, like Valdinoci and Buda, seek refuge in Mexico. As Galleani's factotum and alter ego, his presence at Lynn was indispensable. Without him the paper would have collapsed.

Schiavina's failure to go to Mexico, however, was no reflection on his commitment to revolutionary action. His ardor for individual rebellion remained undiminished, and he cleaved heart and soul to the ultra-militants, whom he counted as his closest friends. Investigators in Youngstown found a photograph of Schiavina, which he had sent to Valdinoci in Mexico. Valdinoci, in turn, sent Schiavina a snapshot of himself with Ella Antolini, taken before her departure for Chicago. With Valdinoci and Buda, Schiavina was a steady correspondent, their letters sometimes alluding to dynamite. Because of this, the Bureau of Investigation branded Schiavina a "very dangerous" character and suspected him of playing a role in the Youngstown conspiracy. According to Finch, the best-informed of the agents assigned to the case, Schiavina was "the leader" of the former exiles in Mexico and "no doubt directly connected up with the shipment of the dynamite to Chicago."[9]

Only in part, however, can this conclusion be sustained. On the one hand, to call Schiavina the "leader" of the activists is to overstate his role in the conspiracy. Men like Valdinoci and Buda recognized no leaders—not even Galleani, much less his youthful assistant, with whom they consorted on equal terms. Schiavina, as far as can be determined, never himself wielded a bomb or engaged in any of the violent acts which his doctrine encouraged and professed. "He was more an intellectual than a man of action," a comrade observed.[10] As Galleani's "bank book," however, he was able to provide material support. That he was privy to the conspiracy there can be no doubt, and he probably took part in its preparation. As planner and coordinator he had no equal. In this respect Finch was correct. All roads led to Schiavina.

. . .

Arrested during the February 22 raid, Schiavina was taken to Boston and charged with failure to register for the draft. Roger Baldwin, head of the National Civil Liberties Bureau and himself an opponent of the war who was later jailed as a conscientious objector, wrote to the young Italian with an offer of legal assistance.[11] Schiavina apparently did not reply. In March 1918 he was tried, convicted, and condemned to a year at hard labor, which he served in the East Cambridge jail. The government recommended deportation on completion of sentence.

Schiavina was followed by others. After the raid on *Cronaca Sovversiva*, Finch and his team sifted through the files in an effort to identify the leading militants. Based on their findings, the Department of Labor's Bureau of Immigration issued about one hundred arrest warrants for Galleanists considered liable to deportation. Nearly half of these lived in New England, mainly in the Boston area. While Sacco and Vanzetti were not among them, a number of their closest comrades were, including Adelfo Sanchioni of East Boston, who had gone with them to Mexico, Ferruccio Coacci of Bridgewater, later accused of participating in the South Braintree holdup, and Vincenzo Brini of Plymouth, owner of the house where Vanzetti had boarded. Also included were Giovanni Fruzzetti, Giuseppe Solari, Tugardo Montanari, Vincenzo De Lecce, Alfonso Fagotti, and Giobbe and Irma Sanchini, all of whom were to be deported with Galleani the following year.[12]

Finch and his men had done their job well. All these individuals were dedicated Galleanists, among the most active in the movement. They wrote for *Cronaca Sovversiva*, collected money for "political prisoners," and took part in other important work. "You will note," wrote Anthony Caminetti to H. J. Skeffington, his immigration commissioner in Boston, "that the above named aliens are apparently active workers for the anarchist newspaper, *Cronaca Sovversiva*, that some are writing articles for this paper, others are taking subscriptions for it and transmitting the proceeds of same by money order, while still others are acting as distributing agents. Some time ago the *Cronaca Sovversiva* was denied the use of the mails, but from evidence now obtained it appears that bundles of the paper are sent out by express to agents at various points, who distribute them to subscribers by hand or mail them under individual wrappers."[13] It is worth noting the wording of this letter, dated May 13, 1918, as passages from it were to be used in preparing new deportation legislation aimed at Galleani and his followers.

Caminetti ordered Skeffington to take the aliens into custody on May 15, or as soon thereafter as possible, and to hold hearings aimed "to establish their anarchistic views and activities. As the *Cronaca Sovversiva* is an acknowledged and established anarchist paper and advocates and teaches anarchy, as well as the unlawful destruction of property, it is especially desired that you endeavor to establish at the hearings the facts that these aliens have been writing articles for the paper, taking subscriptions and transmitting the proceeds of same by mail, or acting as agents in the distribution of it. If these facts can be established, the Department [of Labor] is prepared to interpret the same as advocating or teaching anarchy, or the unlawful destruction of property."[14]

To facilitate the roundup, Agent Finch was temporarily assigned to Commissioner Skeffington's office. "Mr. Finch," wrote Caminetti to Skeffington, "will no doubt be able to render you very valuable assistance, as he is thoroughly familiar with not only these cases, but the anarchistic situation generally, having recently spent considerable time in investigations concerning the same for his Department. The Bureau considers these Italian anarchists very dangerous to this country, particularly at the present time, and is therefore anxious that sufficient evidence be secured to justify their removal from the country. It is suggested that you place your most efficient officers on the cases and instruct them to go into the matter thoroughly."[15]

On May 15, accordingly, the dragnet went out. Over the next few days immigration officials, assisted by local police, carried out arrests throughout New England. Similar roundups occurred across the country. All told, some eighty *Cronaca Sovversiva* militants were apprehended, approximately thirty of them in the Boston area. Adelfo Sanchioni was arrested at his home in East Boston, "a hotbed of anarchists," the investigators called it. Ferruccio Coacci, along with five others, was picked up in Bridgewater by Police Chief Michael E. Stewart, who would figure prominently in the case against Sacco and Vanzetti. Vincenzo De Lecce, detained near his home in Athol, Massachusetts, was found to be carrying a book on the manufacture of explosives (apparently *La Salute è in voi!*). According to the authorities, he was on his way to meet Giovanni Eramo, Giuseppe Solari, and a third comrade, who were planning to blow up a factory in Lynn. Eramo, Galleani's printer, was himself swiftly taken into custody, followed in turn by Solari. A search of Solari's rooms in East Boston yielded hundreds of books, pamphlets, and newspapers, all of them relating to anarchism.[16]

Galleani himself was arrested on May 16, a day after the roundup began. He had previously been questioned by immigration officials following the publication of his article "Matricolati!" At that time, Immigration Inspector John A. Ryder had favored an order for deportation but, owing to the size of Galleani's family, recommended that it be held in abeyance. In August 1917 this recommendation was sustained by Commissioner General Caminetti, who held that deportation was not justified by the evidence. Galleani, whose intelligence and bearing consistently impressed his interrogators, was released until further notice. For the next nine months he remained a free man.[17]

Then came his May 1918 arrest. Taken to the immigration station in East Boston, he was subjected to renewed interrogation. Inspector Ryder, however, still doubted that deportation was in order. "He is independent, belongs to no organization," said Ryder. "There is no organization of [Italian] anarchists in the United States any more than there is of Italian atheists."[18] Galleani, as a result, was set free.

Steps were taken, however, to suppress *Cronaca Sovversiva*, which the Justice Department considered the "most dangerous newspaper published in this country."[19] Excluded from the mails the previous year, it had since managed to appear on a more or less regular basis, distributed by express or by private means. On July 18, 1918, it was finally outlawed by the authorities. Galleani, however, refused to acquiesce. No sooner was the paper shut down than its printing presses were dismantled and secretly shipped to Providence, the site of an active Galleanist group. Two further numbers were to make their appearance, still edited by Galleani himself. "Galleani was a real man, a born rebel," Joseph Moro remarked. "He would never give in. He published two more issues of *Cronaca Sovversiva*, reading every word before it was printed. He was very fussy about it."[20] These issues, both illegal, appeared in March and May of 1919, the second on the eve of Galleani's deportation. He was still working on it, adding the final touches, when orders came down to arrest him.

. . .

Until June 14, 1940, when the Bureau of Immigration was transferred to the Department of Justice, deportation was a function of the Department of Labor, whose Secretary was responsible for its administration. Deportation proceedings could not be conducted by the Justice Department or any other government agency. Alien violators could be arrested only on warrants issued by the Secretary of Labor, who had sole authority in the matter; and though the Department of Justice might furnish evidence and participate in investigations, arrests were carried out by officers of the Bureau of Immigration, often with the aid of local police. Deportation cases, moreover, were heard by immigration inspectors, and aliens could be deported only on orders signed by the Secretary of Labor, a post occupied at the time by William B. Wilson.[21]

The government, it should be noted, took the position that deportation was not a criminal proceeding and involved no punishment. It was deemed purely an administrative matter, an exercise of the right of every sovereign state to determine who shall reside within its borders. As such, the niceties of legal procedure did not apply. An alien in an immigration hearing was not entitled to the constitutional protections that he would have received at a criminal trial. His case was handled by immigration officials, who heard the evidence and rendered a decision. Formal indictment, the right to counsel, the right to a speedy trial— none of these pertained, though in March 1919 Secretary Wilson altered the rules to allow the presence of counsel during interrogation.[22] No judge or jury passed on whether the alien held views or was guilty of behavior specified as grounds for deportation. Nor was there any appeal to a court from the decision rendered. The word of the Secretary of Labor was final.[23]

What this meant, in the eyes of the authorities, was that a foreigner who was expelled from the United States, no matter how long he had lived here, no matter that he must leave his family and possessions behind, no matter if his wife and children were American citizens, was not being subjected to punishment or deprived of constitutional rights. Not everyone accepted this position. In an 1893 deportation case Supreme Court Justice David J. Brewer dissented: "Deportation is punishment. It involves first an arrest, a deprival of liberty; and second, a removal from home, from family, from business, from property." He added that "everyone knows that to be forcibly taken away from home and family . . . and sent across the ocean to a distant land is punishment; and that oftentimes the most severe and cruel."[24]

Civil libertarians agreed. Aliens, they insisted, were "persons" within the Fifth Amendment, which established the principle that life, liberty, and property must not be taken away except by "due process of law." The government's position, however, was upheld by the Supreme Court, which ruled that deportation was an administrative action rather than a judicial proceeding. Criticizing this decision, Judge Learned Hand noted that the alien, as a result, faced dangers that were "inherent in a system where prosecutor and judge are one and the ordinary rules which protect the accused are in abeyance." To Zechariah Chafee of Harvard Law School it conjured up *Alice in Wonderland*: " 'I'll be judge, I'll be jury,' said cunning old Fury; 'I'll try the whole cause, and condemn you to death.' "[25]

The authorities, by contrast, welcomed the Supreme Court's decision. Where aliens were involved, the Department of Justice seized on deportation as the most effective means of rooting out sedition. It did so, moreover, precisely because deportation circumvented judicial procedure, with all its uncertainties and delays. It avoided, as one congressman put it, the "long, slow process of the courts."[26] Through cooperation with the Department of Labor, the Department of Justice sought to eliminate troublemakers without the indictments and trials, without the lawyers and appeals, that criminal cases entailed. To purge the nation of alien radicals was the common object of both departments, and to achieve it they worked hand in hand.

Yet the task was not as simple as it seemed. Even as an administrative process, deportation proved no easy matter. Efforts to exclude foreign radicals had begun in the wake of the Haymarket affair, in which anarchists, mostly foreign-born, had been accused of bombing policemen. In 1888 a resolution was proposed in the House of Representatives calling for "the removal of dangerous aliens from the United States," but it failed to carry. The following year a bill was introduced in the Senate making it unlawful for "an avowed anarchist or nihilist or one who is personally hostile to the principles of the Constitution of the United States or to the forms of Government" to enter the country.[27] It too, however, failed to pass. In 1894, following a wave of assassinations in Europe, further bills were introduced in both houses to regulate the admission of undesirable aliens, but the result once again was the same.

It was only with the assassination of President McKinley in September 1901 that these efforts finally bore fruit. Committed by a self-professed anarchist (Leon Czolgosz), the slaying convinced the authorities, as well as the country at large, that anarchism was an intolerable menace. Theodore Roosevelt, the new president, denounced it in his December 1 message to Congress. "Our present immigration laws are unsatisfactory," he declared,and "we should aim to exclude absolutely not only all persons who are known to be believers in anarchistic principles or members of anarchistic societies, but also all persons who are of a low moral tendency or of unsavory reputation." Linking anarchism with criminality, Roosevelt was echoing a view widely expressed since the Haymarket episode and which he himself would later repeat: "The anarchist is the enemy of humanity, the enemy of all mankind, and his is a deeper degree of criminality than any other."[28]

Responding to Roosevelt's appeal, Congress, on March 3, 1903, enacted an immigration law excluding "anarchists, or persons who believe in or advocate the overthrow by force or violence of the Government of the United States, or of all government, or of all forms of law, or the assassination of public officials." Violators of the law were deportable within three years of their arrival in the country.[29]

Thus Congress, at a stroke, abandoned the American tradition of asylum for political refugees, no matter what their opinions. Nor did attitudes soften with the passage of time. The opposite, indeed, occurred after the outbreak of the European war. The immigration act of February 5, 1917, introduced by Representative John L. Burnett of Alabama, penalized not only persons who believed in or advocated the violent overthrow of government or the assassination of public officials, as provided in the 1903 law and reaffirmed in an act of February 20, 1907, but it enlarged upon these measures to include persons who "advocate or teach the duty, necessity, or propriety of the unlawful assaulting or killing of any officer or officers, either of specific individuals or of officers generally, of the Government of the United States or of any other organized government, because of his or their official character, or who advocate or teach the unlawful destruction of property." The law, moreover, made aliens deportable up to five years after entry, rather than three as stipulated in the 1903 and 1907 acts, or without time limit if found to be advocating the destruction of property or the overthrow of the government by force or the assassination of public officials.[30]

It was under this law that the roundups of May 1918 took place, in which Galleani and his followers were arrested. Held for deportation proceedings, they were charged with nearly every offense deemed punishable by expulsion from the country, namely, advocating or teaching anarchy, the forcible overthrow of the government, the assassination of public officials, and the unlawful destruction of property.[31] Yet even the 1917 law, buttressed though it was with additional clauses, proved inadequate for the requirements of deportation. Had the detainees actually been teaching anarchy? Had they in fact called for the overthrow of the government? Where, specifically, had they done so? Where, moreover, had they preached the assassination of public officials or, for that matter, the destruction of property? Such questions were difficult to answer, and, without tangible evidence, violation of the law could not be established. In such circumstances, even the most hostile immigration inspectors were powerless to act. One by one, to the government's consternation, the anarchists were released on bail pending a review of their cases.

The authorities, however, refused to admit defeat. At once they set about strengthening the law in order to facilitate deportation. During May 1918, in consultation with the Department of Justice, officials of the Bureau of Immigration drafted a bill designed to remedy the deficiencies of the 1917 law. Their chief purpose was to define anarchistic activity with greater precision, as well as to remove the five-year limit on expulsion, so that Galleani and other longtime residents would not slip through the net. On May 25 Secretary of Labor Wilson wrote to Congressman Burnett, chairman of the House Committee on Immigration, and to Thomas W. Hardwick, his counterpart in the Senate, requesting them to introduce the bill, "so as to make it possible for this Department to effectually deal with the problems that have arisen concerning aliens of the so-called anarchistic classes."[32]

Both men agreed to cooperate. Burnett, sponsor of the 1917 law and of similar measures to expel objectionable aliens, acted at once, introducing the bill on June 6. After a perfunctory debate, the measure was overwhelmingly approved. One congressman said: "It seems to me the quicker you can get rid of cattle of this kind the better." Another, Albert Johnson of Washington, wanted to exterminate the "rats gnawing at very foundations of our Government."[33]

Senator Hardwick was slower to respond. After a month went by without any action on his part, the Acting Secretary of Labor, John W. Abercrombie, tried to give him a push. "There are now pending before the Department," he wrote Hardwick on July 1, "a large number of cases of aliens who fall within the provisions of this bill and with respect to the possibility of deporting them under the terms of the existing law there is considerable doubt. The matter is regarded as one of great importance, and the Department trusts that it may be possible for the bill to be enacted into law before Congress takes a recess."[34]

Hardwick, however, failed to comply. It was his last term in the Senate before returning to his law practice in Georgia. Refusing to be rushed, he bided his time until after the summer recess. A frustrated Abercrombie, on September 24, sent him another appeal. "Can not something be done to get this bill before the Senate for final consideration?" he wrote. "The need for the legislation becomes more and more apparent as time passes."[35] Meanwhile, Secretary Wilson had himself been writing to Hardwick's colleagues on the committee, urging them to get the bill through. Nearly all expressed enthusiasm for the measure and promised to redouble their efforts. Senator Borah of Idaho was an exception. He wrote to Wilson: "After a party has been in this country and become in some sense a part of us, dwelling here for a number of years, I am utterly opposed to the banishment of these people without the fullest and most complete public hearing." Borah added, however, that he did not intend to obstruct the bill and was ready to have it put to a vote.[36]

On July 26, in anticipation of the bill's enactment, five officials of the Department of Labor, among them Abercrombie and Caminetti, met to discuss the "disposition of cases of alien anarchists, some of whom are Italian anarchists and others Industrial Workers of the World and Russian Union Workers, now pending before the Department." Out of their discussion emerged a six-paragraph memorandum, outlining new criteria for deportation. Two of these paragraphs, echoing Caminetti's letter to Skeffington of May 13, applied specifically to the Galleani movement:

(5) That, in the cases of Italian anarchists, evidence of their continued subscription to the *Cronaca Sovversiva*, the leading anarchist newspaper in the United States, writing articles for publication in this paper, taking subscriptions for it and transmitting the proceeds to the publishers, acting as distributing agents, receipting for bundles of the paper sent by express after it was denied the use of the mails, contributing to or soliciting and remitting money for the anarchist defense fund, and otherwise by their acts as well as by their words assisting in the spreading of the anarchist propaganda, shall be considered good grounds for deportation on the charge of advocating and teaching anarchy in the United States.

(6) That such of these Italian anarchists as are ordered deported shall be removed from the country to Italy as soon as possible or practicable, but that before such removal the matter shall be taken up with the proper Italian authorities.[37]

The same Draconian spirit permeated the new immigration law, which, to the satisfaction of Abercrombie and his colleagues, swept through Congress on a mounting wave of antiradical feeling. The object of the law, signed on October 16, 1918, was "to exclude and expel from the United States aliens who are members of the anarchistic and similar classes." What constituted such classes was spelled out in unprecedented detail:

(a) aliens who are anarchists;

(b) aliens who advise, advocate, or teach, or who are members of, or affiliated with, any organization, society, or group, that advises, advocates, or teaches opposition to all organized government;

(c) aliens who believe in, advise, advocate, or teach, or who are members of, or affiliated with, any organization, association, society, or group, that believes in, advises, advocates, or teaches:

(1) the overthrow by force or violence of the Government of the United States or of all forms of law, or

(2) the duty, necessity, or propriety of the unlawful assaulting or killing of any officer or officers, either of specific individuals or of officers generally, of the Government of the United States or of any other organized government, because of his or their official character, or

(3) the unlawful damage, injury, or destruction of property, or

(4) sabotage;

(d) aliens who write, publish, or cause to be written or published, or who knowingly circulate, distribute, print, or display, or knowingly cause to be circulated, distributed, printed, or displayed, or knowingly have in their possession for the purpose of circulation, distribution, publication, or display, any written or printed matter, advising, advocating, or teaching opposition to all government, or advising, advocating, or teaching:

(1) the overthrow by force or violence of the Government of the United States or of all forms of law, or

(2) the duty, necessity, or propriety of the unlawful assaulting or killing of any officer or officers of the Government of the United States or of any other government, or

(3) the unlawful damage, injury, or destruction of property, or

(4) sabotage;

(e) aliens who are members of, or affiliated with, any organization, association, society, or group, that writes, circulates, distributes, prints, publishes, or displays, or causes to be written, circulated, distributed, printed, published, or displayed, or that has in its possession for the purpose of circulation, distribution, publication, or display, any written or printed matter of the character in subdivision (d).

The new act, as must be apparent, went far beyond any previous legislation. Under its provisions, deportation need no longer be based on individual actions or beliefs. For the first time mere membership in an anarchist organization or possession of anarchist literature for the purpose of propaganda became grounds for eviction from the country. The law, it should be added, removed the five-year limit on expulsion and declared it a felony for any alien to enter the United States after having once been excluded, punishable by imprisonment for up to five years followed again by deportation.[38]

The October 1918 law gave the government a weapon of immense power with which to suppress the Galleani movement. Prior to its enactment, cases of deportation of alien anarchists had been few and far between. From 1911 through 1918 only fourteen noncitizens had been evicted for their anarchist beliefs. Starting in 1919, however, what Assistant Secretary of Labor Louis F. Post termed the "deportations delirium" manifested itself with a vengeance. Although the war had ended in November 1918, pressures for deportation had continued to mount. For during the preceeding years the public had been whipped up by patriotic propaganda to a pitch of nativist excitement, and such emotion could not be instantly turned off. Instead, wartime hatred of Germans transformed itself into peacetime horror of radicals, especially alien radicals. If only the menace of un-Americanism could be eliminated, it was widely felt, the nation would be cleansed, its difficulties and tensions mitigated.

From all over the country came the demand that radicals be ruthlessly suppressed. The government eagerly responded to the call. In February 1919 the Justice Department announced that it would round up an "army of undesirable aliens" for deportation by the Department of Labor. At least seven thousand were expected to be expelled. Before the end of the month the Bureau of Immigration had shipped thirty-nine radicals from the West Coast to Ellis Island, a move widely applauded by the nation's press. "The United States," exulted the *New York World*, "is to be swept clean of its alien anarchists and trouble makers."[39]

High on the list of undesirables remained the *Cronaca Sovversiva* anarchists. Armed with the October 1918 law, the government renewed its efforts to expel Galleani and his adherents. In March 1919, for example, Andrea Ciofalo, who had been in Mexico with the ultra-militants, was arrested at his home in the Bronx and subjected to deportation proceedings. That same month Pietro Marucco, a miner in the "Demolizione" Group of Latrobe, Pennsylvania, was taken from his home and brought to Ellis Island for deportation on the steamship *Duca degli Abruzzi*. Under unexplained circumstances Marucco died in the middle of the Atlantic and had to be buried at sea. His comrades, among them Vanzetti and Coda, cited the incident as an example of government treachery and accused the authorities of foul play.[40]

The chief target, however, was Galleani himself. On November 18, 1918, barely a month after the passage of the new law, Commissioner General Caminetti recommended a warrant for his deportation. Following a hearing before Inspector Ryder, this recommendation was sustained, and on January 27, 1919, Acting Secretary of Labor Abercrombie signed the necessary order. Legal maneuvers delayed action for several months, during which Galleani remained free on bail. Finally, in June 1919, he was taken into custody and brought to the East Boston immigration station.

Arrested with Galleani were eight of his closest associates, regarded by the Bureau of Immigration as being "among the most dangerous aliens yet found within this country."[41] Ordered to be deported with their mentor, they included Giovanni Fruzzetti, a seasoned militant from Carrara and one of the founders of *Cronaca Sovversiva* at Barre in 1903. He had been in the United States for twenty-six years and was the father of ten children, eight of whom were born in Vermont. Throughout *Cronaca*'s existence, Fruzzetti, who at the time of his arrest lived on a farm near Bridgewater, Massachusetts, where anarchist picnics and gatherings took place, had been a frequent contributor to the paper.[42]

Also detained for deportation was Giuseppe Solari, another veteran of the Barre years. Tugardo Montanari was a third, a resident of the United States since 1902. After *Cronaca* was banned from the mails, he went about on his motorcycle, delivering the paper throughout New England. The rest were Vincenzo De Lecce, age thirty-six, who used the pseudonym "Ebreo Errante" (The Wandering Jew); Alfonso Fagotti, twenty-four, imprisoned for stabbing a policeman during the December 6, 1916, riot in Boston's North Square; Raffaele Schiavina, also twenty-four, who had recently completed his sentence for refusing to register for the draft; and Giobbe and Irma Sanchini, accompanied by their two small daughters, both born in New Britain, Connecticut.[43]

All eight were fervent disciples of Galleani, who had helped keep his paper alive in the face of relentless persecution. At their deportation hearings, however, they insisted that they did "not believe in and had not advocated or taught the destruction of government by forcible means," according to an official summary of their testimony, "but were simply believers in the doctrine that government is an unnecessary institution, and had been teaching this doctrine simply as a philosophy."[44] The authorities rejected this claim. On June 24, 1919, the nine anarchists, having been transferred from Boston to Ellis Island, were deported to Italy. They sailed on the *Duca degli Abruzzi*, the same vessel on which Pietro Marucco had met his death. Galleani, at the time of his expulsion, had been living in the United States for eighteen years. He was never to return. Fifty-seven years old, he left behind his wife and five children, three of whom had been born in this country and were American citizens.

CHAPTER NINE

Go-Head!

IN FEBRUARY 1919, on the heels of Galleani's deportation order, the following circular appeared throughout New England:

GO-HEAD!

The senile fossils ruling the United States see red!

Smelling their destruction, they have decided to check the storm by passing the Deportation law affecting all foreign radicals.

We, the American Anarchists, do not protest, for it is futile to waste any energy on feeble minded creatures led by His Majesty Phonograph Wilson.

Do not think that only foreigners are anarchists, we are a great number right here at home.

Deportation will not stop the storm from reaching these shores. The storm is within and very soon will leap and crash and annihilate you in blood and fire.

You have shown no pity to us! We will do likewise.

And deport us! *We will dynamite you!*

Either deport us or free all!

THE AMERICAN ANARCHISTS[1]

Its signature notwithstanding, this circular was unmistakably the work of Italian anarchists of the Galleani school, against whom the new deportation law was directed. The first of three similar leaflets (the others would appear in June 1919 and September 1920), it plays an important part in our story; and among those responsible for its publication, it seems, were Buda and Valdinoci, who had meanwhile returned to Massachusetts.[2]

The leaflet issued a challenge to the authorities: The anarchists will not tolerate repression. Revolution is on the horizon. The government seeks to forestall it by deporting alien radicals. Such efforts are futile. The storm is gathering and will destroy the existing order. Deportation will avail nothing. We will dynamite you in return.

This was no idle threat. Over the past few years a rash of bombings had taken place for which Italian anarchists were responsible. One need only recall the New York City explosions of 1914 (which Galleani all but attributed to his followers), the police station bombing in Boston in December 1916, and the Milwaukee incidents of November 1917 and April 1918, not to mention the 1916 bombing in San Francisco of which Mooney and Billings were convicted but which may in fact have been committed by Italian anarchists. Galleani himself hinted as much during his November 1918 deportation hearing:

Q. Do you recollect, at any time, writing about the arrest of Mooney, the labor man in San Francisco?

A. I think so; we had a special correspondent in San Francisco for this Mooney affair.

Q. I recollect seeing an article which I believe you wrote, saying that Mooney was innocent and that they had not got the right criminal; is that so?

A. Yes.

Q. Would you mind telling us how you get that impression?

A. It isn't an impression that I have that Mooney is innocent; I have the mathematical certitude that he is innocent.

Q. Do you realize that this is of vital interest to the country if you could prove that he is innocent; the Secretary of this Department has put in lots of time on that case and is vitally interested in getting at the facts?

A. It is a very ticklish affair upon which I do not wish to comment; I am positively sure that it was not Mooney who threw the bomb.

Q. That is your personal conviction without evidence?

A. I believe it absolutely.[3]

Another incident, in Philadelphia, merits attention, as it established the pattern of what was to come. On the night of December 30, 1918, the homes of President of the Chamber of Commerce Ernest T. Trigg, Acting Superintendent of Police William B. Mills, and Judge Robert von Moschzisker were heavily damaged by bombs. The bombs, filled with metal slugs, all went off shortly before midnight and within fifteen minutes of each other. Though none of the intended victims were seriously injured, Superintendent Mills was thrown from his bed by the force of the explosion, and a woman standing at the window of her house across the street was struck above the eye by a slug. (Luckily she was not badly hurt.) At each site leaflets were scattered about, denouncing "the priests, the exploiters, the judges and police, and the soldiers," whose rule was declared to be at an end. Copies of the same leaflet were afterwards found at the Post Office Building and at the Federal Building, where a fourth bomb, placed outside the office of United States Attorney Francis Fisher Kane, failed to go off. Anarchists were immediately suspected. For one thing, Judge von Moschzisker, in 1908, had sentenced four Italian anarchists to long terms of imprisonment, and the incident was apparently not forgotten.[4]

With the appearance of the *Go-Head!* flyer, the pace of events accelerated. On February 22, 1919, members of the Grupo Pro Prensa, Spanish anarchists in New York and Philadelphia, were arrested and held for deportation, accused of plotting to assassinate President Wilson. On February 27 Luigi Galleani, himself awaiting deportation, delivered an incendiary speech at Taunton, Massachusetts. The next evening, at the nearby town of Franklin, four Italian anarchists—Silverio De Chellis, his brother Eustachio, Domenico Palumbo, and Amedeo Nanni—blew themselves up while planting a bomb at the mill of the American Woolen Company, where they worked and where a strike was in progress. Windows in the factory were shattered, as well as those in houses nearby, where several persons were injured by flying glass. Concetta De Chellis, Silverio's twenty-three-year-old wife, was in the kitchen of their company-owned house when the blast occurred. "All the dishes fell from the cupboard and broke," she later recalled. "All four were killed—my husband, his brother, and two comrades—all young men in their twenties. The factory was on strike, and they were determined to shut it down. But the bomb had gone off prematurely. I was left with a seven-month-old son. It was a terrible tragedy."[5]

All four men were ardent Galleanists. They had made donations to *Cronaca Sovversiva*, raised funds to aid "political prisoners," and given their children such names as Gori, Vero, and Germinal. All had attended the lecture in Taunton. This gave rise to the suspicion that Galleani had incited their act. Such was the belief of the Bureau of Investigation, which claimed that one of Galleani's daughters, an architecture student, had sketched a map of Franklin on which the American Woolen factory was marked. "It may be possible," speculated an agent at the Boston office, "that the plans for the alleged attempt to blow up the mill were drawn by her, and in carrying out this diabolical scheme the conspirators met an unexpected death."[6]

Whether Galleani had in fact been involved remains debatable. Joseph Moro, who attended the Taunton meeting, flatly denies any connection. An alternate theory, proposed to Sacco by Saverio Piesco, was that the police themselves had planted the bomb in an effort to discredit the strikers. Had not William M. Wood, president of the American Woolen Company, engineered a similar frameup during the Lawrence strike of 1912? Sacco, however, knew better and dismissed the hypothesis as nonsense.[7]

In the wake of the explosion, federal agents descended on Franklin and began a prolonged investigation. "In no time the town was filled with police," Concetta De Chellis recalled. "Everywhere you went you saw police—policemen were hanging from trees." While Moro and others went into hiding, Concetta herself was detained for interrogation. "I was his wife," she explained, "and they wanted information. They held me for three or four months. They questioned me and questioned me, but I told them nothing. 'If you don't talk we will deport you,' they said. 'Do you want me to tell lies?' I asked them. 'Yes,' they said, 'tell us lies, and we will repeat them after you!' They began deportation proceedings. 'Well, you're going back to Italy,' one of them said. But they had no evidence against me. So here I am!"[8]

. . .

The bombing in Franklin occurred during a period of mounting social turmoil, compounded by the difficulties of economic readjustment after the war. In 1919 a wave of strikes spread across the country—the one at Franklin being a case in point—as wages lagged behind a rapidly rising cost of living. In Seattle, during February, a general strike paralyzed the city for five days. The red-baiting mayor, Ole Hanson, a former Progressive who had supported Wilson in 1916, saw the shutdown as part of a vast revolutionary plan. It signaled, he had no doubt, the beginning of a general insurrection, led by "scoundrels who want to take possession of our American Government and try to duplicate the anarchy of Russia." "The time has come," Hanson declared, "for the people in Seattle to show their Americanism. . . . The anarchists in this community shall not rule its affairs." At Hanson's request, federal troops were called in and swiftly brought the strike to an end. Overnight he became a national hero. Newspapers around the country hailed him as a "red-blooded patriot," a man "with a backbone that would serve as a girder in a railroad bridge."[9]

On the morning of April 28, 1919, a small package arrived by mail in Mayor Hanson's office. Postmarked New York City, it was neatly wrapped in brown paper and bore the return address of Gimbel Brothers, Broadway at Thirty-Second and Thirty-Third Streets. On separate faces of the package the words "NOVELTY" and "SAMPLE" were stamped in red letters. Next to the name of the addressee, which had been typed on the wrapper, was the emblem of a mountain climber with a pack on his back and an alpenstock in his hand.

Hanson was in Colorado when the package arrived, fulfilling a speaking engagement, and it was opened by William Langer, a member of his office staff. Within the brown paper was a cardboard box, seven inches long, three inches wide, and two inches deep, itself wrapped in bright green paper. Inside was a homemade bomb, constructed of a small bottle of acid fastened to the top of a wooden cylinder. Breaking the bottle would release the acid and ignite three fulminate-of-mercury caps resting on a stick of dynamite within the cylinder. The bomb, filled with metal slugs, showed evidence of skillful workmanship and careful preparation. Opening the cardboard box should have loosened a coil spring, causing the acid to leak and detonate the explosive. This, however, did not happen. For Langer, as fate would have it, opened the box from the wrong end. As a result, the bottle of acid, instead of trickling onto the fulminating caps, dropped out intact upon the table. The bomb therefore failed to go off, and Langer summoned the police.[10]

This incident was only the beginning. The next day, April 29, an identical package was delivered to the home of former Senator Thomas Hardwick, whose term as chairman of the Committee on Immigration had recently expired. Hardwick, co-sponsor of the 1918 deportation bill, had since returned to his law practice in Atlanta. He was at his office when the package arrived.[11]

The package, mailed to Hardwick's former home at Sandersville, Georgia, had been forwarded to his apartment in Atlanta. Thinking it was a sample of pencils, Mrs. Hardwick asked her black maid, Ethel Williams, to open it. They were both in the kitchen at the time. As the maid unwrapped the parcel, it exploded and blew off her hands. Mrs. Hardwick, standing nearby, was burned about the face and neck. A metal slug cut her upper lip and loosened some of her teeth. Her husband was informed of the explosion. "During the last week of my term in the Senate," he told reporters, "I introduced a bill to prohibit foreign immigration, and I believe it was my efforts to prohibit and restrict immigration that caused some one to make the dastardly attempt on my life."[12]

The Hardwick bombing made headline news across the nation. Charles Kaplan, a clerk in the parcel post division of the New York General Post Office, had finished his shift at midnight and was reading about it in the early morning newspaper as he rode the subway home to the Bronx. The package containing the bomb was described as being about seven by three inches, wrapped in brown paper, and marked with the return address of Gimbel Brothers. Kaplan was struck with terror. Three days before, he had put aside sixteen such packages for insufficient postage. Rushing from the train, he crossed to the downtown platform and hurried back to the post office, located at Eighth Avenue and Thirty-Third Street. There he found the packages where he had left them, neatly stacked in the basement. He notified the night superintendent, Henry Meier, who telephoned William E. Cochran, chief postal inspector for the New York area. Cochran, in turn, summoned the police.[13]

The next day the parcels were examined and found to be identical with those sent to Seattle and Atlanta. All were wrapped in brown paper, carried the Gimbel Brothers label, were marked "NOVELTY" and "SAMPLE," and bore the alpine climber's emblem. All, moreover, contained bombs of the same construction. Further investigation revealed that the packages had been placed in mailboxes on the west side of Manhattan between Twentieth and Thirty-Sixth Streets, the neighborhood of both Gimbel Brothers and the General Post Office. All had been mailed between April 22 and 26, apparently timed to arrive on May 1.

A general alarm was sounded. Orders went out to all post offices to be on watch for similar packages, and three were shortly intercepted. These were addressed to Senator Lee S. Overman of North Carolina, Senator William H. King of Utah, and Frank K. Nebeker, Special Assistant to the Attorney General. Several others, however, had already left the post office and were on the way to their destinations. On April 29, packages were delivered to San Francisco District Attorney Charles M. Fickert and Assistant District Attorney Edward A. Cunha, who had prosecuted the Mooney-Billings case. By then the Seattle bomb was in the news, and Cunha, realizing that his parcel matched the description of Mayor Hanson's, immediately had it removed. Fickert's was also removed, although not disposed of until several days later, when someone noticed that it was leaking acid.[14]

On April 30 yet another package was delivered, this one to Judge Landis in Chicago. Landis, however, was away, and the package lay unopened on his desk for several hours before being recognized for what it was.[15] That same day, moreover, a package arrived at the Gadsden, Alabama, home of Representative John L. Burnett, co-sponsor with Senator Hardwick of the 1918 immigration law. Burnett narrowly escaped injury when the lid on the box stuck as he tried to open it. His suspicions aroused, he called the police, who identified the package as a bomb. Taken to a nearby river bank, it was detonated with a policeman's bullet.[16] Finally, a bizarre incident occurred when a package addressed to Senator Reed Smoot of Utah was returned to Gimbel Brothers for lack of postage. A shipping clerk, undoing it, opened the box, took out the bottle of acid, and examined the percussion caps and wooden cylinder. Deciding that the device must be a "joke," he rewrapped the package, added the necessary postage, and sent it again on its way. Fortunately for Senator Smoot, it was intercepted by postal officials.[17]

In the end, not a single bomb harmed its intended victim. No one was killed and, apart from Senator Hardwick's maid, no one seriously injured. In Washington, Postmaster General Burleson, himself one of the would-be recipients, attributed the lucky outcome to the vigilance of his department's employees, singling out Charles Kaplan for special praise.[18] In all, thirty bombs were accounted for, addressed to some of the nation's most prominent citizens. The list of recipients ran as follows:

1. A. Mitchell Palmer, Attorney General
2. Albert S. Burleson, Postmaster General
3. William H. Lamar, Solicitor of the Post Office Department
4. Oliver Wendell Holmes, Jr., Associate Justice of the U.S. Supreme Court
5. William B. Wilson, Secretary of Labor
6. Anthony Caminetti, Commissioner General of Immigration
7. Frederic C. Howe, Commissioner of Immigration, Port of New York
8. Lee S. Overman, Senator from North Carolina
9. William H. King, Senator from Utah
10. Reed Smoot, Senator from Utah
11. Thomas W. Hardwick, former Senator from Georgia
12. John L. Burnett, Congressman from Alabama
13. Albert Johnson, Congressman from Washington
14. Kenesaw Mountain Landis, U.S. District Judge, Chicago
15. Frank K. Nebeker, Special Assistant to the Attorney General
16. Charles M. Fickert, District Attorney of San Francisco
17. Edward A. Cunha, Assistant District Attorney of San Francisco
18. John F. Hylan, Mayor of New York City
19. Richard E. Enright, Police Commissioner of New York City
20. R. W. Finch, Special Agent, Bureau of Investigation
21. Ole Hanson, Mayor of Seattle
22. William C. Sproul, Governor of Pennsylvania
23. William I. Schaffer, Attorney General of Pennsylvania
24. T. Larry Eyre, State Senator of Pennsylvania
25. John D. Rockefeller
26. J.P. Morgan
27. William M. Wood, President of the American Woolen Company
28. Theodore G. Bilbo, Governor of Mississippi
29. Walter Scott, Mayor of Jackson, Mississippi
30. Frederick Bullmers, editor of Jackson, Mississippi, *Daily News*[19]

Though none of the above was injured, the presence of bombs in the mail alarmed both the authorities and the general public. The sheer audacity of the scheme, combined with the eminence of the intended victims, aroused widespread fear and indignation. Denouncing the culprits as "human vermin," newspapers clamored for action. To congressmen and public officials it was "the most widespread assassination conspiracy in the history of the country." Mayor Hanson, himself a bomb target, criticized federal policy towards radicals as "skim milk, weak, vacillating and changeable." With his usual bluster he called on Washington to "buck up and hang or incarcerate for life all the anarchists." "If the Government doesn't clean them up," he added, "I will."[20]

Like Hanson, the Department of Justice considered radicals the likeliest perpetrators and viewed the bombs as part of a wider conspiracy to sow panic in preparation for a revolutionary takeover. Radicals and their sympathizers, by contrast, saw the episode as a deliberate "frame-up" by the authorities to provide an excuse for further repressions.[21] To some it seemed inconceivable that anyone but a lunatic or an *agent provocateur* would be indifferent to the fact that men like J. P. Morgan and John D. Rockefeller do not open their own mail, so that the likeliest victims would be their employees, as was the case with Ethel Williams in Atlanta.

The authorities, at all events, mounted a determined investigation. Postal inspectors, Bureau of Investigation agents, the bomb squad of the New York police department, and bomb experts of the fire department combined their energies to locate the culprits. Errors in the names typed on the packages—Mitchell A. Palmer, Oliver Wendel Holmes, Frederick C. Howe—led to the belief that foreigners might be responsible.[22] Additional clues were available: the paper in which the packages were wrapped, the Gimbel address labels, the alpine emblem, the cardboard boxes, the green paper covering them. Not least, there were the bombs themselves, most of which remained intact.

Each day brought significant "new leads," and arrests were declared to be "imminent." In time, the manufacturer of the green paper was found—Louis De Jonge & Company of 69 Duane Street, New York—who supplied officials with a list of customers. It was also discovered where the cardboard boxes had been made. The investigators were making "good progress," the public was told, and would presently run down the assassins.[23] Nothing, however, resulted. Each new clue led to a dead end. The perpetrators were never identified, and the case remained unsolved.

Yet someone had marked thirty individuals for death on May 1. Who was it? A glance at the list of targets reveals the answer. Palmer, as

Attorney General, headed the Department of Justice and its Bureau of Investigation, the nemesis of anarchists and other leftists. Burleson, as Postmaster General, and Lamar, his department's solicitor, had banned radical newspapers, including *Cronaca Sovversiva*, from the mails. Caminetti had recommended warrants for the deportation of Galleani and his associates, and Secretary Wilson had duly signed them. Howe, in the same connection, was the immigration commissioner at Ellis Island, from where most deportations took place.

All of these men, in one way or another, had offended the Galleanists. The same was true of the others on the list. Senator Hardwick and Representative Burnett had introduced the law which made the deportations possible, while Congressman Johnson and Senators Overman, King, and Smoot, all bitter opponents of radicalism and labor, had been its most outspoken supporters, detesting the "rats," as Johnson dubbed alien subversives, gnawing at the foundations of the government.[24]

Burnett, in addition, harbored a special animus against Italians, whom he associated with criminality and sedition. Of the 1912 Lawrence strike he had said: "The educated blackhander led the long procession and stirred them to frenzy and to crime, but behind him was the horde of illiterates with a bomb in one hand and a banner in the other on which was inscribed 'No God, No Law, No Master.' "[25] To remedy the situation, he had called for a four-year moratorium on immigration, which failed, however, to attract much support. Overman, in a similar vein, had introduced a bill—buried in the Senate—under which no one might display the red flag or advocate, in writing or speech, the violent overthrow of the American government or the destruction of industrial property. Overman, moreover, had chaired a subcommittee of the Senate Judiciary Committee which conducted hearings on bolshevism and anarchism. King, a member of the committee, had branded the IWW a "treasonable organization," and Solicitor Lamar had recently testified before the committee on the existence of a radical plot to overthrow the United States government.[26]

As for the remainder of the bomb targets, Justice Holmes, in March 1919, had delivered the opinion of the Supreme Court affirming the conviction of E. V. Debs under the Espionage Act. Judge Landis, in Chicago, was a particular object of loathing for his role in the Antolini and IWW trials the previous year. Frank Nebeker, a corporation lawyer from Utah, had acted as chief prosecutor at the IWW trial, while Fickert and Cunha, as has been noted, had prosecuted Mooney and Billings.

And so on down the list. Mayor Hanson had summoned troops to crush the Seattle general strike. Mayor Hylan of New York had ordered raids on radical meeting halls, including that of the Union of Russian

Workers, an anarcho-syndicalist group. "These alien firebrands with their revolutionary doctrines," he had exulted, "are rapidly being deported and will no longer have an opportunity to pollute the free breezes of America."[27] Richard Enright, Hylan's police commissioner, had supervised the raids, conducting what he called "a determined movement against the anarchists in this city." Enright had also enforced a ban on all displays of the red flag, "emblematic of unbridled license and anarchy," as he put it. "It, like the black flag, represents everything that is repulsive to the ideals of our civilization and the principles upon which our Government is founded."[28]

In Pennsylvania, where Galleani had once been arrested for inciting to riot, Governor Sproul, Attorney General Schaffer, and Senator Eyre had been instrumental in enacting anti-sedition legislation designed to stamp out radicalism in the state. Similar laws had been enacted in Mississippi, where bombs were sent to Governor Bilbo, Mayor Scott, and Frederick Bullmers. As for John D. Rockefeller and J. P. Morgan, they stood as the embodiment of capitalist exploitation, "robber barons" of the American plutocracy, symbols of everything the anarchists opposed. William M. Wood, president of the American Woolen Company, fell into the same category, a *bête noire* since the Lawrence dispute of 1912, when he engineered a frame-up against the strikers.

Although conclusive evidence is lacking, these facts point unmistakably in one direction. Far from being part of a widespread revolutionary conspiracy, the package bombs were the work of a small group of Galleanists, centered in New York and Massachusetts. Precisely which individuals were involved is difficult if not impossible to determine. Possibly Galleani himself, more so Schiavina, had a hand in selecting the victims. Almost certainly, however, they played no role in the physical preparations. This task was left to more practiced hands, such as those of Valdinoci and Buda, who, making good their threat of retaliation, struck back with a vengeance against their tormentors. "You have shown no pity to us! We will do likewise. And deport us! *We will dynamite you!*" Such had been their challenge to the authorities, and now they had begun to act.

Nor did they act at random. Unlike their counterparts in Europe, they did not indulge in indiscriminate violence, such as bombings of crowded theaters and cafés. On the contrary, they chose their victims with utmost care, drawing up an "enemies list," in the terminology of a later era. Each target, as Attorney General Palmer noted, represented "state authority or counter-radical activities of some nature."[29] Nearly all, moreover, had antagonized the Galleanists in some specific and unforgivable way: suppressing their paper, arresting their comrades, and the like. The perpetrators knew exactly whom they were after. No matter that Howe and Holmes were men of liberal and moderate temper, in contrast to the Overmans and Burnetts. In the eyes of the Galleanists there was little to distinguish between conservatives and reformers. All were pillars of the established order, willing servants of government and capital, cogs in the machinery of injustice and repression.

Should any doubt remain concerning the identity of the plotters, the appearance of Finch on the list must serve to dispel it. Why should a lowly Bureau of Investigation operative be selected as a target? The answer seems clear. It was Finch, during the early weeks of 1918, who had arrested Scussel in Youngstown and dogged Valdinoci through the mining camps along the Ohio River. In February 1918, moreover, he had led the raid on *Cronaca Sovversiva* and arrested Raffaele Schiavina. Transferred to New York, he had continued his pursuit of the Galleanists, arresting Andrea Ciofalo in the Bronx.[30] Ciofalo, released on bail, may have been a party to the bomb conspiracy. Like Valdinoci and Schiavina, he bore a special grudge against Agent Finch.

When the parcel bearing his name turned up in the mails, Finch's intrepidity wavered. More than anyone, perhaps, he knew the manner of men with whom he was dealing. Young, full of life, he had no intention of getting himself blown up. He therefore went into seclusion. "By reason of ill health," as his supervisor put it,[31] Finch took refuge in the mountains of southern Pennsylvania. He was not to emerge for several weeks. Remaining incommunicado, he refused to answer mail or have any contact with the outside world. When he finally reappeared, during the summer of 1919, he left the Bureau of Investigation for safer pastures, becoming chief investigator of the Lusk Committee, which was probing sedition in New York State.[32]

. . .

The package bombs had scarcely become news when May 1 arrived, the date on which they were intended to reach their victims. Primo Maggio, "sweet Easter of the workers," as Pietro Gori described it, was a red-letter day on the anarchist calendar. For the Galleanists it was a time not only to commemorate their fallen comrades, the Haymarket martyrs, but also "to unleash the ragged ones" against their oppressors.[33] Disturbances indeed erupted in several cities, most notably Cleveland, New York, and Boston. They were not triggered by anarchists, however, but by patriotic citizens, including ex-soldiers and sailors dressed in their uniforms, who attempted to break up radical meetings. In Cleveland, where a major riot occurred, a May Day parade was attacked by soldiers, civilians, and policemen, who inflicted frightful injuries on the marchers. A detective shot and killed a man carrying a red flag; more than forty others were hurt. The police arrested 106 demonstrators, most of them aliens, and charged them with inciting the trouble. Not a single assailant, either soldier or civilian, was detained.[34]

Comparable rioting took place in New York, where a mob of soldiers and sailors sacked the offices of the socialist *Call* on Fourth Avenue. Breaking furniture and using chair legs as clubs, they beat everybody in sight. Seven members of the staff had to be hospitalized, and the rest were driven into the street. At the same time, men in uniform invaded a meeting for Tom Mooney at Carnegie Hall, while others stormed the Russian People's House on East Fifteenth Street, headquarters of the Union of Russian Workers, and forced a gathering to sing the "Star-Spangled Banner" while they smashed equipment and destroyed newspapers and books.

The worst of the disturbances occurred in Boston, where paraders in the Roxbury district were set upon by indignant bystanders, chased through the streets, beaten, trampled, and kicked. The police assisted the rioters in attacking the marchers, arresting some and clubbing them in their wagons. Shots were exchanged; four men, including two policemen, were struck by bullets. A police captain died of a heart attack during the melee.[35]

All told, 116 paraders were arrested. Among them were William James Sidis, the son of the Harvard psychopathologist Boris Sidis, and H.W.L. Dana, a grandson of Henry Wadsworth Longfellow and Richard Henry Dana, along with Luigi Salvucci of Quincy and Antonio Cesarini of Roxbury, a longtime comrade of Buda and Valdinoci. Tried before Judge Albert F. Hayden of the Roxbury Municipal Court, fourteen demonstrators were found guilty of disturbing the peace and sentenced to prison terms ranging up to eighteen months. After passing sentence, Judge Hayden castigated "these foreigners who think they can get away with their doctrines in this country." It was "foolish to Americanize people who do not believe in our Government," he declared. "If I could have my way I would send them and their families back to the country from which they came."[36] His remarks did not go unnoticed.

CHAPTER TEN

Plain Words

THE SHOCK created by the package bombs had barely worn off when a new round of bombings took place. On Monday night, June 2, 1919, there were explosions in seven cities: Boston, New York, Paterson, Philadelphia, Pittsburgh, Cleveland, and Washington. Unlike the May 1 bombs, which had been sent in the mail, these were delivered by hand to the doors of the intended victims. Moreover, they were much more powerful than the package bombs, each containing about twenty pounds of dynamite. In this respect they resembled the Milwaukee and Philadelphia bombs of the previous year. As in Philadelphia, furthermore, the explosions occurred almost simultaneously, all going off within an hour of midnight. Once again, moreover, copies of a leaflet were found at every site, clearly pointing to an organized conspiracy. The bombings, as one police official put it, were "all done and planned by the same outfit."[1]

The leaflet, printed on pink paper measuring seven by eleven inches, bore the title *Plain Words* and was signed "The Anarchist Fighters." Riddled with errors in spelling and grammar and showing other signs of hasty production, it provided an important clue and occupied a central place in the investigation that followed. In due course, as we will see, it would lead to the identity of the conspirators.

Both in style and in content, *Plain Words* resembled the leaflet *Go-Head!*, which had been circulated in Massachusetts a few months earlier. The signatures—"The American Anarchists," "The Anarchist Fighters"—were similar and their messages essentially the same. You have provoked the fight, *Plain Words* declared. You have jailed, deported, and murdered us. We accept the challenge. The workers have a right to defend themselves; and since their presses have been silenced and their voices muzzled, we mean to speak for them with dynamite. "There will have to be bloodshed; we will not dodge; there will have to be murder: we will kill, because it is necessary; there will have to be destruction; we will destroy to rid the world of your tyrannical institutions." We shall not rest until your downfall is complete and the laboring masses have taken possession of all that rightfully belongs to them. We know how to stand against you and how to take care of ourselves. Your hounds and police will never get us all; and our numbers are growing. "Long live social revolution! down with tyranny. THE ANARCHIST FIGHTERS."[2]

In Boston there were two explosions. Shortly before midnight, a bomb made of iron pipe stuffed with dynamite and shrapnel almost demolished the home of Judge Albert F. Hayden, who had dealt so harshly with the May Day paraders. The severity of the sentences, noted a Bureau of Investigation agent, "undoubtedly furnished the motive for the bomb."[3] The device, placed on the porch, wrecked the front and sides of the house, located at 11 Wayne Street in Roxbury. Copies of *Plain Words* were found amid the debris. The force of the explosion damaged five adjacent dwellings and shattered every window on the street. No one, however, was hurt. Except for Hayden's twenty-year-old son Malcolm, the family was away at its summer house in Plymouth. Malcolm, who had been out for the evening, was on his way home and was only a few hundred feet from the house when the blast occurred. He saw a car speeding away just before the explosion.[4]

Shortly after midnight, a similar bomb tore off the side of a house in suburban Newtonville belonging to State Representative Leland W. Powers. The bomb, which went off at 12:02 A.M., had been planted at the rear of the house near a cellar window. Powers, his two children, and two maids were at home at the time, and his four-year-old daughter Polly was cut on the cheek by flying glass. The injury, however, was not serious. Again copies of *Plain Words* were scattered about.[5]

There were two likely motives for the attack. First, Powers's father, ex-Congressman Samuel L. Powers, was attorney for William M. Wood of the American Woolen Company, at whose mills the strikes at Lawrence and Franklin had taken place. (Woods, as already related, was the recipient of a May 1 bomb.) More important, Powers himself, as a member of the Massachusetts legislature, had introduced an anti-sedition bill prescribing up to three years imprisonment for anyone who, either in speech or print, "advocates, advises, counsels or incites assault upon any public official, or the killing of any person, or the unlawful destruction of real or personal property, or the overthrow by force or violence of the government of the Commonwealth."[6] The bill, modeled on the federal immigration act so odious to the Galleanists, became law on May 28, 1919, five days before the bombing.

Less than an hour after the Powers incident, a nearly identical bombing took place in New York City. At precisely 12:55 A.M.—a clock in the hallway stopped running—an explosion occurred at 151 East Sixty-First Street, an elegant brownstone owned by Judge Charles C. Nott, Jr., of the municipal court. The bomb, planted at the basement entrance, tore the vestibule completely away and blew in sections of the first and second floors. Every window in the house was shattered and furniture was hurled into the street, where copies of *Plain Words* were strewn about. Neighboring houses were badly damaged and windows broken for blocks around.

At the time of the explosion Judge Nott and his three daughters were away at their summer home in Connecticut. Mrs. Nott, however, asleep on the second floor, was thrown from her bed and lay stunned on the floor for several minutes. A caretaker and his family, likewise flung from their beds, suffered from shock and minor bruises. More terrible was the fate of a seventy-year-old security guard, William Boehner, who for the past ten years had been employed as a watchman for a number of private dwellings on the block. He was blown to pieces by the blast.[7]

Immediately following the explosion, New York police officials, having received reports of similar incidents in other cities, sent special details to the homes of prominent citizens who might also be in jeopardy. For this purpose hundreds of officers were pressed into service on short notice. The police were puzzled, however, by the selection of Judge Nott as a target. All the other victims, including the two in Boston, had been involved in recent antiradical activities. This did not seem to be the case with Judge Nott. A highly respected jurist, noted for his fairness on the bench,[8] he appeared to have no particular enemies. Why then had he been marked for assassination? The bombers, police officials speculated, had confused him with Federal Judge John C. Knox, who had presided at several trials involving radicals.

The police, however, were overlooking an important fact. Four years earlier, in 1915, Nott had condemned Frank Abarno and Carmine Carbone of the Bresci Group to long jail terms for conspiring to blow up St. Patrick's Cathedral. It was Nott himself who noticed the connection. "I do not consider this a personal attack on me, but a preconcerted effort on the part of the Bolshevists, I.W.W. and associated radical organizations to terrorize the judiciary and the upholders of law and order in this country," he told reporters. "Of course," he added in a flash of understanding, "the bomb may be the work of friends of the two anarchists who attempted to place a bomb in St. Patrick's Cathedral and were sentenced to prison by me."[9]

This once realized, Amedeo Polignani, the bomb squad detective who had exposed (or entrapped, as the anarchists claimed) Abarno and Carbone, was assigned to the investigation. With Polignani involved, the police announced, "important developments might be expected hourly."[10] It proved to be an idle boast.

Meanwhile yet another bombing had occurred across the river in Paterson, New Jersey, a stronghold of Italian anarchism since the 1880s. The intended victim was Harry Klotz, president of the Suanhna

Silk Company, whose apartment in the fashionable Eastside district of the city was heavily damaged. Klotz, a member of the executive board of the Paterson manufacturers' association, had opposed the granting of a forty-four hour work week to the silk operatives, and this was thought to be the motive for the assault.[11] The bomb went off at 12:20 A.M. Klotz and his family, who occupied the downstairs floor of a two-family house, were away in the country at the time. The upstairs inhabitants, who owned the building, managed to escape injury, though residents in adjacent homes were thrown from their beds. Two men, apparently Italian, had been seen in the vicinity shortly before the explosion, and copies of *Plain Words* were found at the scene.[12]

The rest of the bombings followed the same pattern. In Philadelphia, however, the target was not a private residence but rather the Church of Our Lady of Victory, where a bomb went off in the rectory at 11:15 P.M. Copies of *Plain Words* were scattered on the lawn. About twenty minutes later a second explosion occurred at the home of a jeweler in another section of town, but this seems to have been an unrelated incident (for one thing, no telltale leaflets were found) and was soon dropped from the Bureau of Investigation's list.[13]

In Pittsburgh blasts occurred at the homes of Judge W.H.S. Thompson of the United States District Court and Inspector W. W. Sibray of the Bureau of Immigration, both of whom had presided at cases against alien radicals. Neither man was injured (Judge Thompson indeed was away at the time), though damage to their houses was considerable. *Plain Words* circulars, needless to add, were found at both sites.[14]

At Cleveland a pipe bomb filled with shrapnel partly wrecked the home of Mayor Harry L. Davis. Davis had not only suppressed the recent May Day demonstration but had collaborated in the prosecution of Scussel and Coda the previous year.[15] The bomb exploded at 11:30 P.M. at the rear of the house, while the mayor, his wife, and several friends were seated on the front lawn. The Davis's three-year-old son and a maid were in the house at the time, but neither was hurt. Two men had been seen about the premises shortly before the explosion; one carried a suitcase which police believed contained the bomb. Copies of *Plain Words* were discovered nearby.

The following day an angry mayor instructed his police department to "go the limit" to remove radical agitators from the city. "There is no need to disclose the methods by which this is to be accomplished," he declared, "but we will rid Cleveland of this red terror." Davis, moreover, called on Washington to exert itself towards the same end. "We will get them out of Cleveland," he vowed, "but we want to see the country rid of them. Such things as happened last night and the sending of bombs by post must waken the federal government to the necessity also for tightening up on immigration. This country cannot be made the dumping ground for the Red propagandists of Europe."[16]

. . .

The most sensational of the June 2 bombings occurred in Washington, D.C., at the home of Attorney General Palmer. Palmer occupied a handsome three-story house at 2132 R Street, Northwest. The neighborhood, populated by congressmen, diplomats, and government officials, was one of the most exclusive in the capital. Two doors away lived Senator Claude A. Swanson of Virginia, and Admiral Theodore F. Jewell was directly opposite, flanked by the Norwegian minister, H. H. Bryn, and Assistant Secretary of the Navy Franklin Roosevelt.

Palmer had already been the target of one of the May 1 package bombs. He now had another narrow escape. At 11:15 P.M., as he and his wife were preparing for bed, they heard a thump at the door followed by a tremendous explosion. The entire house trembled, its front was demolished, and all the windows were blown in. Up and down the block, houses shook and windows shattered from the blast. Representative Mansfield of Texas, who had just turned into R Street on his way home, was struck by flying debris. Several residents of nearby houses, including the Norwegian minister's son, were hurled from their beds by the explosion. Palmer himself, dressed in pajamas, had been reading near a front window of an upstairs room and was showered with broken glass. His wife, the sole other occupant of the house besides servants, was in a rear bedroom. Miraculously no one was hurt.[17]

Following the blast, neighbors, some of them in night clothes, rushed from their homes to determine the cause. A pungent acid smell hung like a vapor in the streets. Franklin Roosevelt, after telephoning the police, went to offer Palmer assistance. He reported that the Attorney General, a lifelong Quaker, was so shaken that he had lapsed into the language of his childhood: "He was 'theeing' and 'thouing' me all over the place—'thank thee, Franklin!' and all that." Within minutes an army of policemen, firemen, and federal agents were at the scene. At the same time, policemen and soldiers were placed at the homes of William B. Wilson, Anthony Caminetti, Albert S. Burleson, and other officials in possible danger.[18]

Beginning that night and continuing for two days, the police searched the area around Palmer's residence. At once they made a startling discovery. The bomb had blown to bits the man who had carried it. Fragments of his body were scattered all over the neighborhood. "We could not take a step without seeing or feeling the grinding of a piece of flesh," said Sergeant Burlingame, in charge of the search. "The house across the street was plastered with the pieces."[19] The man's left leg below the knee was discovered on the doorstep of a house opposite the Attorney General's and part of his right leg some fifty feet away. On an automobile parked a block away and smeared with blood another piece of a leg was found. So great was the force of the explosion that part of the torso, mingled with scorched and bloodstained shreds of clothing, was found hanging on the cornice of a house on S Street more than a block away.[20]

Further search revealed additional fragments. Pieces of flesh and bone, sent flying through the air, were found in houses up and down the block. Bits of human debris had penetrated windows across the street, and a section of spinal column fell into the bedroom of the Norwegian minister's son, where it landed after smearing the casement with blood. No fingers or parts of hands were found, eliminating the possibility of fingerprint identification; a supposed thumb picked up in the street turned out to be a toe.[21]

Two theories were put forward to explain the grisly fate of the bomber. The first was that, in his excitement and the darkness of the hour, he had tripped on a coping several feet from the front door, where he had intended to place the bomb, and the impact of his fall had triggered the explosion. According to the second, a defective or improperly timed fuse had set off the bomb prematurely as he touched a match to it. The latter was considered the more likely hypothesis, since not a finger or part of a hand remained intact. Clarence Hall, chief explosives expert of the Bureau of Mines, was "of the positive opinion that the dynamiter did not stumble or fall on top of the explosive." Pointing to the fact that the middle step of three front steps was destroyed by the blast, Hall added: "I think he was on the steps at the time of the explosion, with the explosive probably in his hands. He no doubt was on the step that was broken in two by the impact. He had not timed his fuse properly, and it was a premature explosion."[22]

Spurred by the discovery of the bomber, the police redoubled their efforts to locate evidence. Assisted by firemen, they scoured the entire neighborhood and gathered up all the clues that they could find. These included two handguns (a .32-caliber Smith & Wesson revolver and a .32-caliber Colt automatic), remnants of a black imitation leather grip, an Italian-English dictionary, a tan sandal-type shoe with rubber heel, shreds of a black pinstripe suit, a blue polka-dot bow tie, and a piece of a black derby. Although the revolver was loaded and undamaged, the Colt was picked up in fragments found scattered from one end of the street to the other, the cartridges having exploded in the magazine. The derby was found in a tree in front of Palmer's house. In a hole in the sidewalk the police found a second hat, a grey fedora, size 7-1/4, bearing the label of De Luca Brothers, Hatters, 919 South Eighth Street, Philadelphia.

Because there were two hats and two guns, it was at first thought that two men were involved. Rumor spread, moreover, that two left legs had been found at the scene. (With such pedal equipment, quipped the *Washington Star*, no wonder the bomber stumbled and fell!) Before long, however, the police definitely established that only one person had been killed. Nor was there any evidence of accomplices.[23]

Further clues were discovered: a pair of brown socks; a ribbed undershirt; fragments of a white pinstripe shirt; a piece of a shirt collar, size 15-1/2, bearing the laundry mark "K.B."; a white linen handkerchief with the same laundry mark; two railroad conductor's checks, one purchased on the 7:10 P.M. train from Philadelphia to Washington, the other on an earlier train from New York to Philadelphia; and a bloodstained District of Columbia streetcar transfer, punched at 10:30 P.M.[24] In addition, some fifty copies of *Plain Words* were found scattered about the area.

A final clue, discovered on June 3, proved to be of crucial importance. At daybreak a large segment of the bomber's scalp was found on the roof of a house on S Street and taken down by firemen searching for evidence. The hair, "dark and bushy," as the press described it, aroused more than usual interest. "Almost the entire scalp has been found," announced Police Superintendent Raymond W. Pullman, "and the hair, because of its peculiarity, shows that it was perhaps one of the man's most principal features in his physical make-up."[25]

Taken to a French hairdresser, the scalp was mounted on a wooden block. In front, the hair was six to eight inches long and curly. Before beginning his work, the hairdresser had said: "Show me the man's hair and I will tell you his nationality." After completing his examination he concluded that the man was Italian and was twenty-six to twenty-eight years old.[26]

On the basis of the evidence obtained, the authorities made some deductions. The bomber was a tall, well-set-up young man, possibly Italian, with abundant curly black hair. At the time of the explosion he was wearing a derby hat, a black worsted suit with green stripes, a white shirt with stripes of different colors, a polka-dot bow tie, brown socks, and tan sandals. Having traveled from New York to Philadelphia, where he purchased a grey fedora at De Luca Brothers, he boarded the 7:10 P.M. Baltimore & Ohio train for Washington on June 2, arriving at Union Station at 10 o'clock. Armed with a Smith & Wesson revolver and a Colt automatic, he carried a black grip containing some twenty pounds of dynamite. The grip also contained an Italian-English dictionary, a supply of *Plain Words*, and a fedora hat, which he had changed on the train for the derby. (The conductor's check was found in the hatband of the fedora.) From Union Station he went directly to Palmer's residence, taking a Connecticut Avenue streetcar. At about 11 P.M. he was seen alighting at R Street, a few blocks from the Attorney General's home. There his destiny awaited him.

· · ·

Although the authorities had not identified him, the dead man was Carlo Valdinoci. Only twenty-four years old, he had been a marked man since 1917. Indicted as publisher of *Cronaca Sovversiva*, hunted for his role in the Youngstown conspiracy, he had eluded the grasp of his pursuers. A deportation warrant had been issued for him, but he could not be found and apprehended.[27] Among his comrades he had thus become a legend. His ability to avoid capture had endowed him with a mantle of invincibility and was a source of inspiration and pride. Despite his youth, he was referred to in terms bordering on veneration. To Giuseppe Sberna he was "one of the best in the movement," ready to help his comrades in any way. Rosina Sacco considered him "a great anarchist."[28] That the great anarchist should have met such a terrible end is an unexpected irony of our story. Courageous, resourceful, he had led a seemingly charmed life. His luck, however, had run out. Valdinoci was no more; only the legend remained.

When last heard from, Valdinoci had been in West Virginia, with Special Agent Finch in hot pursuit. That was in February 1918, sixteen months before his death. Making good his escape, he apparently doubled back and headed for Milwaukee, where on April 15 the attempt was made to blow up the house of District Attorney Zabel. A day or two later Valdinoci returned to Massachusetts, finding sanctuary with Augusto Rossi.

Rossi, a building contractor in Newton, where he lived at 304 Adams Street, was an "angel" of the Galleani movement. Thirty-eight years old, a native of Pesaro in the Marche, he furnished shelter, jobs, and money to help his comrades. In 1916, for instance, he had put up $1,200 bail for Mario Buda, arrested in the North Square demonstration. The following year he provided travel funds (sixty dollars each) for comrades going to Mexico. When Galleani was arrested for publishing "Matricolati!" it was at Rossi's house that the *Cronaca Sovversiva* subscription list was concealed. Schiavina, it might be added, received his mail at the Rossi home, where he prepared the paper for distribution.

Rossi's house, as the Bureau of Investigation later described it, was "a well-known rendezvous for Italian anarchists."[29] A haven for militants on the run, it was a natural place for Valdinoci to take refuge. Rossi's twelve-year-old daughter, Fiorina, instantly fell in love with him. "He was a handsome fellow with dark hair," she recalled many years later. "We had three vacant rooms in the front. He and his brother and sister came to live with us."[30] Joining them was Domenico Ricci, their *paesano* from Gambettola, who had previously shared their quarters in Roxbury and Somerville.

It was in Boston and its suburbs that plans for the 1919 bombings were laid. Mario Buda, having likewise returned from the midwest, joined forces with Valdinoci to resume their vendetta against the authorities. Although the complete story of the bomb plot remains to be unraveled, the following seems a plausible reconstruction. Originating with Valdinoci and Buda, it centered in the Gruppo Autonomo of East Boston, which met in the hall of the Italian Independent Naturalization Club on Maverick Square. The members of this group, some forty or fifty strong, came from all over the Boston area—Coacci from Quincy, Sacco from Stoughton, Vanzetti from Plymouth, and so on. In one way or another, nearly all of them took part in the conspiracy. Apart from Valdinoci and Buda, however, the most important participant appears to have been Nicola Recchi, a twenty-nine-year-old bricklayer from the Marche, who had lost his left hand while making bombs.[31]

Once preparations had been completed, Valdinoci left Boston and traveled south, stopping in New York, Paterson, and Philadelphia, before going on to Washington. We may assume that he carried bombs for every location.[32] He also brought a supply of *Plain Words*, to be deposited at the site of each explosion. These—the bombs and the leaflets—he left with local comrades, with whom the scheme had been coordinated and who, at the appointed hour, were to carry out the actual bombings. In New York, it seems probable, these consisted of members of the Bresci Group, including Ciofalo, Sberna, and Conti, who had been with Valdinoci in Mexico. In Paterson his likeliest confederates were Ruggero Baccini and Filippo Caci, members of a group of direct-actionists called "Gli Insorti" (The Insurgents).[33] Baccini, a baker by trade, hailed from the province of Rome, while Caci, like Valdinoci, was a carpenter from the Romagna and may have been his principal contact. Washington, the climax of the whole venture, Valdinoci had reserved for himself. Handsomely dressed, armed to the teeth, he could hardly have foreseen what lay ahead.

As Valdinoci traveled south, another Boston anarchist—most probably Buda—went west on a similar mission. He too carried bombs, as well as a bundle of *Plain Words*, stopping at Pittsburgh and Cleveland. Chicago, it appears, was also to have been the scene of a bombing, Judge Landis being the probable target. The authorities, however, apparently were tipped off. For on May 29, four days before the explosions, a meeting of Italian anarchists in Chicago was raided by the police, nipping the *attentat* in the bud.[34] Among those arrested was Umberto Colarossi, a comrade of Valdinoci and Buda's. Buda himself, however, managed to slip away.

The foregoing account must be regarded as tentative, given the scarcity of reliable evidence. Yet its general outlines may be accepted as accurate. That an organized bomb plot existed is beyond dispute; the simultaneity of the explosions in widely separated locations, coupled with the presence of *Plain Words* at each, constitutes sufficient proof. Anarchists who had been in Mexico played a key role in the conspiracy, Buda and Valdinoci among them. Though evidence is lacking, one suspects that Coda and Scussel were similarly implicated, possibly in Pittsburgh or Cleveland.

Much, however, remains obscure. How many people were involved in the conspiracy? Was Galleani himself among them? What, if any, was the role of Schiavina, or, for that matter, of Sacco and Vanzetti? Where were the bombs made? What was the relationship between the May 1 and June 2 bombings? Were they carried out by the same individuals?

Definitive replies are lacking. To the last question, however, the answer is yes, if Giuseppe Sberna may be credited. Both sets of bombings, he told an undercover informant, were "only one affair, done by the same people." The authorities shared this view. "The same gang," said Acting Police Superintendent William Mills of Philadelphia, "prepared the bombs used here and in Washington. The bombs mailed in New York undoubtedly were the product of this crowd."[35] Mills went further, claiming that the group had also been responsible for the December 1918 bombings in his city, of which he himself had been a target. Sberna would not have contradicted him.

As for the number of conspirators, as many as fifty or sixty may have been involved. Their roles, however, varied greatly. Some made bombs (for example, Recchi); some planted them (Valdinoci). Some wrote and printed leaflets. Others provided shelter (Rossi) or a place where the bombs could be made (Luigi Falsini). Still others furnished moral and financial support. A few, of course, performed several of these functions—Valdinoci and Buda, for instance. Others confined themselves to offering advice or taking part in the selection of targets.

Whatever their roles, all lived in constant fear of detection, of being discovered by federal agents or local police. Forced into an underground existence, they were wary of strangers, of informants and spies, who might seek to infiltrate their ranks. They never forgot Detective Polignani; their fear of penetration was ever present.

At the same time, however, they relished the excitement of underground life and took satisfaction in outwitting the authorities. A mere handful of determined men, tilting with the state apparatus, they habitually went about armed in case of trouble. It was an unequal struggle, to be sure, a lashing-out of the weak against the strong. Yet, despite their insignificant forces, it might still be possible to strike a damaging blow, weakening and disorganizing the government. The romanticism of clandestine action had a fatal attraction for these ultra-militants, who boldly courted martyrdom and danger. There were some for whom the impulse to violence was especially strong, who were ready to immolate others as well as themselves in the service of what they believed to be just. Buda and Valdinoci fell into this category. Inspired by Galleani's rhetoric and by the hope of imminent redemption, they confronted death with defiance and exaltation.

To men of this stamp the use of violence was no crime; it was a justifiable response to persecution. They considered themselves at war with the forces of government and capital; and if they resorted to bombs it was as the government used bombs, for the purposes of war. Capitalism, as they saw it, was a gigantic system of banditry and killing; by comparison the violence used to combat it seemed trivial. A few innocent people might suffer, but in warfare this was unavoidable. Violence, in any event, was one of the few weapons at their disposal, a necessary means of self-defense. How else were they to retaliate against their tormentors? As Vanzetti expressed it: "I would my blood to prevent the sheading of blood, but neither the abyss nor the earth, nor the heavens, have a law which condemns the self-defense."[36]

It is certainly true that, by its repressive and often illegal actions, the government bore no little responsibility for creating the conditions for armed retaliation. Mounting persecution intensified the zeal of the Galleanists and strengthened their determination to resist. Each deportation and each round of arrests and imprisonments, often after farcical trials, provoked further attempts to exact vengeance. "Death for death," declared Vanzetti. "We fight for the triumph of a cause—not to be crushed by the keepers—we will never win without vanquishing them. They are mercenary, we idealist; should a free man or a rebel allow them to do what they please to him?"[37]

· · ·

Was Vanzetti himself involved in the conspiracy? Though the evidence is far from satisfactory, the answer almost certainly is yes. The same holds true for Sacco. Both were ultra-militants, believers in armed retaliation. They carried guns; they had gone to Mexico; they were associated with known participants in the plot. Buda reckoned them the "best friends" he had in America, and they were equally close to Valdinoci, whom Rosina Sacco hailed as "a great anarchist." After his death, it is worth noting, his sister Assunta went to live with the Saccos and remained with them for many years.[38]

Sacco and Vanzetti lived at once a legal and a clandestine existence—one of earning a living and devotion to family, on the one hand, and of underground insurgency, on the other. Of the two men, Sacco is usually regarded as the more militant. "He loved flowers," noted Gardner Jackson. "He loved birds. . . . He was also a terrific hater."[39] Counting himself among the "good soldiers" of the revolution, he was ready to do battle for his cause. "I have try to hit at the centres of this decrebid society," he later declared. As his comrade Aldino Felicani put it: "Sacco was a man of action, more of a violent anarchist [than Vanzetti]. He was capable of throwing a bomb. I would say yes to that without any hesitation. But not Vanzetti."[40]

Felicani was not alone in this assessment. "I never saw Vanzetti with a gun," said Beltrando Brini. "There were no guns in our house—and certainly no dynamite. His room was an open book. There was no paraphernalia or equipment for carrying out violent deeds. I never saw him perform any act other than what I would describe as gentle and considerate."[41] To the civil libertarian Roger Baldwin, who visited both men in prison, Vanzetti seemed "such an innocent really," an "open, naive fellow." Sacco, by contrast, was "passionate, suspicious and militant."[42]

Yet such a distinction is misleading. Those who perceived Vanzetti as a mere dreamer, as a chatterer rather than a man of action, saw only one side of his complex personality. He liked to talk, it is true. But he was every bit as militant as Sacco. He was also better acquainted with Galleani, who told Edward Holton James that he knew Vanzetti well but had met Sacco only twice.[43] The Bureau of Investigation had obtained a photograph of Vanzetti together with his mentor. Being self-employed and without domestic encumbrances, Vanzetti was better able to participate in the conspiracy than Sacco, the family man and steady worker. And it was Vanzetti, according to one of the numerous unsubstantiated rumors that swirled about the case, who made the bomb that blew up Judge Hayden's house in Roxbury.[44]

The rumor is cited by Upton Sinclair in his "documentary novel" *Boston*. In 1923, at defense attorney Fred Moore's urging, Sinclair visited Vanzetti in prison and thought him "a wise and gentle working-class philosopher." He was "one of the wisest and kindest persons I ever knew," wrote Sinclair, "and I thought him as incapable of murder as I was."[45] Four years later, after the executions of Vanzetti and

Sacco, Sinclair returned to Boston to gather material for his novel about the case. He interviewed scores of people and visited all the relevant scenes, checking and rechecking the smallest details. He also enlisted young writers associated with the Defense Committee—Catherine Huntington, Tom O'Connor, Creighton Hill—to verify facts and provide additional data. His research was "impressively thorough," as his biographer put it, and the resulting book was distinguished by a factual accuracy and an understanding of the characters unsurpassed in later works, historical and fictional alike. More than sixty years after its appearance, it remains a classic treatment of the case. As Sinclair himself rightly thought, "the novel will outlive me."[46]

Sinclair came to Boston convinced that Sacco and Vanzetti had been merely "philosophical anarchists" and that there was "no possibility of either being guilty of any crime," as he wrote to Creighton Hill.[47] In the course of his research, however, he found that he had been mistaken. Collecting his data and "talking to everyone who had been close to the case," including many of Sacco and Vanzetti's comrades, he concluded that, far from being pacifists, both men "believed in and taught violence." Of this Sinclair was "absolutely certain."[48] "I became convinced from many different sources," he wrote, "that Vanzetti was not the pacifist he was reported under the necessity of defense propaganda. He was, like many fanatics, a dual personality, and when he was roused by the social conflict he was a very dangerous man."[49]

The same applied equally to Sacco. Both, Sinclair was convinced, had been involved with dynamite. He had learned this from their comrades in Boston. On his way back home to California, Sinclair stopped at Denver to confer with Fred Moore, who corroborated his findings. Sinclair was faced with a dilemma. He had no wish to tarnish the image of Sacco and Vanzetti by connecting them with bombs. During their years in prison he had sought to obtain justice for the two men; it would be hard to exaggerate the intensity of his feelings or the degree of his outrage over their persecution. Their execution he called "the most shocking crime that has been committed in American history" since the assassination of Lincoln. It would "empoison our public life for a generation," he said. "To the workers of the whole world it is a warning to get organized and check the bloodlust of capitalism."[50] But his chief obligation was to the truth. "Men commit acts of violence in the class war, and they deny it, and the radical movement defends them," he wrote to Hill. He could not follow suit. Refusing to perpetuate "the legend of Sacco and Vanzetti as pacifists,"[51] he proceeded to tell what he knew.

Having received his information in confidence, Sinclair refrained from documentation. His conclusions, however, are unassailable. Nevertheless, when *Boston* came out in 1928, Sinclair was taken to task by sympathizers of the executed men for suggesting that they had been dynamiters. Among the harshest critics were the anarchists. *The Road to Freedom*, an anarchist journal in New York, complained that the book would be read by thousands of people entirely unfamiliar with anarchist ideals who would be led to accept "the definition of the police and paid scribes of the yellow press that the cardinal creed of anarchism is physical force." Sinclair replied that he had the facts for every statement in his book, but were he to provide them they would not be printed and he would be accused of counterrevolutionary conduct. Would you like me, he asked the editor, to contribute to your columns an article of intimate revelations on the subject of "Anarchists I have known and their attitude to dynamite"?[52] *The Road to Freedom* did not respond.

That Sacco and Vanzetti were involved in the 1919 bombings is, indeed, a virtual certainty, and further evidence of their complicity will emerge in later chapters of this book. Their precise roles, however, remain unclear. Questioned about this, their comrade Joseph Moro refused to answer. "It can only hurt the movement," he said.[53] Concetta De Chellis was more forthcoming. "Well, they were both in Mexico," she answered. "They were all activists there. They were both strong with the Idea. They didn't stop to think what might happen to them. 'If I die, I die, but that's what I wanted to do.' That was the way they felt. They were different types: Sacco was excitable; Vanzetti was calm, thoughtful, and explained everything. But both were militants and were ready to do whatever was necessary to achieve their beautiful Idea."[54]

PART THREE

Repression

CHAPTER ELEVEN

Manhunt

THE BOMBINGS of June 2, 1919, triggered a wave of fear and anger across the land. These obviously coordinated explosions, their shocking, outrageous character, the bloodthirsty language of the leaflets ("There will have to be bloodshed; we will not dodge; there will have to be murder: we will kill . . . we will destroy to rid the world of your tyrannical institutions") fueled passions that had been building for months and gave a powerful impetus to the unfolding Red Scare. Nor did federal spokesmen allay the panic. The Department of Justice, on the contrary, contributed to it by declaring the bombings to be part of an organized conspiracy, nationwide in scope, to overthrow the American government. Further explosions were predicted. A campaign had been launched, as one official put it, to start "a reign of terror in the United States."[1]

Yet the notion of a powerful conspiracy was only a myth. For all the labor militancy of the period, for all the widespread strikes and disturbances, the chances of a nationwide rising were remote. No radical organization—least of all the anarchists—presented a serious threat; and it was folly to believe that the planting of a few bombs heralded a full-scale social upheaval. Still, the fear of revolution gripped public opinion. Citizens and congressmen alike lumped all radicals—anarchists, communists, IWWs—into a single "red menace" and demanded appropriate action. "All the forces of government," declared Senator Overman regarding the bombers, "should be utilized to run these fellows down and hang them."[2]

The hue and cry was taken up in the press, which called for "a few treatments in the electric chair." Blaming the explosions on alien radicals, the *Buffalo Evening News* declared that "the time has come to teach these foreigners a little Americanism." When the Attorney General of the United States becomes the target for assassination, echoed the *New York Times*, "it is time for the federal government to employ every resource at its command to find out who these venomous miscreants are, to trace them to their hiding places, to destroy them."[3]

Palmer himself, having come close to losing his life, needed little persuasion to act. At once unnerved and infuriated by the bombing of his house, he vowed to bring the perpetrators to account. On June 3, the day after the explosions, he issued the following statement: "The outrages of last night indicate nothing but the lawless attempt of an anarchist element in the population to terrorize the country and thus stay the hand of government. This they have utterly failed to do. The purposes of the Department of Justice are the same today as yesterday. These attacks by bomb throwers will only increase and extend the activities of our crime detecting forces. We are determined now, as heretofore, that organized crime directed against organized government in this country shall be stopped."[4]

Palmer was as good as his word. That very day he set in motion a sweeping reorganization of the Justice Department's antiradical operations. His first step was to name Francis P. Garvan, the department's Alien Property Custodian, a post previously held by Palmer, as Assistant Attorney General in overall charge of the investigation and prosecution of subversives. To direct the Bureau of Investigation, Palmer recruited William J. Flynn, former head of the Secret Service and a well-known private investigator. Palmer hailed Flynn as "the greatest anarchist expert in the United States," one who "knows all men of that class" and can "pretty nearly call them by name."[5] Frank Burke, manager of the Secret Service's New York office, was named as Flynn's assistant, with the title of "Chief." At the same time John T. Creighton, who had headed the investigative section of the War Trades Board, became Special Assistant to the Attorney General to help Garvan.

With the aid of these experienced investigators, Palmer began drawing up plans for an all-out crusade against radicalism. On June 6, referring to the recent bombings, he promised to end once and for all "these lawless attempts to intimidate and injure, if not destroy, organized government in this country."[6] To accomplish this goal, he asked Congress for a special appropriation of $500,000, beyond the $1,500,000 already appropriated for fiscal year 1920. To justify his need for additional funds, Palmer claimed to have information of an imminent attempt by radicals "to rise up and destroy the government at one fell swoop."[7] The date on which this was to occur, rumored to be July 4, would mark the beginning of a revolution throughout the country of which the June 2 bombings had been the prelude. July 4 came and went without incident, yet Congress granted Palmer the money.

Palmer was now able to beef up the Justice Department, and especially the Bureau of Investigation, which conducted the department's criminal probes. When created in 1908, the Bureau was a minor agency with only twenty-four operatives, authorized to investigate interstate commerce and antitrust cases only. America's involvement in the war and attendant concerns about espionage and subversion spurred the Bureau's expansion, both in size and activity. At war's end the number of agents approached six hundred, assigned to branches throughout the country.[8] Under Palmer, who took office in March 1919, this trend accelerated, the complement of agents being augmented by immigration officials, postal inspectors, treasury investigators, and the like. By 1920 the Bureau of Investigation was on its way to becoming the powerful FBI of J. Edgar Hoover fame.

Hoover himself, at the time of the bombings, was a twenty-four-year-old clerk in the Justice Department's Alien Registration Section. Young, energetic, ambitious, he was already known as an expert on radicalism. Looking for men with his qualifications, Palmer, on Garvan's recommendation, promoted him to the rank of Special Assistant to the Attorney General, assigned to the dynamite investigation. Hoover's principal task was to head the General Intelligence Division (also known as the Radical Division), created by Palmer as part of his shake-up of the department's investigative services.

Under Hoover's supervision, the General Intelligence Division, which he would direct until his appointment as head of the Bureau of Investigation in 1924, became the fastest-growing unit in the department. Its purpose was to gather and coordinate information on radicalism around the country. To facilitate this task, Hoover oversaw the creation of an index file of names of more than 200,000 radical agitators, groups, and publications. Radical literature of all kinds—books, pamphlets, newspapers, flysheets—was systematically collected, almost "by the bale," as Palmer put it. More than 600 periodicals—251 of them classified as "ultra-radical"—were filed and indexed. Many were rendered into English by a corps of forty translators, who prepared daily reports on their contents.[9]

The chief object of all this activity was to track down the bomb conspirators. Flynn, as head of the Bureau of Investigation, was charged with accomplishing this mission. Swinging into action, he directed his agents to launch "a vigorous and comprehensive investigation of anarchistic and similar classes, Bolshevism and kindred agitations advocating change in the present form of government by force and violence, the promotion of sedition and revolution, bomb throwers and similar activities." Agents and informers were instructed to report "all information of every nature, whether hearsay or otherwise."[10]

To help in the search Flynn enlisted the support of immigration officials, local police, and private individuals and groups. In response, officers with experience with radicals, among them Detectives Polignani and Correlli of the New York City bomb squad, were at once dispatched to the capital.[11] On June 29 Flynn spoke before a conference of police chiefs from eastern and midwestern cities, who met to discuss cooperative measures. Assuring them that the bomb plotters would be found, he in turn was assured of their assistance. Before long more than sixty suspects had been taken into custody for questioning. "There is not an anarchist haunt that is not under federal or local surveillance," boasted Flynn.[12]

Though Flynn remained nominally in command, the investigation soon came under the direction of Hoover, with the General Intelligence Division as its nerve center. All reports and correspondence dealing with the bombings ended up on Hoover's desk. Even when addressed to Flynn, they were labeled "Attention Mr. Hoover" and afterwards marked "Noted J.E.H." Hoover, as one of his biographers put it, was "in complete charge of planning the attack on radicalism during the summer and fall of 1919."[13]

To Hoover, as to Flynn and his assistants, anarchists seemed the likeliest perpetrators of both the May and June 1919 bombings. According to the General Intelligence Division, there were four especially dangerous groups: L'Era Nuova of Paterson, Pro Prensa of Philadelphia, the circle around Emma Goldman and Alexander Berkman, and the followers of Luigi Galleani, "the notorious Italian anarchist," as Hoover called him.[14] All these groups, it was felt, were capable of the dynamite conspiracy.

Before long, however, suspicion focused primarily on the Galleanists, and especially those in eastern Massachusetts. It was the consensus of the investigators, noted Special Agent William J. West of Boston, that Galleani was "the moving spirit of Italian anarchists in this section of the country" and that "if it is believed the present bombing outrages were the work of Italian anarchists, that Galleani would surely be acquainted with the perpetrators of these outrages." Another agent went even further, suggesting that Galleani himself had "conceived and directed" the plot.[15] It is surprising, then, that Palmer should have made no attempt to stop Galleani's deportation, scheduled for June 24. On June 23 Bureau of Investigation agents appeared at the East Boston immigration station and questioned Galleani and his eight associates. Nothing was learned, however. They admitted only that they were anarchists, and "believed in the overthrow of the government and did not believe in church or state."[16] Thereupon the expulsions proceeded as planned.

While this was taking place, Bureau of Investigation operatives scoured the country for Galleanists who had previously been involved with explosives. John Scussel, in August, was located in Philadelphia, where he had lived before going to Mexico. Appearing at his door, an agent, without identifying himself, asked for the whereabouts of Carlo Lodi, claiming to have "an important message" for him. Scussel, of course, said nothing. Two months later, Emilio Coda was found, employed in a coal mine in western Pennsylvania. Approached by an agent from the Pittsburgh office, he "evaded all questions and seemed very hostile."[17] In an effort to avoid detection, Coda had grown a goatee and mustache, which only made him more conspicuous. Soon afterwards he shaved off the beard, keeping the mustache for the rest of his days.

In the meantime a determined effort was made to identify the Washington bomber. Agents set out to trace remains found at the scene: his bow tie, a shoe, a piece of his suit, his shirt collar, a handkerchief, two hats, two guns, and an Italian-English dictionary. The tie, with its unique design, seemed a good clue, and the manufacturer was soon found in New York. He said that he had made up an even dozen to test their selling potential. A single haberdasher had purchased the lot. When agents visited his shop they found that he had disposed of only one. Unfortunately he could give only a vague description of the buyer.[18]

Meanwhile other agents were working on the shoe, a sandal with a rubber heel. The heel had recently been repaired, and the agents found the cobbler who had fixed it. A description of the wearer was obtained, which tallied in part with that supplied by the haberdasher. While this was going on, investigators determined that the cloth in the bomber's suit had been made at the Livingston Wool Mills in New York. Eventually an East Side tailor was found who recalled making a suit of such material. He remembered the customer well and provided a good description. In general it matched the other two.[19]

The other leads proved less fruitful. At De Luca Brothers in Philadelphia no one could recall the purchaser of the grey felt hat. As for the derby, it was found to have been bought at Lamson & Hubbard of Boston, but no record of the customer had been preserved. Nor could the shirt collar and handkerchief, both bearing the "K.B." laundry mark, be traced; and the Italian-English dictionary (published in Milan in 1913) likewise led nowhere.[20]

An investigation of the handguns yielded similar results. The Smith & Wesson revolver, recovered intact, had been sold by the manufacturer to a hardware store in Philadelphia, which shipped it to another store in South Carolina. There, apparently, it was sold, but no record of the sale could be found. The Colt automatic likewise led to a dead end. Blown to pieces in the explosion, it was painstakingly reassembled and the serial number (276442) recovered. The Bureau of Investigation traced it to the Iver Johnson Sporting Goods Company of Boston, where it was sold on April 20, 1918. Records listed the purchaser as Luigi Caliseri of 24 Wright Street, Medford, who gave his occupation as carpenter. No such address existed, however, and no one of that name could be found.[21]

Despite these setbacks, the inquiry proceeded apace. On September 2, 1919, the police chief of Newton, Massachusetts, turned over to Agent West of Boston a package of index cards containing the names and addresses of the subscribers to *Cronaca Sovversiva*. This subscription list, which the Bureau of Investigation had been unable to find during its raid in February 1918, had been found concealed in a barn on the property of Augusto Rossi, who had left Newton a month before.[22] Though no revelations were obtained, the discovery lifted the morale of the investigators.

Particular efforts were made to trace the origin of *Plain Words*, the sole piece of evidence linking all of the bombings together. Identical in color, paper, and type, the flyers obviously had a common source. The task, however, was to find it. Isabel Tuska, a linguist for the War Department, subjected the text to a careful analysis. Construction of the sentences, she noted, indicated a Latin origin; the word "pedestal" was spelled "piedistal," as in the Italian *piedistallo*; the words "vulgar" and "usurped" were used in the Italian manner; and the phrase "the history of every day" was a literal rendering of the Italian expression *la storia di ogni giorno*, meaning an everyday occurrence. From such evidence, she concluded, the leaflet "appears to be either translated from the Italian or to have been written by one whose native tongue is Italian."[23] This bolstered the suspicion that Italians were responsible for the bombings.

Beyond this, however, no significant progress was made. By the fall of 1919 the investigation had begun to flounder. From time to time reports appeared in the newspapers that the case was nearing solution, the plotters were known, and arrests were in the offing. But the arrests never came. For all the abundant leads, the identity of the culprits remained a mystery.

The difficulty, at least in part, lay within the Department of Justice itself. In spite of Palmer's reshuffling, the investigative services remained inadequate. For one thing, the quality of the operatives left much to be desired. A few competent agents stood out—Clabaugh, De-Woody, West, and above all Finch. But men of their caliber were rare. The majority, ill trained and informed, seemed as unable to distinguish between anarchists, communists, and socialists as the public at large, lumping them together and associating them with a monstrous assault on American society. All too often, moreover, they filed wordy and exaggerated reports, if only to show how vigorous they were in carrying out their assignments.

These reports, conspicuous for the unfounded gossip, rumors, allegations, and sheer nonsense that they contained, poured into Washington from every section of the country. So vast was the quantity of material, and so indiscriminately was it collected, that it proved beyond the powers of the General Intelligence Division to absorb it. Important documents were lost or mislaid. A case in point was *La Salute è in voi!*, Galleani's dynamite manual, a copy of which had been seized in 1918 and was needed in the investigation. Try as he might, Hoover was unable to locate it, and feverish efforts to find another were unavailing.[24] A related problem was the lack of personnel equipped with Italian, so that significant material went unnoticed and key names were garbled and confused (Nicola Recchi became "Giuseppe" Recchi, who was mistaken for Domenico Ricci). As for Hoover's vaunted card file, it proved of limited use, both because of the volume of material and the shortcomings of the agents.

Above all, perhaps, the investigation lacked a guiding intelligence sufficiently honed and informed to put all the pieces together. Neither Garvan nor Flynn was adequate to the task. Nor, for that matter, was Hoover. As coordinator of the enterprise he comes off badly. Dogged and tenacious though he was, he lacked the sophisticated knowledge and depth of understanding that might have led to a swift resolution. As it was, the investigation lagged and threatened to peter out entirely.

Then suddenly the outlook brightened. From undercover informants the Bureau of Investigation received information that pointed to one of two men as the Washington bomber, Umberto Colarossi or Carlo Valdinoci. Both were active disciples of Galleani. Both were about the same age (Colarossi was a few months older than Valdinoci), both had been in Mexico, both had black hair and wore sandals. Agent Feri Felix Weiss of the Boston office thought it possible that Colarossi was the man who bought the Colt automatic at Iver Johnson's and that the clerk, unfamiliar with Italian names, recorded it as "Caliseri."[25] (The theory later proved erroneous.) Weiss, accompanied by Frank Bellucci, a confidential informant, inquired after Colarossi at his last suspected place of residence in Roxbury. They presented themselves as undertakers, seeking to identify a certain dead body as that of Colarossi, in order to obtain insurance money for his family. No information was secured. Using a similar ruse, Agent M. R. Valkenburgh interviewed Ercole Valdinoci at his place of employment in Cambridge. Ercole denied knowing Colarossi, even though former neighbors in Somerville had told Valkenburgh that the two were "very close friends." He was equally silent regarding his brother.[26]

Colarossi was eliminated as a candidate when agents learned that he had been arrested in Chicago a few days before the Washington bombing; still very much alive, he was being held in custody awaiting deportation. Suspicions now concentrated on Valdinoci. From informants it was established that he not only fit the description of the bomber, but he had vanished without a trace after telling a friend, about a week before the explosion, that he was planning a trip to Washington. One undercover agent, about whom more will be said later, reported being told by Italian anarchists in New York that it was definitely Valdinoci who had blown himself up at Palmer's house.[27]

By the spring of 1920 the Justice Department felt confident enough that it had identified the bomber for Palmer to so inform the Congress.[28] Although definite proof was never obtained, evidence secured over the next two years confirmed the identification beyond any doubt. Regarding the Colt automatic, for example, Agents West and DiLillo made an important discovery. Although the address given by the purchaser, 24 Wright Street, Medford, did not exist, there was, as it happened, a lot at 24 Rye Street, which had been assessed in 1917 in the name of Domenico Ricci. Ricci, at that time, lived with Valdinoci in Somerville, and the two were partners in a consortium of Italian construction workers, mostly anarchists from the Romagna, who had bought the lot as a site for houses. The buyer of the pistol, apparently Ricci or Valdinoci, had given the Rye Street address to the salesman. As for the buyer's name, Caliseri, it turned out to be the surname of Ricci's uncle in Gambettola and was listed on immigration records as that of his nearest relative.[29]

In the opinion of Agent West, it was Valdinoci himself who had purchased the automatic. West further believed that the laundry mark "K.B." found on the bomber's shirt collar and handkerchief could have been "used by a person unfamiliar with the Italian language as the initials of Carlo Valdinoci." In addition, West emphasized, reports submitted after the Washington explosion indicated that the person killed was a tall Italian "with black, bushy hair," a description matching that of Valdinoci obtained during the Youngstown investigation.[30]

Encouraged by these findings, West continued his search for evidence, devoting considerable time and energy to the task. In November 1922 his efforts bore fruit. More than three years after the bombing, he located Assunta Valdinoci, then living with Rosina Sacco and her children. Having abandoned Stoughton following the trial, they now occupied a house in Millis, where Assunta worked at the Herman Shoe Company. It was there that West went to see her. Questioned about her brother, Assunta responded warily. She had not seen him in several years, she stated. "She further said," reported West, "that since her brother CARLO VALDINOCI left this vicinity no one, including herself and family, had heard anything from him; admitted it seemed strange that no one in her family had received even a post-card from him, because he usually communicated with them, but could not account for his failure to communicate with her in the United States or his family in Italy." West then asked whether it was not a fact that Carlo was dead. Assunta replied, as West recorded, that "she did not believe that he was dead, had never heard that he was dead, and thought he might be in South America or some other country." Asked to describe him, she said that he was "a tall, young man, 27 or 28 years of age, clean shaven, with very black, curly hair." This description, noted West, "coincides with that sent out at the time of the bomb explosion." These facts, West concluded, offered substantiation "that the person killed in Washington, D.C., on June 2, 1919, was CARLO VALDINOCI."[31]

.   .   .

The dynamite conspiracy, in the meantime, had revived the old stereotype of the anarchist as bomb thrower and assassin. Ever since the Haymarket affair, the image of the anarchist as a wild-eyed, foreign-looking maniac, with a bomb in one hand and a pistol in the other, had been embedded in the popular mind. Berkman's shooting of Frick, followed by Czolgosz's assassination of McKinley, had reinforced this image, as had the Mooney-Billings and Lexington Avenue explosions. Anarchism, in the same connection, was widely associated with immorality and crime. A movement which professed its unyielding opposition to accepted values was painted by the authorities as inherently lawless, capable of every depravity and vice. Its adherents, far from seeking to transform society for the benefit of the workers, were nothing but madmen and fanatics bent on the desecration of law and order. As Attorney General Palmer put it: "The Red Movement is not a righteous or honest protest against alleged defects in our present political and economic organization of society. . . . It is a distinctly criminal and dishonest movement in the desire to obtain possession of other people's property by violence and robbery." "Each and every adherent of this movement," he added, "is a potential murderer or a potential thief, and deserves no consideration."[32]

The fact that most anarchists were foreigners intensified feelings against them. Nativist sentiment ran high, accentuated by the European war. In 1915 President Wilson had warned of "hyphenated Americans" who "have poured the poison of disloyalty into the very arteries of our national life. . . . Such creatures of passion, disloyalty and anarchy must be crushed out." Palmer now echoed these views. "Out of the sly and crafty eyes of many of them," he said of radical aliens, "leap cupidity, cruelty, insanity and crime; from their lopsided faces, sloping brows, and misshapen features may be recognized the unmistakable criminal type."[33]

Articulated in these words were all the fears and hatreds, all the prejudice and paranoia, that equated foreign-born radicals with subversives. Such feelings were far from uncommon. Small wonder that, following the June 2, 1919, explosions, a renewed outcry went up for wholesale deportations. One clergyman called for the expulsion of alien revolutionaries "in ships of stone with sails of lead, with the wrath of God for a breeze and with hell for their first port." In the same vein, a California speaker suggested that "these murderous wild beasts of our otherwise blessed Republic should be given a pint of meal and a bottle of water and shoved out into the ocean on a raft, when the wind is blowing seaward." Senator McKellar of Tennessee even favored sending native-born Americans with radical beliefs to a penal colony in Guam.[34]

Palmer and Secretary of Labor Wilson were eager to oblige, at least as far as aliens were concerned. On June 10, 1919, Wilson wrote to Palmer proposing a conference between officials of their departments to work out "the best means of effecting thorough co-operation."[35] A week later Palmer held an all-day meeting with Garvan, Flynn, and their assistants at which a strategy of mass deportations was devised. After the meeting Palmer spoke to the press. The recent bombings, he declared, were part of a plot by "alien anarchists" to overthrow the government. Those, he said, "who can not or will not live the life of Americans under our institutions . . . should go back to the countries from which they came."[36]

The scene was thus set for the notorious "Palmer raids." Before going into action, however, the Attorney General made a last attempt to dispose of alien radicals through criminal prosecution. In July 1919 he brought conspiracy charges against three Spanish anarchists of the Ariete Group of Buffalo, New York, which had issued a leaflet urging American workers to rise up and overthrow the government. ("Proclaim yourselves openly an anarchist," it read. "Let the revolution come! Hail to the immaculate and redeeming anarchy!")[37] Palmer's efforts backfired. On July 24 U.S. District Judge John R. Hazel threw out the case on grounds that the leaflet constituted propaganda, not conspiracy. Failing in the courts, Palmer reverted to deportation as the best means to eliminate the radical menace. He vowed to "tear out the radical seeds that have entangled American ideas in their poisonous theories," warning that revolution was "licking at the altars of the churches, leaping into the belfry of the school bell, crawling into the sacred corners of American homes, seeking to replace marriage vows with libertine laws, burning up the foundations of society."[38]

Starting in November 1919, the Department of Justice launched a series of nationwide roundups of alien radicals with a view towards expelling them from the country. Assisted by local police, Bureau of Investigation agents swooped down on meeting places and private homes, seizing papers and possessions and arresting everybody in sight. The raids were carried out with utter indifference to legality. Thousands of aliens were taken into custody and subjected to brutal treatment. More often than not, the arrests were made without warrants. Men were beaten without provocation. Locked in overcrowded jails and detention centers, they were held for weeks, and in some cases months, while their families suffered anxiety and hardship. In Detroit some eight hundred suspected radicals were kept under abominable conditions in the city's antiquated Federal Building, only to be cleared of any wrongdoing. One Pittsburgh man was missing for almost a month before he was located, having been arrested without warrant and held incommunicado without explanation or bail. In some instances those who tried to visit the prisoners were themselves thrown behind bars on the theory that they too must be subversives.[39]

Between November 1919 and February 1920, when the arrests tapered off, about three thousand aliens underwent deportation proceedings. Of these some eight hundred, including many anarchists, were ultimately evicted from the country, though few had ever committed a criminal offense. On December 21, 1919, 249 deportees, among them Emma Goldman and Alexander Berkman, were put aboard the *Buford* and shipped to Russia. Some left behind wives and children, who attempted to break through the Ellis Island ferry gates to join them. The press nevertheless rejoiced. "It is to be hoped and expected," said the *Cleveland Plain Dealer*, "that other vessels, larger, more commodious, carrying similar cargoes, will follow in her wake."[40]

This statement echoed the feelings of the general public. In many quarters the repression of radicals, however brutal, at whatever cost to civil liberties, was reckoned a necessary expedient. America was threatened with subversion, and in such an emergency national safety took precedence over finicky concern for constitutional rights. As a prominent legal scholar, Dean John H. Wigmore of Northwestern University Law School, remarked: "When you are trying to protect the community against moral rats you sometimes get to thinking more about your own trap's effectiveness than of its lawful construction." Citing the same grounds, other jurists favored at least a partial suppression of legal safeguards. "There is only one way to deal with anarchy and that is to crush it," one law journal declared, not with "a slap on the wrist, but a broad-axe on the neck."[41]

Not everyone agreed, however. At no time in living memory had there been such a ruthless invasion of civil rights. Roundups of innocent people, detention without warrant, denial of counsel, secret testimony of undercover informants, seizure of property, extortion of confessions—such practices were not easily tolerated by those who cherished American traditions of personal liberty and fair play. For encouraging them, said H. L. Mencken, Palmer was "perhaps the most eminent living exponent of cruelty, dishonesty, and injustice." Mencken accused the Department of Justice of maintaining "a system of espionage altogether without precedent in American history, and not often matched in the history of Russia, Austria, and Italy. It has, as a matter of daily routine, hounded men and women in cynical violation of their constitutional rights, invaded the sanctuary of domicile, manufactured evidence against the innocent, flooded the land with *agents provocateurs*, raised neighbor against neighbor, filled the public press with inflammatory lies, and fostered all the worst poltrooneries of sneaking and malicious wretches!"[42]

Many such protests were heard. Such blatant contempt for the Constitution on the part of the very officials entrusted with protecting it turned the stomachs of concerned citizens. Francis Fisher Kane, the United States Attorney in Philadelphia and himself the target of an anarchist bomb, resigned his office in protest. Another would-be bomb victim who spoke out was Frederic C. Howe, the commissioner of immigration at Ellis Island. The recipient of a Gimbel Brothers "novelty," he nonetheless sympathized with the plight of the deportees and showed leniency to those in his charge. Even more, he traveled to Washington and urged Labor Secretary Wilson to reopen doubtful cases. In vain. "Things that were done," he later wrote, "forced one almost to despair of mind, to distrust the political state. Shreds were left of our courage, our reverence. The Department of Justice, the Department of Labor, and Congress not only failed to protest against hysteria, they encouraged these excesses; the state not only abandoned the liberty which it should have protected, it lent itself to the stamping out of individualism and freedom."[43]

As time went on, cooler heads began to prevail. In March 1920, with Secretary Wilson ill, Assistant Secretary Louis F. Post took charge of deportation matters. A liberal and single-taxer like Howe, he too was concerned for the fate of the aliens and opposed expulsions without due process of law. Accordingly, he set about reviewing all deportation cases. In the process he found that many of those arrested had been denied proper counsel and that the evidence against them, often illegally obtained, was insufficient to justify expulsion. Appalled by the gross violations of legal procedure revealed by his review, he canceled more than two thousand warrants that he had found to be deficient and ordered the prisoners set free.

While Post was thus engaged, a committee of twelve distinguished lawyers, including Felix Frankfurter, Zechariah Chafee, and Dean Roscoe Pound of Harvard Law School, joined the chorus condemning Palmer's "frenzied activities." In a report sponsored by the National

Popular Government League, an organization of progressives and reformers, they denounced "the utterly illegal acts which have been committed by those charged with the highest duty of enforcing the laws—acts which have caused widespread suffering and unrest, have struck at the foundation of American free institutions, and have brought the name of our country into disrepute."[44] Yet another blow was struck in June 1920, when Federal Judge George W. Anderson of Massachusetts, ruling against the government in a deportation case, declared that the existing system of expelling aliens was based on the theory of "hang first and try afterwards." "A mob is a mob," said Judge Anderson, "whether made up of government officials acting under instructions from the Department of Justice, or of criminals and loafers and the vicious classes."[45]

Palmer, looking towards the 1920 Democratic presidential nomination, lashed back indignantly at his critics, dismissing Howe, Post, and their ilk as "friends of the anarchists." Howe, accused of coddling the deportees at Ellis Island, resigned his position, while Post, a "moonstruck parlor radical," as Palmer described him, "with an habitually tender solicitude for social revolutionists and perverted sympathy for the criminal anarchists of the country," was hailed before the House Committee on Rules for impeachment proceedings, which collapsed after his eloquent defense.[46]

Palmer, until the end, denied any impropriety in his treatment of aliens. "I apologize for nothing that the Department of Justice has done in this matter," he declared on the eve of his departure from office. "I glory in it. I point with pride and enthusiasm to the results of that work; and if some of my agents out in the field . . . were a little rough and unkind, or short or curt with these alien agitators, whom they observed seeking to destroy their homes, their religion and their country, I think it might be well overlooked in the general good to the country which has come from it."[47]

Nor did Palmer lack for defenders. Dean Wigmore, for one, assailed civil libertarians who defended personal freedom to the point where it endangered American institutions. "Prompt measures were vital," he said, referring to the Palmer raids. "Ordinary long-drawn-out judicial proceedings would have been suicidal. Individual mistakes, of course, were made, but the individual is nothing when a nation's life is at stake. If some of the deportees were victims of their own ignorance or of subordinate officials' harshness—well, evey soldier knows that such things will happen in war; and this was really war against an enemy. Mr. Palmer saved the country, in my opinion."[48]

CHAPTER TWELVE

The Spy

DESPITE THE DRAGNET arrests of alien radicals, progress in the bomb inquiry was slow. Apart from Valdinoci, the names of the culprits remained unknown, and clues to their identity were getting cold. Other methods having failed, the authorities pinned their hopes on secret informers, who had been infiltrating anarchist groups throughout the country. One such individual, Eugenio Ravarini by name, succeeded beyond their wildest expectations. Acting alone, he penetrated almost to the heart of the conspiracy, wreaking havoc on the militant circles. When he departed from the scene in the spring of 1920, the Galleani movement was a shambles.

Ravarini, about whom information is sketchy, possessed the qualities of a master informer. Forty-one years old, a smooth talker and clever dissembler, he had been born in the Piedmont town of Saluzzo, in Cuneo province, not far from Vanzetti's Villafalletto. Apparently he had anarchist family connections; since the turn of the century a Luigi Ravarini of the same town, three years younger than Eugenio, had been under surveillance for his anarchist affiliations.[1] Whether Eugenio shared Luigi's convictions is not known, though he was certainly familiar with anarchist ideas.

As a young man, Ravarini left for Milan to study sculpture, but abandoned this to enlist as a *carabiniere*, serving two three-year stints. Then, restless, dissatisfied, he wandered through France and Germany, finally emigrating to the United States. This was in 1911, when he was thirty-three years old. For the next eight years we know nothing of his activities, though he continued to move about, living in Pennsylvania, Massachusetts, and New York. In the summer of 1919 he was approached by Alfred L. Becker, a former deputy attorney general of New York State, who during the war had acquired a certain prominence for his investigation of German espionage plots. Returning to his law practice, Becker began a private inquiry into the May 1 and June 2 bombings, for which he enlisted Ravarini as an informer. Through contacts in Washington, Becker managed to get Ravarini on the payroll of the Bureau of Investigation, which assigned him the code name "D-5." His mission was to infiltrate the Italian anarchist movement with the object of locating the bomb conspirators.[2]

Ravarini carried out his assignment over a seven-month period, from September 1919 to March 1920. Moving from place to place, he posed as a direct-actionist of the most violent type, disdaining the brand of anarchism "which is to be applied in the distant future," as he put it, "that of the thirtieth century, for instance."[3] Revolution, he maintained, was on the horizon, and the time for action was now. Professing unbounded admiration for the likes of Ravachol and Clément Duval, he wormed his way into the confidence of the ultra-militants, from whom he learned some of their most carefully guarded secrets—for example that Valdinoci was the Washington bomber and that the May and June bombings were "only one affair, done by the same people." These he communicated to Becker, who passed them on to Hoover and Flynn.[4]

Given their suspicion of strangers, the readiness with which the anarchists opened their hearts to Ravarini is nothing short of astonishing. That he was able to penetrate both the Gruppo Autonomo of East Boston and the Bresci Group of East Harlem bears witness to his gifts as an informer. Wherever he went—Boston and Providence, Paterson and New York—he succeeded in establishing useful contacts. In Boston he spoke to Vanzetti and Felicani about reviving *Cronaca Sovversiva* under their editorship and offered them sufficient money for the purpose. He seemed to have an unlimited supply of funds. What was more, he was continually asking for names and addresses on the pretext of distributing anarchist literature. He spent much time rummaging in Italian print shops, looking for the kind of type with which *Plain Words* had been printed and for traces of the Gimbel address labels.

Despite all this, suspicions were not aroused. Ravarini, indeed, had further successes. In January 1920 he not only infiltrated the Gruppo L'Era Nuova of Paterson, an anarchist bastion since the 1880s; he even managed to secure lodgings in the home of Firmino Gallo, one of the most active figures in the group.[5] On the basis of information provided by Ravarini, Bureau of Investigation agents, led by Frank R. Stone of the Newark office, raided the headquarters of L'Era Nuova and arrested twenty-nine of its members. The raid occurred on the night of February 14, 1920, and took the anarchists by surprise. Weapons and literature were seized, and eighteen of the men arrested were removed to Ellis Island on warrants of deportation, although thirteen of the warrants were afterwards canceled by Assistant Secretary of Labor Post, who ruled that mere membership in a radical group was insufficient grounds for expulsion from the country.[6]

In the wake of the Paterson raid, Ravarini finally fell under suspicion. From comrades in New York as well as Paterson, Carlo Tresca, editor of *Il Martello*, learned that Ravarini had been snooping about and asking questions and was suspected by some of being the cause of the arrests. Tresca at once issued a warning. On guard! he announced in his paper. Ravarini may be a spy.[7] On reading this Ravarini called on

Tresca to demand that the accusation be withdrawn, insisting that it was totally baseless. When Tresca refused, Ravarini requested a tribunal of comrades—including Sberna, whose confidence he still enjoyed—to hear the case. This, too, Tresca rejected, lest the authorities use the occasion for another roundup. When Ravarini left his office, Tresca's suspicions were keener than ever. Another Polignani, he conjectured, recalling the case of Abarno and Carbone.[8]

In March 1920 these suspicions were further strengthened when N. Morgillo, the owner of a printing shop in East Harlem, called on Tresca for advice. Morgillo said that federal agents were watching his shop and had questioned him about *Plain Words*. Morgillo suspected that Ravarini was behind the surveillance. Ravarini visited the shop often and was urging him to print material of an inflammatory character. Tresca advised Morgillo not to print anything unless Ravarini agreed to sign it. That put an end to the matter. Ravarini's visits to the shop ceased.[9]

Tresca continued to gather information about Ravarini, convinced that he had nailed a rat. But others were slow to believe it. Vanzetti, taken in by his *paesano*'s blandishments, wrote Felicani that he wanted "T" to disavow publicly what he has "so lightly divulged."[10] Tresca refused. On the contrary, he repeated his allegation in the May First issue of *Il Martello*, buttressed with additional evidence. The skeptics now opened their eyes, and no further protests were heard.

Tresca's denunciation made life too hot for Ravarini, and soon afterwards he disappeared. He returned to Massachusetts, where he found shelter with his mother and sister, who lived in Quincy. But he considered himself a marked man. Since the time of the Paterson raid, he informed Agent Mortimer J. Davis of the Boston office, he had feared that he had been "turned up" and might become a target for reprisal. Davis conveyed this information to his superiors, recommending that informer "D-5" be returned to New York, as his services were no longer needed in Massachusetts.[11] After this Ravarini vanished from sight.

But the damage had already been done. During the February raid in Paterson, agents discovered a supply of pink paper of "the same tint and texture" as that on which *Plain Words* had been printed.[12] The paper was found in the shop of Beniamino Mazzotta, where *L'Era Nuova* had been printed until its suppression in 1917. Agent Emmett T. Drew, active in the Paterson bombing investigation, proceeded to question Mazzotta. Mazzotta denied any connection with *Plain Words*. He told Drew, however, that the same kind of paper had been used by a printer in Brooklyn named Roberto Elia, editor of a clandestine journal called *L'Ordine*. If anyone in the New York area printed *Plain Words*, said Mazzotta, most probably it was Elia.[13]

Meanwhile the identical information had been obtained from another Paterson anarchist, Ludovico Caminita. Caminita, a former editor of *L'Era Nuova*, had been getting out a successor, *La Jacquerie*, illegally printed in Mazzotta's shop and delivered by hand to its subscribers, who included both Sacco and Vanzetti.[14] After the February 14 raid, *La Jacquerie* was suppressed and Caminita removed to Ellis Island. "Caminita arrested?" wrote a comrade in New York when news of his detention got out. "Woe to us!"[15] Such apprehensions proved justified. For Caminita was not one to remain silent. Questioned by Hoover, who went to Ellis Island for the interview, he talked freely for several hours. Naming names (Elia, Caci, Sberna, Recchi, Felicani), he supplied, as Hoover put it, "some very valuable information" concerning the bomb plot.[16]

At last, then, solid progress was being made. The next task was to locate Roberto Elia. Neither Mazzotta nor Caminita knew his address, so Frank Stone, the Bureau head in Newark, sent an agent to Brooklyn to make inquiries. By questioning postmasters throughout the borough, he found that Elia worked at a printing shop at 255 Fifth Avenue. He immediately notified Stone, who telephoned Agent Charles J. Scully, in charge of the New York office, and urged him to bring in Elia as soon as possible.[17]

Scully wasted no time in responding. That very day, February 25, he dispatched two subordinates, Agents V. J. Valjavec and Joseph A. Barbera (who was fluent in Italian) to the Brooklyn address. Accompanying them was Detective Cornelius Browne of the New York Police Department bomb squad, in the event a formal arrest should be required. They found the premises occupied by the Brooklyn Art Press, owned by an Italian named Goffredo Canzani. A family man with two teenage children, he handled mostly commercial accounts and enjoyed a good reputation in the neighborhood. Elia, a forty-eight-year-old compositor, was at work at the time. Summoned by Canzani, he was questioned by the agents but made no incriminating statements. A search of his locker, however, uncovered a quantity of anarchist literature as well as a stock of pink paper like that used for the *Plain Words* leaflet. Thereupon he was asked to take the agents to his place of residence where a further search might be conducted.[18]

Elia, a bachelor, occupied a room at 757 Union Street. Here the agents and Detective Browne found additional anarchist publications, including copies of Elia's *L'Ordine* and of another journal, *La Frusta*, edited by Giobbe Sanchini in Italy. Wrapped in a newspaper, moreover, they discovered a U.S. Army revolver, for which Elia had no permit. This was a boon for the agents, as they had no federal warrant. He was arrested by Detective Browne and brought to Brooklyn police head-

quarters, where he was kept overnight and his photograph and fingerprints were taken. The next day he was arraigned before a magistrate
and charged with possession of an unregistered handgun, in violation
of the Sullivan law of New York State. Detective Browne asked the
judge to fix a high bail, explaining that Elia was being held at the request of the Department of Justice. The judge complied, setting bail at
$10,000, and Elia was remanded to the Raymond Street jail.[19]

At the jail, on February 28, Elia was questioned by Agents Barbera
and Harry C. Leslie. He denied having printed *Plain Words* or knowing
Valdinoci, Colarossi, or other suspects in the June 2 bombings. The
revolver found in his room, he claimed, he had bought two months
earlier from an ex-soldier for eighteen dollars. He did not believe in
violence, he said, though he admitted to being an anarchist. "Do you
believe in the overthrow of the present form of government?" he was
asked. "I am in favor of it," he replied, "but I know that it is impossible
in this regime of capitalism. Theoretically it is possible, but practically
impossible." Elia, the agents learned, had been born in the Calabria
region of southern Italy and emigrated to the United States in 1906. At
different times he had worked on *Cronaca Sovversiva* for Galleani, *La
Plebe* for Tresca, and *L'Era Nuova* for Caminita. Caminita, however, he
had not seen for several years, since "he and I did not get along very
well, due to personal reasons." In 1913 Elia had come to New York and
worked first for Morgillo and then for Canzani, where he had been for
the last three or four years.[20]

On March 2, two days after his interrogation, Elia's case came up in
the Brooklyn Court of Special Sessions but was adjourned because the
prosecutor was not ready. On March 8 it came up again, and Elia
pleaded guilty to unlawful possession of a firearm. Meanwhile, at the
request of the Department of Justice, a deportation warrant was issued
against him. The judge, informed that Elia might have information of
value to the federal authorities, imposed a suspended sentence and
turned him over to Agents Leslie and Reid, who were present in the
courtroom. Elia accompanied the agents to the offices of the Bureau of
Investigation on the fourteenth floor of a building at 15 Park Row in
lower Manhattan, a stone's throw from City Hall.[21] There he remained
for the next eight weeks while his fate was being decided.

·   ·   ·

On his very first night at the Park Row building Elia was interrogated
again. The focus, as before, was the dynamite conspiracy. In an effort
to get him to talk, his inquisitors, Agents Greene and Palmera (who
spoke Italian), told him that the type used for the *Plain Words* leaflet

had been found in Canzani's shop. Eliciting no reaction, they then showed him a bloodstained sandal and piece of clothing that they said had been worn by the man blown up in Washington. They also showed him one of the package bombs intercepted in the mails the previous April. Elia all the while remained silent.[22]

In the midst of the questioning, another agent, Frank Francisco, came into the room with his coat off and sleeves rolled up. In a menacing voice he ordered Elia to remove his eyeglasses. Elia obeyed. He thought he was about to be beaten. But nothing happened. Francisco, gesturing angrily, stalked out of the room. Soon afterwards, however, Elia heard a commotion next door. Someone cried out in pain. Elia recognized the voice as that of Andrea Salsedo, a comrade and fellow employee at Canzani's. He was being given the "third degree," and Elia could hear his screams.[23]

Earlier that day, Salsedo, thirty-eight years old, had been arrested by Agents Barbera and Gurevich at his apartment on 113 Street in East Harlem. His wife, Maria, had been at work in a shirtwaist factory, and Salsedo was at home with the children, a boy of eight and a girl of two. Like Elia, he had been a close associate of Galleani and had worked at *Cronaca Sovversiva* for several years. A native of Pantelleria, an island off the coast of Sicily, he had met his mentor as a youth when Galleani was confined there in the 1890s. Captivated by his eloquence, he became a devoted disciple. Thereafter his loyalty to Galleani never wavered. In 1902 he followed him to the United States and worked on *Cronaca Sovversiva* as a typesetter.[24]

It was there that Salsedo first met Elia, with whom he formed a close friendship. By 1919 both men had moved to New York and were working at Canzani's, Elia as a compositor and Salsedo as a typesetter. During their off hours they published an illegal journal called *Domani*, intended as a small-scale successor to *Cronaca Sovversiva*. After the June 2 bombings they changed the title to *L'Ordine* but continued to follow the Galleanist line, denouncing the plutocrats of Wall Street as "modern-day bandits." Vanzetti, under the pen name "Il Picconiere," was among its contributors.[25]

Together with Salsedo, Agents Barbera and Gurevich also seized his books and papers and brought them to the Park Row office. Soon after their arrival the third degree began. Salsedo's interrogators, Agents Scully, Francisco, and Leslie, put intense pressure on him in an effort to unlock the secrets of the dynamite conspiracy. As with Elia, they showed him the sandal and fragment of cloth found in Washington and asked if he knew whose they were. "You see this blood?" one of them said. "This is the blood of the man who was blown up. Tell me whose blood that is." When Salsedo said he did not know, Francisco and

Scully struck him repeatedly in the face and head with the heel of the sandal. Salsedo began to scream, but Francisco and Scully continued to work him over. He was on the point of fainting when Agent Leslie, who had not taken part in the beating, intervened and stopped it.[26]

The agents later denied that Salsedo had been beaten. In affidavit after affidavit they insisted that they had not used physical force, that their conduct had been beyond reproach. "He was never mistreated at any time and never was struck, intimidated, or threatened," they maintained.[27] But Salsedo's was not an isolated case. There were many testimonials to such brutality—threats, verbal abuse, beatings with fists and blackjacks, shoving and kicking—by aliens detained by the Bureau of Investigation during this period.[28] Take the example of Gaspare Cannone, arrested in March 1920 on a tip from Ravarini. An acquaintance of Salsedo and Elia, he was seized without warrant at his home in Brooklyn and taken to the Park Row office. There, he claims, while being questioned about the bomb plot, he was beaten so badly that both his eyes were black for two weeks.[29] Salsedo sustained comparable injuries. According to a lawyer who saw him the day after his interrogation, he "had blackened eyes, his face was all bruised, and he was in a condition of collapse." Salsedo's wife offered a similar description.[30]

The arrest of Salsedo and Elia was the first big break in the investigation, and Director Flynn came up from Washington to examine them. On March 9, the day after Salsedo's beating, Flynn installed himself in an office at 116 Nassau Street, around the corner from the Park Row building. Early that afternoon Elia was taken there for questioning. Now, however, he had an attorney, Narciso Donato by name. Fluent in both English and Italian, Donato occupied offices on the eleventh floor of the same building on Park Row in which the Bureau of Investigation was located. Who had retained him was never made clear, but he appeared on behalf of Salsedo as well as Elia and seems to have been hired by their friends.[31]

As Elia awaited Flynn's summons, Salsedo came into the office. His face and forehead were badly bruised from the beating he had received the night before. He had red spots and scratches on his cheeks and temples, and his eyes had a vacant look. "He was depressed," Elia noted. "I never saw him normal during all the time after that that we were together."[32] Presently the men were brought before Flynn. Donato, indicating Salsedo's condition, asked if his clients might not rest before undergoing further interrogation. Flynn assented and postponed the examination until the following day.

The next day, March 10, the examination began and continued on March 11. The 11th marked a turning point in the interrogation. Questioned by Flynn in the presence of Donato, Scully, and other agents,

Elia and Salsedo began to talk. Both men admitted that they were anarchists and had been so for many years. Salsedo confessed that he had printed *Plain Words*, turning out seven hundred copies. He had done so at the request of Nicola Recchi, who brought the manuscript to Canzani's in May 1919.[33] A few days later Recchi returned, and Salsedo gave him the finished leaflets. He took them away, along with the original manuscript.

Elia confirmed Salsedo's story. He had been present when Recchi came to the shop and discussed the leaflet with him. He had also been present when Recchi returned to fetch it. He denied, however, having had anything to do with the Gimbel address labels on the package bombs, or with the alpine climber's emblem, though he admitted that he had once seen such an emblem in a printer's catalogue.[34]

With this the examination was concluded. After their statements were read back to them and signed, the men asked Flynn what would happen to them. "Deportation," he said, "within a couple of weeks." Warrants for both men had been issued by the Department of Labor but had not yet been served, he explained. In the meantime, he suggested, they might remain at the Bureau of Investigation office while the information furnished by them was verified and the other persons involved in the plot located. Flynn warned Donato that, if he sought to have them released, the men would immediately be arrested and charged with violation of the New York State sedition law. Donato explained this to his clients. Given the choice of being held at Park Row or going to prison, they chose the former.[35]

So it came about that for the next two months Salsedo and Elia, without warrant or other legal pretext, were kept in detention by the Department of Justice. Though threatened with deportation, they were not turned over to the Department of Labor, as the customary procedure required. Nor, during all this time, were they given a hearing, indicted on any criminal charge, or put in jail. They were in effect private prisoners, practically incommunicado, held secretly in the offices of the Bureau of Investigation. Only their families and close friends knew of their confinement, which lacked any basis in law. The Department of Justice, while insisting that the men had "voluntarily" agreed to remain in the Park Row building, laundered its files to remove evidence of illegal detention. In a Bureau of Investigation report on the case a reference to Elia and Salsedo's being kept "in custody" was crossed out and replaced with "under surveillance." Similarly they were being "watched"—substituted for "held"—pending the arrest of their confederates.[36]

Nor did their lawyer assist them. At their first meeting on Nassau Street, Flynn told Donato that he desired his cooperation in obtaining information regarding the bomb plot, and Donato replied that he would do whatever was consistent with his professional ethics and his clients' interests. Yet he protested at nothing that was done to them. He did not take the simple legal step of obtaining a writ of habeas corpus that would have secured their release. On one occasion, indeed, he even assisted in the interrogation, as we learn from George F. Lamb, the Bureau's New York division superintendent. "At no time," said Lamb, "did he ever express any dissatisfaction with the way his clients were being treated."[37]

Because of Donato's timidity, friends of Elia and Salsedo later accused him of having been an accomplice of the Justice Department, whose offices were in the same building. The truth is more complex. In 1914, it seems, Donato had been forbidden to appear before the Department of Labor in immigration cases, having charged his clients excessive fees. The rules prescribed that charges must not exceed ten dollars; Donato, however, had demanded of a client an additional forty-five dollars. The matter was brought to the attention of Ellis Island officials by Fiorello LaGuardia, at that time president of the New York City Board of Aldermen, and Donato was excluded from immigration practice.[38]

The Justice Department was fully aware of these facts and made sure that Donato knew it; hence his lack of assertiveness in behalf of Salsedo and Elia. At the same time, however, he was loath to antagonize their anarchist comrades, by whom, it appears, he had been hired. "It is quite apparent," noted Superintendent Lamb, "that Donato feared the anarchists, and he has openly admitted that if he were to make a statement it might result in his death."[39]

Donato, then, was caught in a vise from which he was unable to extricate himself. His solution was to do nothing. Pressed by his clients, he kept putting them off, as the days and weeks slipped by. "What is our status?" Elia demanded. "I want to know where I am." Donato remained noncommittal. "I do not want to compromise your case by insisting to Flynn," he said. "I will wait until he sends for me."[40] The summons, needless to say, never came.

So matters continued for two months. The men, however, were not mistreated. Once they had confessed, a room (number 1406) was fitted out for them with two comfortable beds, and they were given ample opportunity to wash and bathe. They were taken to the barber for haircuts and shaves and received regular changes of linen. For their meals agents took them to public restaurants, most often the W&G Restaurant on Nassau Street. After dinner, weather permitting, they were taken for walks in Battery Park. Sometimes they went to the aquarium and once even to the movies. To while away the time, moreover, they were supplied with playing cards, tobacco, and Italian newspapers and magazines ("other than those considered radical"). Nearly every day Donato came to see them, as did Salsedo's wife. On occasion their employer Canzani turned up for a visit.[41]

There were no more beatings, moreover, and no further formal interrogations. From time to time the men were asked to identify photographs of suspected Galleanists and to provide information about them, which they did.[42] In return, to ease their anxiety, they were assured that no harm would befall them: they would soon be deported to their homeland or released under government protection. One agent said: "If we find where Sberna is, you'll be free." On Easter Sunday, Elia recalled, they were told by Flynn's assistant that "we would be sent to a beautiful farm in California where we would be tranquil."[43] Such, however, was not to be. Their confinement, on the contrary, ended in tragedy.

CHAPTER THIRTEEN

Death of Salsedo

WITHIN DAYS of the arrest of Elia and Salsedo, word of their detention leaked out. Disquieting reports reached their fellow anarchists: the men had been apprehended; they were not in the custody of immigration officials but of the Department of Justice; they were being held incommunicado; and Salsedo had been beaten to extract information. The longer the two remained in confinement, the more nervous their comrades became. How much, if anything, had they told? How many secrets had they revealed? Had they disclosed the names of their accomplices? Who might be in peril because of them? These were questions which the Galleanists asked each other.[1]

In Boston, the focus of the bomb plot, the arrests aroused particular concern. Felicani and Vanzetti were "much worried" and "really desperate" to help.[2] At last, in late March or early April, Salsedo managed to smuggle out a letter to Vanzetti, informing him of his plight. He and Elia were "under grave charges," but they had told the authorities only what "by common agreement we have decided to say." (They had, of course, said much more.) In a second letter to Vanzetti, sent through Luigi Falsini, Salsedo urgently requested money. He and Elia had only one lawyer, and a feeble one at that. Their situation was desperate.[3]

On April 17, a Saturday, Vanzetti relayed this information to Felicani. The next day both men attended a meeting of the Gruppo Autonomo in East Boston and discussed the matter with their comrades. Some twenty other members were present, among them Buda, Orciani, and Sacco. Pending further developments, there was not much that they could do. For the moment, however, they began collecting money in response to Salsedo's plea.[4]

From this point on Vanzetti was continually on the move. A close friend of Elia and Salsedo, he bent all his efforts to assist them. Shuttling back and forth between Plymouth and Boston, he gathered information, consulted with friends, and raised funds for their defense. Often spending the night in Boston, he stayed with Vincenzo Colarossi, Umberto's bachelor cousin, who occupied a room in the North End. He too, like Vanzetti, was alarmed by the plight of his comrades and did all that he could to help.

On Sunday, April 25, the Gruppo Autonomo held another of its weekly meetings at Maverick Square. Vanzetti and Colarossi attended, along with Felicani, Sacco, Orciani, Falsini, and a dozen others.[5] Buda, however, was not present, for reasons which will be explained in the next chapter. As before, the detention of Elia and Salsedo dominated the proceedings. Following intense discussion, it was decided that someone must go to New York to find out what was happening. The choice fell upon Vanzetti. Being self-employed and having no family obligations, he was better able to travel than the others. By now, in any event, he was the main liaison with the prisoners; being in direct contact with Salsedo, he knew the most about the circumstances of his arrest, a token, perhaps, of his own involvement in the bomb plot.

Vanzetti departed without delay. That same night he boarded a train for New York, arriving at Grand Central station early Monday morning. From there, after visiting an old comrade, he went to see Carlo Tresca, a good friend of Felicani's, in the offices of *Il Martello* on East Twenty-Third Street. Vanzetti himself knew Tresca, "not well, but he knew him,"[6] and asked for any help that he could give.

Tresca, an anarcho-syndicalist, differed fundamentally from the Galleanists on matters of tactics and organization. Yet their fellowship overlapped broadly. As adherents of the same general movement, they shared a deep antipathy towards capitalism and government and, until the 1920s at any rate, dealt with each other on more or less amicable terms. Although they competed for the allegiance of Italian workers, the lines between them were not as sharply drawn as in later years, and they could count on each other's help in moments of adversity. Thus Tresca, in 1915, served on the Abarno-Carbone defense committee, side by side with such anti-organizationists as Mandese and Sberna. In 1917, after Galleani's arrest, he expressed his profound concern; and two years later, in *Il Martello*, he severely condemned Galleani's deportation.[7] Galleanists, by the same token, demonstrated for Tresca during the Mesabi strike of 1916, for which Sacco, among others, was briefly arrested.

Tresca was indefatigable in his defense of persecuted comrades, regardless of their place in the anarchist spectrum. During the tenure of Attorney General Palmer, he was in the forefront of legal battles to aid victims of government repression. Should an anarchist be arrested, he knew lawyers and immigration officers and had contacts to raise bail money. He was always ready to help in an emergency, organizing protests, forming committees, and gathering funds.[8]

Such was the case when Elia and Salsedo were arrested. No sooner did Tresca learn of it than he set about making inquiries. Hard as he tried, he was unable to see the two men, but he conferred with Donato about their situation. Bureau of Investigation agents, keeping the lawyer under surveillance, notified their superiors of Tresca's visits. "The inference is unavoidable," complained Superintendent Lamb, "that Donato, while ostensibly aiding the Government, was secretly keeping Tresca fully informed of the developments of the case."[9] This seems an overstatement. True to his cautious nature, Donato in fact told Tresca very little. But whatever Tresca had managed to learn he now confided to Vanzetti. One thing in particular he made clear: he lacked any confidence in Donato, whom he suspected of being in league with the authorities. At all events, new counsel was badly needed.

Having spoken at length with Tresca, Vanzetti next consulted with Luigi Quintiliano, whom he visited on April 27. Quintiliano, a tailor by trade, was secretary of the Italian Committee for Political Victims, organized by Tresca at the onset of the Palmer repressions. Like Tresca, with whom he was closely associated, he was to play an active role in behalf of Sacco and Vanzetti, just as he did now for Elia and Salsedo.[10] Following Vanzetti's visit, Quintiliano conferred with Walter Nelles, whom he had engaged as counsel for the Italian committee. What should Vanzetti, on his return to Boston, advise his associates to do?

In contrast to Donato, Nelles was a well-trained and highly capable attorney. A native of Kansas, he received both his bachelor of arts and law degrees at Harvard before entering practice in New York City. In 1912 he voted for Theodore Roosevelt and for Woodrow Wilson in 1916, but in 1918 he joined the Socialist Party, which he soon abandoned, however, becoming convinced that "its futility was incurable."[11] Nelles, as his Harvard classmate Roger Baldwin described him, was "a scholarly lawyer with an explosive sense of humor and a capacity for deep indignation." Shocked by the persecutions accompanying American participation in the war, he resigned his conservative practice and entered the firm of Hale, Nelles & Shorr, which specialized in defending alien radicals.[12] At the same time, he volunteered his services as counsel for the National Civil Liberties Bureau, and for its successor the American Civil Liberties Union, founded in January 1920 as a result of the Palmer raids. He later served as a professor at Yale Law School, to which he was appointed in 1926. He died in 1937 at the age of fifty-three.[13]

Had Nelles, instead of Donato, represented Elia and Salsedo, their fate might perhaps have been different. As it was, he could only respond to Quintiliano's appeal for advice. The Justice Department, he said, feared that May 1 might bring a repetition of the bombings and disturbances of the previous year and was preparing to take preventive action. He warned Quintiliano that more raids might be coming and advised him to tell his friends to dispose of radical literature and other incriminating material in their possession.[14] This advice Quintiliano relayed to Vanzetti, who saw him again on April 28. Thus forewarned, Vanzetti hastened to depart.

On April 29 Vanzetti took the night boat to Providence, returning to Plymouth the following day. The first thing he did on reaching home was to send a fifty-dollar money order to Quintiliano.[15] He then boarded the train for Boston and went to see Felicani. What he had learned in New York had "operated very bad" on his mind. The men were in grave peril. It was essential to secure competent counsel as well as to awaken public attention to the case. Alarmed, Felicani gave Vanzetti forty dollars from his pocket to send to Quintiliano's committee.[16]

May 1 came and went without incident. In Boston the police were on alert. Machine guns had been mounted on patrol cars and deployed around the city. But nothing happened. The disturbances had failed to materialize: no bombs, no riots, no assassinations. Vanzetti, back in Plymouth, spent the afternoon digging for clams. In the evening he returned to Boston, staying as usual with Colarossi. The next day, a Sunday, the Gruppo Autonomo would meet, with Vanzetti due to report on his trip.[17]

In addition to Vanzetti and Colarossi, the usual crowd turned out for the afternoon gathering at Maverick Square: Sacco, Falsini, Orciani, Felicani, and the rest. (Buda once again was absent.) Vanzetti repeated the advice given to Quintiliano by Walter Nelles: to dispose of their anarchist literature, which would be damaging evidence in case of raids. (The immigration law of October 16, 1918, authorized deportation for those who "knowingly have in their possession for the purpose of circulation, distribution, publication, or display any written or printed matter, advising, advocating, or teaching opposition to all organized government.") To accomplish this, it was agreed that three of the men present—Sacco, Vanzetti, and Orciani—would meet with Buda, who owned a car, to gather up and conceal such material. Vanzetti then reported that additional money must be collected to engage a new attorney for their comrades. For this purpose, it was decided to arrange a public meeting in Brockton for the following Sunday, May 9, at which Vanzetti would be the speaker.[18] This settled, the meeting adjourned.

· · ·

In New York City, meanwhile, matters had taken a turn for the worse. Ever since his confession, Salsedo had become increasingly despondent. By acknowledging his role in the conspiracy, he had violated the anarchist code of honor, whose chief article forbade giving information to the authorities. Even worse, he had informed on his comrades, a cardinal sin in the anarchist lexicon, the most hateful offense a Galleanist could commit.

Salsedo was conscience-stricken at having betrayed his comrades. At the same time he was fearful of reprisals, in particular at the hands of Nicola Recchi. He had heard, perhaps, that Tresca was talking to Donato and that Vanzetti had come to New York to make inquiries. At any rate, as a Bureau of Investigation report noted, he showed "evidence of being in deadly fear of an attack by his comrades who were implicated in the matter with him." (One day, while agents were looking over his mail, they found written in Italian on the inside of a newspaper wrapper, "Arm yourself, don't talk.")[19] It was mainly for their own protection, insisted the Bureau, that he and Elia had consented to remain at the Park Row office. "They wanted to stay here," said Superintendent Lamb. "They were afraid of their anarchist friends, afraid that something would happen to them if they were out, and we were glad to keep them here to get information." Elia later denied this. "No one ever made any threat or sign to us," he declared. "We were never in fear of our compatriots or friends."[20]

Salsedo, nevertheless, was plainly frightened. His wife on her visits endeavored to calm him, all to no avail. "He was always nervous and worried when I saw him," she said. Nor did his depression abate. He groaned all night, refused to eat, and complained of pains in his stomach and head. "He showed clear signs," said Elia, "of an unbalancing mind."[21]

As the detention dragged on, Salsedo's mental state continued to deteriorate. He became increasingly morose and suspicious, telling Elia that their playing cards were being tampered with, their conversations recorded, and their movements watched from the Woolworth Building across the street. In addition, he stopped talking to Agent Palmera, although they had gotten along well before.[22]

By May 1 Salsedo was in a state of near collapse. His eyes bulged, said Donato, who visited him that day, his talk was incoherent, and he appeared to be "under a tremendous nervous strain."[23] The following day, May 2, saw no change in his condition. In the evening he walked a bit with Elia in the hallway, then went to bed at 9 o'clock. Elia sat down outside with the agents, who were smoking and telling stories. At 11 P.M. he entered the room with Palmera and switched on the light. Salsedo begged him to turn it off. "I have a terrible headache," he complained. "That cigarette you gave me hurt me." Elia did as he was asked, then he too retired for the night. For a long time he heard Salsedo groaning and lamenting. At last Elia fell asleep. He heard nothing more until awakened by the watchman early the next morning. "Your comrade is dead," he was told. "He has jumped from the window."[24]

Salsedo had committed suicide. At 4:20 A.M., when all was quiet, he had gotten out of bed. Without disturbing Elia, asleep across the room, he made his way to the window, climbed on a chair, and jumped out. William Harding, a policeman from the Oak Street station two doors away, saw a body flash down and hit the pavement in front of the building. Harding narrowly escaped being struck. On questioning the porter, he was told to inquire at the Justice Department offices on the fourteenth floor. There he told Agent Henry Dotzert that a man had plunged from a window and was lying on the sidewalk in his underclothes. Dotzert and Agent G. J. Crystal went to room 1406, turned on the light, and saw Salsedo's bed vacant and the window open. They rushed outside and found his crushed body on the pavement. Dotzert at once telephoned Scully, who hurried to the office. At this point Elia was awakened and told what had happened. Putting his hands to his head, he exclaimed, "Oh, my; oh, my—it's too bad!"[25]

The responsibility for Salsedo's death at once became a matter of controversy. Did he jump from the window or was he pushed out by his captors? His comrades, among them Emilio Coda, pointed the finger at the Department of Justice; the "men of Palmer and Flynn," as Coda put it, had seen to it that Salsedo was " 'suicided' by falling from the fourteenth floor, remaining a mass of unrecognizable flesh and bones on the sidewalk below."[26] From Italy Galleani lamented the death of his longtime disciple, whose friendship he had cherished for twenty-two years. "I knew him in Pantelleria," said Galleani, "and afterwards in the United States—a faithful husband, the father of two children, and a dedicated worker and comrade. Taken from his home by the authorities, he was tortured day and night and finally murdered." Vanzetti was of a similar opinion. "I don't believe Salsedo committed suicide," he wrote. "I believe he was murdered by the Federal police in New York. If he committed suicide it was because they drove him to it."[27]

The anarchists were not alone in this belief. Louis F. Post, branding it "the Salsedo homicide," wrote as follows: "Nothing is clear about that homicide except that Salsedo was lawlessly a prisoner, that he was held incommunicado in a secret prison controlled by detectives of the Department of Justice, that this prison was fourteen stories above the street, and that his body struck the pavement with an impact that turned it to pulp."[28]

The Justice Department rejected these charges. If Salsedo was pushed, officials argued, surely Elia, asleep in the same room, would have been awakened by the commotion. Besides, why should the agents have killed him when he was providing them with valuable information? As a department memorandum expressed it, Salsedo "put an end to the arrangement" by taking his life. "It is my judgment," said Attorney General Palmer, "that he was in terror of the results of having given information to the Government, that his knowledge of the facts which he had not disclosed was preying on his mind, that he knew Tresca was informed of his whereabouts and probably of his disclosures, and these things, together with his ill-health, caused him to commit suicide."[29]

Palmer's analysis cannot be faulted. That Salsedo took his own life is beyond dispute, and allegations that he was pushed lack any substance. And yet the Justice Department cannot be absolved of responsibility. For it was Salsedo's illegal detention and the confession which it produced that led him to his desperate act. He had been "driven insane," as Walter Nelles put it, "by six weeks of incessant cross-examination and terror."[30] Had proper legal procedures been observed, at worst he would have been deported.

On the basis of this argument, Salsedo's widow brought suit for $100,000 against Palmer, Flynn, Lamb, Scully, and Francisco, charging them with causing her husband's death. With Nelles to represent her, she alleged that they had "lawlessly and wrongfully arrested and seized his body and held him in confinement and captivity without process of law and against his will; they assaulted him; they inflicted upon him blows and grievous bodily injuries; they subjected him against his will to repeated interrogations and inquisitions." Despite promises to set him free, moreover, they had caused him to live in constant fear and thereby "to lose control of his mind" and become "suicidally despondent," with the result that "he projected his body from a window of his chamber of confinement."[31]

Maria Salsedo lost the case, and the U.S. Circuit Court of Appeals affirmed the decision, ruling that the suicide was "not a result naturally and reasonably to be expected from the acts of misconduct alleged to have been committed by the defendants." One judge, however, disagreed. In his dissenting opinion he said: "If a man is confined against his will for two months and continuously and grievously injured and, at the same time, continuously threatened with death, can it be said as a matter of law that the wrongdoer should not have foreseen that the infliction of such wrongs continuously over a long period of time might naturally and probably lead to loss of mind and that self destruction might follow?"[32]

Aided by her husband's comrades, Maria Salsedo returned to Italy with her children. In the meantime, Carlo Tresca, on behalf of the Committee for Political Victims, asked the Italian consulate in New York to demand an investigation of Salsedo's death, Salsedo being an

Italian subject. The consulate responded by conducting an inquiry of its own, and the matter was also raised in the Italian parliament, but without result. In the United States, too, the case quickly melted away, although it revealed, in the words of the *New York Call,* "the existence of a system which secretly and silently takes suspected men from their homes, spirits them away to secret chambers and there keeps them for months in an effort to obtain confessions of guilt from them."[33]

One of these men was now dead. Faced with the sudden glare of publicity, the Department of Justice removed the other from its Park Row offices and hustled him off to Ellis Island for deportation proceedings. This took place on May 5, scarcely two days after Salsedo's plunge, causing Louis Post to remark that the Justice Department seemed more anxious to get Elia "out of the country than into the dock or the witness chair of a criminal court."[34] Yet it was Post himself, ironically, who signed the deportation order. Walter Nelles, who had meanwhile replaced Donato as Elia's counsel, told his client that if he was able to deny being an anarchist he might avoid expulsion. Elia declined. "This is my only title of honor," was his reply.[35]

On August 7, 1920, Elia was deported on the S.S. *Patria* bound for Naples. Returning to his native Calabria, he plunged anew into the anarchist movement. At a conference in January 1921 he was chosen to edit a new journal, *Pane e Libertà,* together with the anarchist poet Bruno Misefari.[36] But his health soon afterwards began to fail. When he died, in 1924, Mussolini was firmly ensconced in power; and in America Sacco and Vanzetti languished in prison.[37]

CHAPTER FOURTEEN

The Arrest

ELEVEN MONTHS had elapsed between the bombings of June 2, 1919, and the death of Salsedo on May 3, 1920. During this interval, which marked the height of the Red Scare, the Galleanists were put to rout. Some, covering their tracks, went into hiding, while others fled the country. In July 1919 Ercole Valdinoci sailed for Italy, returning to his native town of Gambettola. At the same time, as has been noted, his sister Assunta moved in with the Saccos at Stoughton. The following month Augusto Rossi, their former host at Newton, abandoned his home and moved to Needham; after a few months he too returned to Italy.[1] Bit by bit the movement was breaking up.

Plans for further bombing operations were suspended. Valdinoci's terrible death had cast a pall over his comrades, leaving them stunned and demoralized. The Palmer raids, combined with the broadening investigation of the bomb plot, also put a damper on militant action. For the moment, then, the anarchists lay low, and no new explosions occurred.

The authorities, however, pursued the anarchists relentlessly. On tips from Ravarini and Caminita, activists were arrested in several cities and held for deportation. Among those expelled in connection with the bombings were Ferruccio Coacci (April 18), Vito Mariani (June 29), Umberto Colarossi (July 15), and, as we have seen, Roberto Elia (August 7). Efforts failed, however, to deport Ella Antolini, Vincenzo Brini, and Gaspare Cannone, their warrants being canceled by Louis Post. Others for whom warrants had been issued chose to flee the country rather than allow the government to evict them. Ruggero Baccini, suspected of complicity in the Paterson bombing, sailed without a passport on January 10, stowing away on the S.S. *Canopic* in New York harbor. Two weeks earlier seven of his comrades had left on the S.S. *America*, having bribed some sailors. On February 7 Alfredo Conti of the Bresci Group departed on the *Dante Alighieri*, using his brother's passport. Andrea Ciofalo, seized by agents in the Bronx, jumped into a construction pit and escaped. Soon afterwards he returned to Italy.[2]

With the arrest of Elia and Salsedo the trickle became a flood. During the two months in which they were held in custody, noted Attorney

General Palmer, a "large number of anarchists" fled the country. Among them were Nicola Recchi, Giuseppe Sberna, and Filippo Caci, all key figures in the bomb plot.[3] Sacco and Vanzetti were also planning to leave. During the February 1918 raid on *Cronaca Sovversiva* material had been seized identifying both men as active Galleanists. Not only had they subscribed to the paper, itself sufficient reason to come under suspicion; they had contributed articles, notes, and money, as well as assisting in its distribution. Furthermore, both had been in Mexico with Valdinoci, automatically making them suspects in the bomb plot, and both had been tagged by Ravarini as direct-actionists. Small wonder that their names were in the files of the Bureau of Investigation as those of "Radicals to be watched."[4]

Thus far Sacco and Vanzetti had avoided Palmer's dragnet, but the bomb inquiry had begun to cross their path. Sometime in March 1920 George Kelley told Sacco that he was under investigation; a Bureau agent—probably Mortimer Davis—visited the Three-K factory and questioned Kelley about Sacco's activities.[5] There were other ominous signs. On March 19 Agent Davis interrogated Aldino Felicani, a close friend of Vanzetti's, in the Bureau's Boston office. Felicani, according to Attorney General Palmer, "stated in substance that he was an alien and a subject of Italy, that he did not believe in marriage nor the church, and that he did not believe in authority or the observance of the laws of the State, and that he was an anarchist." On March 22 another agent (Anderson by name) spent the day in Stoughton checking the post office and factories for the whereabouts of Assunta Valdinoci. He was unable to find her, though she was living with the Saccos at the time.[6] The net, at all events, was tightening.

By now Sacco had begun to consider returning to Italy. His decision to do so was hastened when, on March 23 or 24, a black-bordered letter arrived from his brother Sabino, carrying news that their mother had died.[7] Sacco's wife was now expecting a baby (a daughter, Ines, would be born in the fall). The time, they felt, had come for them to leave, and in late March or early April Sacco went to the Italian consulate in Boston to inquire about getting a passport. Vanzetti, too, was planning to go. "I have saved up enough to be able to return to Italy," he wrote his father, "in case the necessity to do so should arise."[8]

Sacco worked for the last time at Three-K on Saturday, May 1, a half-day. On Sunday he attended the meeting of the Gruppo Autonomo at which Vanzetti reported on his trip to New York. The next day, the 3rd, he stopped at the factory to pick up his tools and work clothes and say goodbye. He planned to leave for New York on May 8, with the pregnant Rosina and seven-year-old Dante, to board a ship for Italy.[9]

Five more days and he would have been safely off to his native land, and there would have been no "Sacco-Vanzetti case."

. . .

On May 3 Vanzetti took a train to Stoughton and stayed overnight at Sacco's house. The next morning the men opened the newspapers and read of Salsedo's death. "Suicide Bares Bomb Arrests," proclaimed the *Boston Herald*. "Salsedo Gave Names of All Terrorist Plotters Before Taking Death Leap." A similar story appeared in the *Boston Globe*. According to the articles, Salsedo and Elia had turned informer, revealing that the "Galleani group of bombers" had staged the June 1919 "death conspiracy." Salsedo had confessed to printing the pink circulars found at the sites of the explosions, and both men, naming Nicola Recchi among the principal conspirators, had been aiding the government "to trace the men who tried to kill Palmer and the others."[10]

The news of Salsedo's death threw Sacco and Vanzetti into a panic. It was, as Felix Frankfurter later put it, "a symbol of their fears and perhaps an omen of their own fate."[11] Their worst forebodings had been realized. Salsedo and Elia had talked, admitting to complicity in the bomb plot. Worse still, they had implicated their accomplices. At any moment fresh arrests might be expected. The situation brooked no delay.

That very day, May 4, Sacco went to Boston for his passport, leaving Vanzetti to wait at his house. Passport in hand, Sacco rode the elevated to Hyde Park to meet Riccardo Orciani, a foundry worker and fellow anarchist whom he had known since his years in Milford. Orciani, a "rough, blunt, open-hearted, hard-working, manly type," as Edward Holton James described him,[12] drove his comrade to Stoughton on his motorcycle, Sacco sitting in the sidecar. Greeting Vanzetti, they sat down to decide their next move. With Salsedo's death, the disposition of incriminating evidence had acquired a new urgency. The men agreed to meet the following day, together with Mario Buda, to remove such material to a safe hiding place. Orciani thereupon returned to Boston, Vanzetti remaining with the Saccos.

The next day, May 5, Sacco and Vanzetti set out on the mission that led to their arrest. At half past four in the afternoon, Orciani arrived at Sacco's house on his motorcycle, with Buda in the sidecar. Buda's automobile, in need of repairs, had been left at the Elm Square garage in West Bridgewater, where it was now ready to be picked up. After supper Orciani and Buda left on the motorcycle, having agreed to meet Sacco and Vanzetti at the garage. Sacco and Vanzetti caught the 7:20 streetcar for Brockton, where they waited for the Bridgewater car. The two men had coffee in a lunchroom. Taking out pencil and paper, Vanzetti drafted a notice of the May 9 meeting in Brockton, no longer to raise money for Salsedo, now dead, but to assist his widow and children, as well as to aid Elia, now being held for deportation. The notice read as follows:

> Workers, you have fought all the wars. You have worked for all the bosses. You have wandered over all the countries. Have you harvested the fruit of your labors, the price of your victories? Does the past comfort you? Does the present smile on you? Does the future promise you anything? Have you found a piece of land where you can live like a human being and die like a human being? On these questions, on this argument, and on this theme, the struggle for existence, Bartolomeo Vanzetti will speak. Hour——Day—— Hall——. Admission free. Free discussion. Bring the ladies with you.[13]

Vanzetti handed the text to Sacco, who put it in his pocket to take to the printer.

When Sacco and Vanzetti got off the streetcar in West Bridgewater, they walked until they saw the light of Orciani's motorcycle. Finding the garage locked for the night, the four men went to the house of the proprietor, Simon Johnson, who lived nearby. Buda asked for his car. Johnson, replying that it lacked 1920 license plates, advised him against driving it. At first Buda wanted to take the car anyway, but he changed his mind and told Johnson that he would return with valid plates the next day. Then he and Orciani rode off on the motorcycle, while Sacco and Vanzetti left on foot. At 9:40 P.M. they boarded the streetcar for Brockton. Twenty minutes later, as the car drew into the town, a policeman got on and placed them under arrest. When asked why, he replied, "Suspicious characters." Sacco and Vanzetti looked at each other. "Another deportation case," they thought.[14]

. . .

But Sacco and Vanzetti were mistaken. Theirs was not another deportation case. Nor were federal officials involved. How then did they come to be arrested?

The answer rests with Michael E. Stewart, chief of the Bridgewater police. On the morning of December 24, 1919, four men had made a bungled attempt to rob the payroll of the L. Q. White Shoe Company in Stewart's town. One of the men—the "shotgun bandit," as he was later called—fired at the moving payroll truck. The driver, swerving around a streetcar, managed to escape, whereupon the bandits jumped into an automobile which sped down a side street and got away. No one was injured, and the $30,000 payroll remained intact.

On April 15, 1920, another holdup, this one successful, occurred in the town of South Braintree. Shortly after 3 P.M. Frederick Parmenter and Alessandro Berardelli, employees of the Slater & Morrill Shoe Company, were shot dead and robbed of the company's payroll. Two men armed with handguns did the shooting. A car carrying other men then approached, picked up the killers, and carried them to a safe getaway. The money, $15,776.51, was never recovered.

The following day, in a seemingly unrelated matter, Inspector O. L. Root of the Bureau of Immigration in East Boston telephoned Chief Stewart in Bridgewater. Root asked Stewart to help him check on Ferruccio Coacci, an Italian anarchist and shoe worker. In May 1918 Stewart had arrested Coacci in the roundup following the Justice Department raid on *Cronaca Sovversiva*. At that time Coacci was marked for deportation and released on $1,000 bond. Since late 1919 he had been living at Puffer's Place, a small house in West Bridgewater, with his wife Ersilia and two children. The house had been rented by Mario Buda, who shared it with the Coaccis. Behind the house was a shed in which Buda kept his car, a dark green 1914 Overland.[15]

While awaiting deportation, Coacci had worked first at L. Q. White in Bridgewater and then at Slater & Morrill in South Braintree. Early in April 1920 he received notice to report for deportation to the East Boston immigration station on the 15th, on which date his bond would expire. Coacci failed to appear. The next day he telephoned the station to say that his wife was sick and he needed some time to take care of her. Suspicious, Inspector Root called Stewart and suggested that he accompany him to Coacci's that evening. Stewart could not go since he was rehearsing a part in a play, but he agreed to send his patrolman, Frank LeBaron.

When Root and LeBaron arrived at Puffer's Place, they found Coacci packing a trunk. There seemed to be nothing wrong with his wife. Root nevertheless offered to postpone deportation for a week. Coacci, surprisingly, refused. He now insisted on going at once. Root took him to the immigration station, from which he was transferred to Ellis Island. On April 18 he was put on board a ship for Italy, leaving Ersilia and the children behind.

After his rehearsal Chief Stewart returned to police headquarters and spoke to Officer LeBaron, who told him what had happened. Stewart mulled things over. Suddenly he had a hunch. "Something hit me," he later recalled, "the dates involved, April 15th and 16th, the bond, and the phoney illness."[16] In a flash he felt he had solved the South Braintree holdup. Coacci had not turned himself in on April 15 because he was committing robbery and murder. Hence, too, his eagerness to leave the country.

Pondering further, Stewart remembered an informant's story, passed on to him by Pinkerton detectives. According to the story, the earlier assault of December 24 had been the work of a gang of Italian anarchists who had hidden the bandit car in a shack near Bridge-water.[17] Both holdups, Stewart now conjectured, must have been the work of the same men, Coacci being one of them. The next day, April 17, the car used by the South Braintree bandits, a stolen Buick sedan, was found abandoned in the Manley Woods, less than two miles from Puffer's Place. Stewart's suspicions were now thoroughly aroused. Though Coacci had been removed for deportation, he decided to go to his house and look around.

On April 20, accompanied by Officer Albert L. Brouillard of the Massachusetts State Police, Stewart paid a visit to Puffer's Place. Coacci's family had moved away, but Mike Boda (i.e., Mario Buda), a man unknown to Stewart, let him in. Buda, who described himself as a salesman of Italian foods (he was actually now a bootlegger of whiskey), showed Stewart and Brouillard around the house. Stewart asked him if Coacci had owned a gun, and Buda said that he kept one in a kitchen drawer. Though Stewart found no weapon, the drawer contained a manufacturer's diagram of a .32-caliber Savage automatic. When Stewart asked Buda if he himself had a gun, Buda produced a .32-caliber Spanish automatic. After looking through the house, Stewart asked Buda if he could examine the shed. It was empty. Buda said that he usually kept his car there but that it was now at the Elm Square garage being repaired. Stewart and Brouillard then left.[18]

The more Stewart pondered, the more plausible his theory appeared. In the Manley Woods the tracks of a second car had been found, not far from the abandoned Buick. Stewart surmised that this car was Buda's. Early the next morning he returned to Puffer's Place with further questions. Buda was eating breakfast in the kitchen when he glimpsed the chief's car coming down the road. Before Stewart had knocked Buda had slipped out the back door. Stewart knocked again, peered through the window at the dishes on the table, and went away. The following evening he returned. This time the house was vacant, stripped of its furnishings. Stewart drove to the Elm Square garage and found that Buda's Overland was still there. He asked Simon Johnson to call him if anyone should come to fetch it. It was a serious matter, he explained.[19]

It was thus that the trap had been set. On May 5 Buda, accompanied by three other men, appeared at Johnson's house and asked for his car. While Johnson spoke to Buda, his wife went next door and telephoned the police. By the time Stewart arrived the men were gone, so he called the Brockton police and told them to pick up two foreigners on the streetcar from Bridgewater, who had tried to steal an automobile. The trap set by Stewart sprang shut. It closed, however, on two men of whom he had never heard: Sacco and Vanzetti. Informed of their arrest, he at once went to Brockton to question them.

On reaching the Brockton police station, Stewart learned that both prisoners had been armed at the time of their arrest, Sacco with a .32-caliber Colt automatic, Vanzetti with a .38-caliber Harrington & Richardson revolver. Both weapons were fully loaded. Sacco, moreover, had twenty-three extra cartridges in his pockets, and Vanzetti carried several shotgun shells. Two heavily armed Italians, acting suspiciously, seeking a car at night—to Stewart this meant holdup men. He questioned them about their movements, where they had been, whom they had seen. He gave no hint, however, that they were under suspicion of robbery and murder and asked nothing that related either to the South Braintree crime or to the earlier holdup at Bridgewater. Instead he focused on their radical affiliations. Are you an American citizen? he asked. Do you belong to any clubs or societies? Are you a communist? An anarchist? Do you believe in this government of ours? Do you believe in changing the government by force? Do you subscribe to anarchist literature?[20]

In response, both men gave false or evasive answers. They lied about their political beliefs, about the guns that they carried, about the purpose of their visit to West Bridgewater (they claimed they had intended to visit a friend). They had seen no motorcycle, they insisted, and denied that they had been to the Johnson house or knew anyone named Buda or Coacci. Questioned the following day by District Attorney Katzmann, Sacco and Vanzetti repeated these lies, with the result that Katzmann was convinced that he had the right men. His hypothesis was identical with Chief Stewart's: Both the Bridgewater and South Braintree holdups were committed by the same men. Puffer's Place was the bandit headquarters, its shed concealing the stolen Buick. Buda was the leader of the gang; a food salesman, he knew the roads and had a car. Coacci took the money to Italy in his trunk. Sacco, Vanzetti, and Orciani were confederates. Vanzetti, who had shotgun shells in his pocket when arrested, was the "shotgun bandit" at Bridgewater. Sacco, with his Colt automatic, was one of the shooters of the victims at South Braintree.

Such became the theory of the prosecution, from which neither Katzmann nor Stewart thereafter deviated. Problems, however, arose. To begin with, no one of Buda's description (5'2", 120 pounds) had been observed at either of the holdups. Furthermore, the contents of Coacci's trunk, when intercepted by the Italian police, revealed nothing. Most important, Orciani, arrested on May 6 (having been traced by his motorcycle registration), was released because he was found to have been at work on the dates of both crimes. Sacco, too, to the dismay of the prosecution, was able to prove that he had been at work on December 24. Records showed, however, that he had not worked on April 15, when the South Braintree murders took place. Vanzetti, being a fish peddler, had no factory alibi at all.[21]

In spite of these holes in their theory, Katzmann and Stewart refused to discard it. With Sacco and Vanzetti in custody, they proceeded with the case, arguing that the men's lies, evasions, and generally suspicious behavior on the night of May 5 revealed a "consciousness of guilt" in connection with the South Braintree crime. Fueled by this argument, the legal machinery that was to execute Sacco and Vanzetti was set in motion. At their trial in Dedham, their behavior at the time of their arrest weighed heavily against them. To Judge Thayer, who presided, it constituted the strongest evidence of their guilt. He laid great stress on it in his charge to the jury and in his subsequent denial of a defense motion for a new trial. "The evidence that convicted these defendants," he asserted, was "evidence that is known in law as 'consciousness of guilt.' This evidence, corroborated as it was by the eyewitnesses, was responsible for these verdicts of guilty."[22]

Thayer, to be sure, had a point. On the night of their arrest Sacco and Vanzetti had indeed displayed a consciousness of guilt, and this undoubtedly figured in their conviction. Of what guilt, however, were they conscious? According to the prosecution, their lies betrayed their involvement in the South Braintree holdup. Yet this was not necessarily the case. There is another, more plausible explanation—namely, that the men thought they had been arrested for their radical activities and therefore lied to protect their friends as well as to avoid criminal prosecution.

This explanation, unlike any other, accords with all the known facts. From the news accounts of Salsedo's death, published only the day before, the men had reason to fear arrest on political charges. "Salsedo Gave Names of All Terrorist Plotters," the *Boston Herald* had announced. Thus the authorities might be after them at any moment. When apprehended, then, they would have assumed they were being held as suspected bombers, or at any rate as anarchist militants. Their interrogation by Chief Stewart could only have strengthened this belief, focusing as it did on their political associations. Stewart's questions, as has been seen, had nothing to do with the Bridgewater or South Braintree crimes, nor were Sacco and Vanzetti informed of the charges against them. It seems reasonable, then, to conclude that the guilt of which they were conscious was that of anarchism, not of robbery and murder.

Nor was this all. At their trial Sacco and Vanzetti testified that they had gone for Buda's automobile in order to move radical literature to a safe hiding place. This, however, was an evasion. "Radical literature," Upton Sinclair tells us, was a euphemism for explosives. Fred Moore, chief counsel for the defense, told Sinclair that "Sacco and Vanzetti admitted to him that they were hiding dynamite on the night of their arrest, and that that was the real reason why they told lies and stuck to them." Moore's statement tallied with information that Sinclair had obtained from Italian anarchists in Boston, so that he had "sufficient reason" to believe it.[23]

The defendants, of course, could not reveal the true purpose of their nocturnal expedition, much as it would have explained their consciousness of guilt. On the subject of dynamite they remained silent, outraged though they were at the charges against them, at being regarded as ordinary gangsters. To go to prison for anarchism was one thing, for robbery and murder quite another. Sacco could barely contain his indignation. "If I was arrested because of the Idea I am glad to suffer," he said. "If I must I will die for it. But they have arrested me for a gunman job."[24]

. . .

Of the five men suspected of the South Braintree holdup, the fate of all but one has been accounted for: Coacci was deported, Sacco and Vanzetti jailed, Orciani arrested and released. Never indicted, Orciani attended the Dedham trial as a spectator. For a time he acted as chauffeur for Fred Moore, the head of the defense team. Then, in early 1922, he returned to Italy.

But what had become of Mario Buda? On April 21, 1920, he was eating his breakfast at Puffer's Place when he saw Stewart's car driving up, and he slipped out the back door. He knew that Stewart would come back. With the help of a friend he got his belongings together and left that afternoon for Boston. He never returned. He had escaped just in time to avoid the fate of Sacco and Vanzetti.

For the next three months Buda remained under cover with an Italian family in East Boston (hence his absence from the April 25 and May 2 meetings of the Gruppo Autonomo). Then, in July, he moved to Portsmouth, New Hampshire, where he stayed for two months with a colony of fellow Romagnoli. The police were unable to find him, nor was he marked for deportation, although his situation remained precarious. On May 6, while still in East Boston, he had read in the papers of the arrest of Sacco and Vanzetti. Since then their plight had worsened. On June 11 Vanzetti was indicted for the Bridgewater holdup and was swiftly brought to trial and convicted. Judge Thayer, who presided, meted out the maximum sentence of twelve to fifteen years to a defendant with no previous criminal record and for a crime in which no one had been hurt and nothing stolen.

Worse was still to come. On September 11 indictments were returned against both Vanzetti and Sacco, charging them with the South Braintree murders. At this Buda went into action. The persecution of his comrades—"the best friends I had in America"[25]—called for retaliation. Leaving Portsmouth, he returned to Boston and began to prepare a response. From there, having chosen his target, he proceeded to New York.

On reaching New York, Buda acquired a horse and a wagon, in which he placed a large dynamite bomb. The bomb, equipped with a timer, was filled with heavy cast-iron slugs. On Thursday, September 16, Buda drove the wagon to the corner of Wall and Broad Streets, the symbolic center of American capitalism. Here, on the north side of Wall Street, stood the Sub-Treasury Building and next to it the United States Assay Office. Opposite them were the firm of J. P. Morgan and Company and an excavation where the New York Stock Exchange was to build an annex. Buda parked his horse and wagon at the curb in front of the Assay Office, directly across the street from the House of Morgan. He then climbed down from his seat and disappeared.

A few moments later a tremendous explosion occurred, sending a hail of metal fragments in every direction. According to the clock in the Assay Office, which stopped as a result of the blast, the time was 12:01 P.M. Trinity Church, at Broadway, was not yet done tolling the hour. The horse and wagon were blown to bits. Glass showered down from office windows, and awnings twelve stories above the street burst into flames. People fled in terror as a great cloud of dust enveloped the area. In Morgan's offices Thomas Joyce of the securities department fell dead on his desk amid a rubble of plaster and glass. Outside scores of bodies littered the streets. Blood was everywhere.[26]

The bomb, timed to go off at noon when the streets of the financial district were crowded, had taken a terrible toll. Ambulance men counted thirty dead, and more than two hundred were injured seriously enough to be taken to the hospital. During the next forty-eight hours three more died of their wounds. The number of victims, large though it was, cannot convey the extent of the inferno produced by the explosion, the worst of its kind in American history. Property damage exceeded $2 million; much of the interior of the House of Morgan was wrecked. J. P. Morgan—the recipient of a mail bomb the previous year—was in England at the time, and Thomas W. Lamont and Dwight Morrow, two of his principal associates, were safe in a conference room at the far end of the building.[27] The victims of the blast, far from being the financial powers of the country, were mostly runners, stenographers, and clerks. Buda was surely aware that innocent blood might be spilled. He was a man, however, who stopped at nothing.

In the wake of the blast a widespread investigation was launched, extending into every section of the country. It was generally assumed that radicals were responsible. According to Attorney General Palmer, the incident was part of a "gigantic plot" to overthrow the capitalist system. The New York Chamber of Commerce called it an "act of war," demanding that Governor's Island be garrisoned with federal troops to deal with any similar emergency.[28] On September 17, a day after the bombing, Director Flynn of the Bureau of Investigation went to New York to oversee the investigation. Flynn attributed the explosion to the Galleanists. "The plot," he told the press, "was conceived by the same group of terrorists who planned and executed the June 2, 1919, outrages."[29] The motive, Flynn was convinced, was revenge for the prosecution of Sacco and Vanzetti, a view widely held within the Bureau. Accordingly, an Italian-speaking informer was placed in a cell next to Sacco in hopes of extracting information. Sacco, however, became suspicious, and the plan had to be abandoned.

There were, however, other promising leads. Around the time of the explosion, a letter carrier emptying a mailbox at Cedar Street and Broadway, a short distance from the scene, discovered five copies of a radical leaflet. Rubber-stamped in red ink on yellow paper, the leaflet warned of further reprisals:

REMEMBER
WE WILL NOT TOLERATE
ANY LONGER
FREE THE POLITICAL PRISONERS
OR IT WILL BE
SURE DEATH FOR ALL OF YOU
AMERICAN ANARCHIST FIGHTERS[30]

The signature, combining those of *Go-Head!* ("The American Anarchists") and *Plain Words* ("The Anarchist Fighters"), bore the trademark of Galleanist insurgency. On Flynn's orders, investigators canvassed stores which might carry sets of rubber stamps of the kind used to print the leaflets. In due course a Boston agent found a dealer who had sold such a set in late July or early August.[31] The clue, however, led no further.

Meanwhile the inquiry continued. Rewards totaling $100,000 were posted. For weeks and months detectives and federal agents followed up every lead. Investigators visited nearly five thousand stables along the eastern seaboard in a vain effort to trace the horse. In New York, however, police found the maker of the horseshoes, a blacksmith on Elizabeth Street in Manhattan's Little Italy section, who recalled that the day before the explosion a man had driven such a horse and wagon into his shop and had a new pair of shoes nailed to the hooves. He described his customer as a Sicilian.

The Bureau of Investigation gathered together more than three thousand photographs of radicals and showed them to the blacksmith. After examining them for two weeks he picked out five which he said resembled the driver of the wagon. From these a composite photograph was made and sent to every police chief in the country. Hundreds of individuals were questioned and a number of suspects detained. All, however, were released for lack of evidence. In the end, the investigation came to nothing. The bomber was never found.[32]

For the last time, then, Buda had planted "the poof." It was his final act of reprisal in America. The biggest of them all, it had gone off without a hitch. His mission accomplished, Buda left New York for Providence. There, shedding his pseudonym "Mike Boda," he secured a passport from the Italian vice-consul. A few weeks later he sailed on a French ship bound for Naples. By the end of November he was back in his native Romagna, never again to return to the United States.

CHAPTER FIFTEEN

Epilogue

BUDA LANDED in Italy at the tail end of the *biennio rosso*, the two "red years" of labor militancy and rural unrest which followed the First World War. He was happy to be back. For not only had he escaped prosecution by the American authorities, but he had long yearned to return to his homeland, where "great changes," he was convinced, were in the offing, changes in which he hoped to play a part.[1] No sooner had he arrived in Savignano than he set about organizing an anarchist group, arranging lectures and distributing literature as before. Wearing his broad-brimmed black hat and flowing black tie, he spoke at meetings for Sacco and Vanzetti. "I know Sacco and Vanzetti as well as I know you," he told audiences in his native district. "I will risk my life that they are innocent."[2]

To earn a living, Buda started a small shoe manufacturing business in partnership with Amleto Fabbri, a native of nearby Santarcangelo, who had abandoned the United States during the Palmer repressions. Before long, Fabbri returned to America and became secretary of the Sacco-Vanzetti Defense Committee. Buda remained in Savignano, operating the shoe business on his own. In leisure moments he frequented the café of Giovanni Poggi, a friend whom he had known in Roxbury. To Poggi's son Charles he recited the poems of Pietro Gori and explained the philosophy of anarchism.[3]

Buda meanwhile reestablished contact with other friends and comrades from America, above all Galleani and Schiavina. Deported in 1919, they had returned to Italy nearly a year and a half before, when the *biennio rosso* was at its height. Convinced, no less than Buda, that the final struggle with capitalism had begun, they had thrown themselves into the work of propaganda, their most important task being the revival of *Cronaca Sovversiva*. This they accomplished in Turin in January 1920, aided by donations from America.[4] Giobbe Sanchini, deported with Galleani and Schiavina, started his own paper, *La Frusta* (The Whip), for which Emilio Coda raised funds in Massachusetts and Ercole Valdinoci acted as distributor in the Romagna.[5]

But anarchists, as soon became clear, were no more welcome in their native country than they had been in the United States. This was especially true of Galleani and Schiavina. From the moment their ship docked their movements were monitored by the police. Persecuted in

America, they were now persecuted in their homeland, followed, harassed, and detained. In October 1920 *Cronaca Sovversiva* was suppressed, never again to be revived. In Washington these developments were noted with approval, the Bureau of Investigaton keeping track of the "two notorious anarchists," erstwhile "leaders of the individualist-terrorist Italian anarchists in the United States."[6]

On Mussolini's accession to power in 1922, matters went from bad to worse. Il Duce, fearing an attempt on his life by the anarchists, ordered their movement suppressed. J. Edgar Hoover, promoted to Director of the Bureau of Investigation in 1924, assisted the fascist police by supplying reports on Galleani and his associates, funneled through the American embassy in Rome.[7] Galleani was presently arrested, convicted of sedition, and sentenced to fourteen months in prison. On his release he returned to his old polemic against Saverio Merlino, publishing it in *L'Adunata dei Refrattari*, the organ of his disciples in America, who also issued it as a booklet under the title of *La Fine dell' anarchismo?* Errico Malatesta, whose conception of anarchism diverged sharply from that of Galleani, hailed the work as a "clear, serene, eloquent" recital of the communist anarchist creed.[8]

The publication of *La Fine dell'anarchismo?* did not endear Galleani to the Mussolini government. Arrested again in November 1926, Galleani was locked up in the same cell in which he had spent three months in 1892 and found it "as dirty and ugly" as before.[9] Soon afterwards he was banished to the island of Lipari, off the Sicilian coast, from which he was later removed to Messina and condemned to serve six months in prison for the crime of insulting Mussolini.

In February 1930 Galleani, now in failing health, was allowed to return to the mainland. Retiring to the mountain village of Caprigliola, he remained under the surveillance of the police, who seldom left his door and followed him even on his solitary walks in the surrounding countryside. On November 4, 1931, returning from his daily walk, Galleani collapsed and died. His anarchism, to the end, had burned with an unquenchable flame. Ever hopeful for the future, despite a life of bitter experience, he had remained faithful to the Ideal that had inspired him for half a century.

To escape a similar fate, more than a few Galleanists went into exile. The most prominent of these was Schiavina, who fled in March 1923 to Paris. On the eve of his departure he saw Buda for the last time in Rimini. Then, stopping at his family home near Ferrara, he tossed a few pebbles at a window to attract the attention of his mother and sister. Looking out, they waved goodbye, never to see him again.[10]

Coacci was another to leave. Deported from the United States in April 1920, he had returned to his native village in the Marche, where his wife Ersilia and their daughters rejoined him. Eugene Lyons, traveling in Italy in 1921, visited Coacci in his mud-colored house nestled in the hills beyond Jesi. "The man's shelves," noted Lyons, "were lined with brochures on the home manufacture of bombs, and he professed himself a terrorist of the Galleani school." Ersilia, by contrast, wept for "the vanished glories of life in a New England shoe town, snatched from her by the ardor of Mitchell Palmer's agents." It was a life to which she would never return. A year before the fascist takeover, Coacci and his family found sanctuary in Argentina. Settling in Buenos Aires, he joined forces with Severino Di Giovanni, the legendary dynamiter and expropriationist, who was to die before a firing squad in 1931.[11]

Nicola Recchi followed a similar path. Returning to his home in the Marche, he fled to France in 1923 after Mussolini launched his crackdown on the anarchists. From France he went on to Argentina, where he had lived before coming to the United States. In Buenos Aires, like Coacci before him, he joined the circle around Di Giovanni, which specialized in holdups and bombings. Though he had lost a hand making explosives, Recchi managed to support his wife and three daughters (Idea, Aurora, and Alba) by working as a bricklayer. After the execution of Di Giovanni, however, he was jailed and brutally tortured. At length he was deported to Italy, leaving his family behind to shift for themselves. In Italy he was immediately arrested but survived until Mussolini's fall from power. After the Second World War he returned to Buenos Aires and was reunited with his wife and children.[12]

Buda's fate was entirely different. Surprisingly, he remained in Italy, plying his shoemaker's trade and circulating (albeit surreptitiously) anarchist literature.[13] This activity ceased in 1927, when he was arrested as a "dangerous anarchist" and condemned to a five-year term on the island of Lipari, where Galleani had preceded him. Charles Poggi encountered him at the railroad station on the day that he was taken away. "He was standing there in handcuffs, a *carabiniere* on either side, smoking a *toscano*, a half-stogy," Poggi recalled. "His manner was calm and collected. As I greeted him he gave me a smile and said goodbye."[14]

In February 1928 Edward Holton James of Boston secured Mussolini's permission to visit Buda on Lipari and question him about the South Braintree holdup, of which Buda maintained his innocence. In April 1932 James returned to Italy, this time accompanied by Dante Sacco, and visited Buda again on the island of Ponza, to which he had been transferred. Buda put his arms around Dante, whom he had known as a child in Massachusetts, and kissed him warmly on both cheeks.[15]

Four months later Buda was released and allowed to return to Savignano. Soon afterwards, according to his police dossier, he went to work as a spy for Mussolini, infiltrating antifascist groups in Switzerland and France. It is hard to imagine Buda in this role, in view of his long history as an anarchist militant, and there is no evidence of his having given anyone away. His career as an informer was brief, lasting only a few months. Possibly he accepted the task as a means of avoiding further confinement. Be that as it may, he was later rewarded for his services by having his name expunged from the list of subversives maintained by the Mussolini government.[16]

. . .

In the United States, meanwhile, as in Italy, the Italian anarchist movement was on the wane. Though by the end of 1920 the Red Scare had largely subsided, irreparable damage had been done. *Cronaca Sovversiva* had been suppressed, and many of its most dedicated adherents had been deported or fled the country. Nor were there fresh recruits to replenish the ranks. For the atmosphere of intolerance persisted into the 1920s, when the desire to protect America from alien radicals found expression in new immigration laws that sharply discriminated against southern and eastern Europeans. The movement, in addition, plagued by incessant rivalries and disputes, became too fragmented to exercise a sustained influence; and its advocacy of violence, even as a retaliatory measure, isolated it from the great majority of Italian-Americans.

Italian anarchism, as a result, never recovered its former place in the radical spectrum. By the 1920s and 1930s the fears which it once engendered had been transferred to the communists, still basking in the glow of the Russian Revolution. Yet the anarchists by no means vanished from the scene. On the contrary, they concerned themselves with the whole range of issues that confronted the world between the wars, not least the rise of the communist and fascist dictatorships. To Vanzetti, languishing in prison, the Bolshevik regime, far from advancing the cause of liberty and equality, represented "an increased perfectioned exploitaton of the proletariat." What was more, as Vanzetti saw it, bolshevism and fascism, for all their mutual recriminations, resorted to the same authoritarian methods and were therefore doomed to the "same results."[17]

From 1920 to 1927 the plight of Vanzetti and Sacco was itself the chief preoccupation of the Italian anarchists, who threw themselves into the campaign to save their comrades. The day after their arrest, Felicani set about organizing the Sacco-Vanzetti Defense Committee, the prisoners' main source of legal and moral sustenance throughout their seven-year ordeal. Among the members of the committee were some of their oldest and closest associates, several of whom (notably Coda) had been with them in Mexico and taken part in the subsequent bomb plots.

The efforts of the committee, however, proved unavailing. When, on May 12, 1926, the Supreme Judicial Court of Massachusetts upheld the defendants' conviction and denied their motions for a new trial, their legal means seemed exhausted. Sacco and Vanzetti now called for direct action. In the June 1926 issue of *Protesta Umana*, an organ of the Defense Committee, the front page headline proclaimed: "As the Day of Execution Approaches, the Prisoners Warn: LA SALUTE È IN VOI!" The article which followed, signed by Sacco and Vanzetti, carried an appeal for retaliation. "Remember," it concluded, "LA SALUTE È IN VOI!"[18]

What this meant, as their comrades understood, was a resumption of bomb attacks against the authorities. Until their death on August 23, 1927, the prisoners often returned to this theme. "If we have to die for a crime of which we are innocent," declared Vanzetti, "we ask for revenge, revenge in our names and in the names of our living and dead." "I will make a list of honor of the perjurors who murdered us," he said. "I will try to see Thayer death. . . . I will put fire into the human breaths."[19] Sacco was equally vehement. In the spring of 1927, when Armando Borghi visited him in Dedham jail, his eyes glittered with hate as he echoed "the bold protests of Henry and Angiolillo, of Paolino Pallas and Bresci." "We are proud for death," Sacco wrote on August 4, after Governor Fuller refused clemency, "and fall as the anarchists can fall. It is up to you now, brothers, comrades!"[20]

Their comrades did not disappoint them. On June 1, 1926, a bomb exploded at the home of Samuel Johnson in West Bridgewater. Whoever planted it apparently mistook Johnson's house for that of his brother Simon, whose call to the police had led to the arrest of Sacco and Vanzetti. On May 10, 1927, a package bomb addressed to Governor Fuller was intercepted in the Boston post office. No one was injured and there was no arrest. Three months later, on August 6, bombs exploded in the New York subway, in a Philadelphia church, and at the home of the mayor of Baltimore. On August 15 an explosion demolished the East Milton, Massachusetts, home of Lewis McHardy, a juror in the Dedham trial. McHardy, his wife, and three children were thrown from their beds but escaped serious injury.[21]

Nor did the bombings cease with the execution of the two men. At the funeral parlor on Hanover Street a floral piece proclaimed, "*Aspettando l'ora di vendetta*"—Awaiting the hour of vengeance. Vengeance came on the night of May 17, 1928, when a bomb exploded at the Richmond Hill, New York, home of Robert G. Elliott, the executioner. No one was hurt, but the house was badly damaged. The final act of reprisal occurred on September 27, 1932, when a bomb wrecked the home of Judge Thayer in Worcester. After this Thayer moved to his club in Boston, where he remained until his death seven months later. There were no further explosions, and none of the bombers were caught.[22]

After the execution of Sacco and Vanzetti, the menace of fascism became the overriding concern of the Italian anarchists. In Little Italys throughout the country the anarchists emerged in the forefront of the antifascist struggle, heckling pro-Mussolini speakers, disrupting rallies, and engaging in fistfights and gunplay. On occasion they also employed dynamite, attacking fascist clubhouses and Italian consulates. In July 1927, a month before the execution of Sacco and Vanzetti, Calogero Greco and Donato Carillo, both militant Galleanists, were accused of murdering two Italian Blackshirts in New York. Clarence Darrow, the celebrated criminal attorney, agreed to take the case, not only because he "detested Mussolini and everything he stands for," but because he had seen in the Sacco-Vanzetti affair how "prejudice and passion" could result in a questionable verdict.[23] Greco and Carillo were acquitted.

The anarchists fought the fascists with words as well as deeds, notably in Tresca's *Il Martello*, Felicani's *Controcorrente*, and Schiavina's *L'Adunata dei Refrattari*. *L'Adunata*, conceived as a successor to *Cronaca Sovversiva*, was founded in 1922, the year in which Mussolini came to power. Apart from rallying the Galleanists, scattered and demoralized by government repressions, its dual aim was to assist Sacco and Vanzetti and to combat the forces of fascism, both in Italy and the United States. For the next two decades the paper was feared by Mussolini and his agents because of its uncompromising militancy and belief in direct action.

These fears sharpened in 1928, when Schiavina became the editor. Five years had now elapsed since he fled Italy for Paris. There he had plunged into the antifascist movement and joined the campaign for Sacco and Vanzetti, editing the journals *La Difesa per Sacco e Vanzetti* (1923) and *Il Monito* (1925–1928) as well as publishing an important book on the case.[24] With the aid of Emilio Coda, Schiavina smuggled himself back into the United States and, under the pseudonym of Max Sartin, took up the editorship of *L'Adunata*, a position in which he continued until 1971, when the paper ended its fifty-year existence. *L'Adunata*, in the wake of the Sacco and Vanzetti executions, needed an articulate spokesman to lift its readers' spirits. In Schiavina it found one. For forty-three years he prepared each weekly issue, wrote much of the copy, did all the editorial work, then gave the material to Andrea Ciofalo, his trusted comrade, who took it to the printer. Ciofalo, having also returned illegally to America, lived quietly in the Bronx with his family. Unmolested by the authorities, he served as administrator of *L'Adunata* until his death in the 1960s.

Schiavina had lost none of his militant fervor, nurtured during his years with Galleani. "For Schiavina," noted a comrade, "the use of dynamite remained the pinnacle of revolutionary action." He was "stern in his ideas," remarked another.[25] On Schiavina's initiative, *L'Adunata* sent funds to Severino Di Giovanni in Buenos Aires to support him in his bombing escapades. In 1931 he furnished similar aid to Michele Schirru, an anarchist from the Bronx, who went to Italy to blow up Mussolini, but was arrested before the deed could be carried out. Although he was an American citizen and had not killed anyone, the United States government failed to intervene in his behalf. No embassy representative so much as visited him in jail, let alone offered any help. On May 29, 1931, Schirru was executed by a firing squad in Rome.[26]

The Spanish Civil War, which broke out in 1936, provided the last field of physical combat for the Galleanists. Apart from furnishing financial and moral support, *L'Adunata* raised a scattering of volunteers who went to fight against Franco. Some died, among them Michele Centrone, a veteran militant of fifty-seven, who had distributed *Cronaca Sovversiva* in San Francisco. For the survivors, the victory of Franco came as a devastating blow. The coming of the Second World War seemed to many the ultimate madness, yet they managed to cling to their ideals.

But time was taking its inexorable toll. By the end of the 1930s the Italian anarchist movement in America was merely a shadow of what it had been two decades earlier. Its adherents, mostly in their forties and fifties, had seen better days, while their children, born and raised in the United States, were entering the mainstream of American life. A few of the older comrades had already passed from the scene. Augusto Rossi, who had returned from Italy and resumed his work as a building contractor in Needham, died in 1926 in his forty-seventh year, leaving a wife and ten children. In 1932 Nestor Dondoglio (alias Jean Crones), who sixteen years before had poisoned the Chicago archbishop's soup and had since been sheltered by an Italian family in Connecticut, fell ill and was taken to the hospital. Rightly convinced that he was dying, he sent for Emilio Coda, who lived in Needham. By the time Coda arrived, however, Dondoglio had slipped into a coma and died without regaining consciousness.[27]

Three years later, in 1935, another longtime fugitive passed away. Clément Duval, the anarchist burglar who had escaped from French Guiana in 1901, died in the Brooklyn home of an Italian shoemaker named Olivieri. He was eighty-five years old. Before moving in with Olivieri, Duval, whose memoirs Galleani had serialized in *Cronaca Sovversiva* and later published as a thousand-page book, had lived with Schiavina and his companion, Fiorina, a daughter of Augusto Rossi. Fiorina Rossi recalls: "Duval was small, old, disfigured from arthritis. But he exercised every morning. A French comrade, a doctor, used to come to our house to examine him. We called him 'Nonno' (Grandpa), and the neighbors thought he was Bruno's [Schiavina's] father. He lived with us for a few months. He felt he was going to die and did not want to cause us trouble, Bruno being illegal. So he went to live with Olivieri where he died two days later."[28]

Meanwhile the centers of the movement were also dwindling. Both the Gruppo Autonomo and the Bresci Group disbanded in the wake of Palmer's repressions. In Massachusetts the focus of activity shifted to Needham, where the Gruppo Libertà, formed in 1925, built a clubhouse on Sachem Street and attracted some thirty members. Among them were such seasoned militants as Luigi Falsini, Domenico Ricci, Emilio Coda, and John Scussel, all involved in the 1918–1919 bomb plots. One suspects that the bombings of the homes of Juror McHardy in 1927 and Judge Thayer in 1932 originated among the Needham anarchists, including Coda and Scussel.

In the early 1940s yet another militant of old standing joined the Needham group. This was none other than Ella Antolini, who had taken part with Scussel and Coda in the Youngstown conspiracy of 1918. Following her release from prison in 1920, Ella had lived for several years in Detroit, where she married a Sicilian tailor, had a son, and was active in the local branch of the Sacco-Vanzetti Defense Committee.[29] In 1927 she returned to New Britain, then moved on to Hartford and Boston, where her husband opened a tailor shop. Ella herself went to work for Priscilla Wedding Gowns as a seamstress, a trade she had learned at the Missouri State Penitentiary twenty years before. In her spare time she haunted the Boston Public Library and the Museum of Fine Arts, ever hungry for learning and culture, a taste also acquired at Jefferson City, under the tutelage of Emma Goldman and Kate O'Hare.

In March 1940, while living in East Boston, Ella learned that Goldman had suffered a stroke. Goldman, then seventy, was living with friends in Toronto, and Ella wrote her a get-well letter. "My beloved comrade," it began, "the news of your illness caused me much grief—and I am wishing with all my heart that you may be well on the way to recovery." Harking back to their days together in prison, Ella added: "I am still the little person you knew—tho sadder and a bit wiser, and your wonderful personality stands out very clearly in my memory. Always, Ella."[30]

Meanwhile Ella and her husband had drifted apart, and Ella went to settle in Needham. "She was still a beautiful lady," Fiorina Rossi recalls. "All the young fellows were crazy about her." In Needham Ella was reunited with Coda and Scussel, the three occupying adjacent houses. In January 1946, however, Coda was struck and killed by an automobile while walking home from work. Ella delivered the eulogy at his funeral. Not long afterwards, his house was sold to a friend, who discovered a cache of dynamite under the stoop.[31] Scussel survived his comrade by little more than a year, dying in 1947 of tuberculosis. Both men were sixty-five at the time of their deaths, "two of the most remarkable figures in our movement," wrote Schiavina.[32]

A few years later Ella moved to Florida, where she worked as a fitter in a dress shop. As in Boston, she habituated the libraries and museums, cultivating her taste for literature and art. In 1982 she suffered a stroke, which left her partially paralyzed. Yet she was able to drive her car and managed to get around, visiting the library once or twice a week. "She was an interesting person," a comrade recalls. "She had a lot to say but did not indulge in small talk. She never pulled her punches; she called a spade a spade; and she kept a lot of her anarchism to the end."[33]

In 1983 Ella developed cancer. She was now eighty-four years old. Her son, who lived in Miami, telephoned Schiavina to tell him that she was dying and received a letter of sympathy in return. Schiavina himself was almost ninety. "I have known her a long time," he wrote, "since 1916–1917. We have never lived in the same place for any long period of time—but we have never forgotten one another. Tell your mother that she remains very much in my heart and mind—and Fiorina also loves her and wishes her well. And you—could you tell me what I should do or say or write to give her a moment of relief from her pains? Kiss her for me and Fiorina and you try to keep us informed about her condition."[34] Two weeks later, on January 23, 1984, Ella died in Hialeah Hospital. Her body was cremated, and her son, following her wishes, took the ashes in his boat and scattered them in Everglades National Park.

By now only a few of the old guard remained, among them Sacco's widow Rosina. Two years after the execution, she became the companion of Ermanno Bianchini, a comrade and supporter of Sacco and Vanzetti, who had fallen in love with her during the time of her husband's imprisonment. In 1943 they married, living in West Bridgewater, where they operated a small poultry farm. From time to time, until the

1970s, Rosina would see her old comrades. "She was quiet, friendly," one of them later recalled. "She and Bianchini were very devoted to each other."[35] After Bianchini's death Rosina moved into a nursing home in Brockton. Now in her ninety-fifth year, she refuses to talk about the case. Because of her opposition to religion, she would not attend her daughter's church wedding or her son's religious funeral (Dante died in 1972).[36]

One by one the others passed away: Amleto Fabbri and Giobbe Sanchini, Adelfo Sanchioni and Aldino Felicani, Domenico Ricci and Tugardo Montanari, to mention only a few. Mario Buda died in Savignano in 1963, Nicola Recchi in Buenos Aires in 1975.[37] It was left to Schiavina to record their passing. He himself was among the last to go, dying in 1987. For fifty-nine years he had lived in conditions of clandestinity, moving from place to place to elude the authorities. On the surface he showed an imperturbable coolness, yet there were inner tremors that he struggled to keep in check. He had nightmares about J. Edgar Hoover and his menacing "bulldog face." In 1972, after a pacemaker was implanted in his chest, he woke up in the hospital trembling with fear. "He thought he was in prison," the daughter of a comrade recalls. "I was there and saw him. He had an abnormal fear of being discovered. He was very secretive."[38] Later the same year, having recovered from his operation, Schiavina felt well enough to attend a lecture. A young historian, Professor Nunzio Pernicone, spoke on "The Italian Anarchist as Rebel and Outlaw," a subject close to Schiavina's heart. After the lecture, also attended by me, I approached him and began to introduce myself, but he fled in terror at being recognized by a stranger. To my eternal regret, I made no further effort to speak to him, respecting his desire to remain anonymous.

With Schiavina's passing the Galleanist movement lost its last important spokesman. His final work, completed with the assistance of Robert D'Attilio, was an English translation of Galleani's *La Fine dell'anarchismo?*, published in 1982. With its trumpet-call for militant action, it was intended for those in the younger generation who were unable to read Italian. "Galleani's little book," wrote Schiavina in his introduction, "will be of great help today, tomorrow, and forever, until . . . the scourges of oppression, exploitation, and ignorance are erased from the face of the earth."[39] Such had been the goal of Sacco and Vanzetti, when they started on their anarchist career. Such, too, had been the goal of Valdinoci, Schiavina's model of the activist hero. Valdinoci, however, in contrast to Sacco and Vanzetti, remained an unheralded martyr of the movement, seldom mentioned or even acknowledged to strangers. His name lives on only in Justice Department records and in the memories of a few surviving comrades.

Notes

The following abbreviations are used in the notes:

BI   Bureau of Investigation
DJ   Department of Justice
FBI   Federal Bureau of Investigation
INS   Immigration and Naturalization Service
OG   Old German files, Bureau of Investigation

All such materials, unless otherwise indicated in parentheses, are housed in the National Archives, Washington, D.C.

INTRODUCTION

1. *The Sacco-Vanzetti Case: Transcript of the Record of the Trial of Nicola Sacco and Bartolomeo Vanzetti in the Courts of Massachusetts and Subsequent Proceedings, 1920–7*, 6 vols. (New York: Henry Holt, 1928–1929), V, 5065. Hereafter cited as *The Sacco-Vanzetti Case.*

2. Herbert B. Ehrmann, *The Untried Case: The Sacco-Vanzetti Case and the Morelli Gang* (New York: Vanguard, 1933).

3. *The Sacco-Vanzetti Case*, V, 5378l.

4. *The Nation*, November 23, 1921.

5. Edmund Wilson, *Letters on Literature and Politics* (New York: Farrar, Straus & Giroux, 1977), p. 154.

6. John N. Beffel to Esther Travaglio, May 18, 1966, Beffel Papers, Tamiment Library, New York University.

7. The proclamation is reproduced in Upton Sinclair, *Boston: A Documentary Novel of the Sacco-Vanzetti Case* (Cambridge, Mass.: Robert Bentley, 1978), pp. 797–799.

8. Ferris Greenslet, *Under the Bridge: An Autobiography* (New York: Literary Classics, 1943), pp. 179–180.

CHAPTER ONE
ITALIAN CHILDHOODS

1. Eugene Lyons, *The Life and Death of Sacco and Vanzetti* (New York: International Publishers, 1927), pp. 14–15; Lyons, "Torremaggiore: A Glimpse of Sacco's Birthplace," *The World Tomorrow*, September 1921.

2. See Frank M. Snowden, *Violence and Great Estates in the South of Italy: Apulia, 1900–1922* (Cambridge, Eng.: Cambridge University Press, 1986).

3. The olive oil business still exists, operated by relatives of the Sacco family. A few years ago, a cousin of Nicola Sacco's from Massachusetts visited Torremaggiore and returned with a jar of olive oil "so thick that you couldn't pour it without diluting it." Telephone interview with Michael Sacco, West Upton, Mass., September 26, 1987.

4. Nicola Sacco and Bartolomeo Vanzetti, *The Letters of Sacco and Vanzetti*, ed. Marion Denman Frankfurter and Gardner Jackson (New York: Viking, 1928), p. 33.

5. Ibid., pp. 28–29, 60.

6. Ibid., p. 11.

7. Ralph Colp, Jr., "Sacco's Struggle for Sanity," *The Nation*, August 16, 1958.

8. Ibid.; *Il Messaggero*, February 1, 1976; *The Letters of Sacco and Vanzetti*, p. 4; interview with Gemma Diotalevi, Milford, Mass., September 19, 1987.

9. *The Letters of Sacco and Vanzetti*, pp. 15–16.

10. John Dos Passos, *Facing the Chair: Story of the Americanization of Two Foreignborn Workmen* (Boston: Sacco-Vanzetti Defense Committee, 1927), p. 65; *The Sacco-Vanzetti Case*, II, 1817.

11. *The Sacco-Vanzetti Case*, II, 1875–1876. See also Dr. Abraham Myerson, "Nicola Sacco—Examination of April 7, 1927," Herbert B. Ehrmann Papers, Harvard Law School Library.

12. *The Letters of Sacco and Vanzetti*, p. 10.

13. Lyons, "Torremaggiore"; *The Sacco-Vanzetti Case*, II, 1818.

14. Telephone interview with Frank Calzone, Jr., Milford, Mass., September 11, 1987; Francis Russell, *Tragedy in Dedham: The Story of the Sacco-Vanzetti Case* (New York: McGraw-Hill, 1962), p. 79; Lyons, *The Life and Death of Sacco and Vanzetti*, p. 16.

15. Bartolomeo Vanzetti, *The Story of a Proletarian Life*, tr. Eugene Lyons (Boston: Sacco-Vanzetti Defense Committee, 1923), p. 5; Lyons, *The Life and Death of Sacco and Vanzetti*, p. 11. See also Hugo Rolland, "Una gita a Villafalletto," *Controcorrente*, April 1962.

16. *The Letters of Sacco and Vanzetti*, pp. 156, 170–174.

17. Ibid., p. 172.

18. Ibid., p. 171.

19. Jessica Henderson to Elizabeth Glendower Evans, July 17, 1923, in Evans, *Outstanding Features of the Sacco-Vanzetti Case* (Boston: New England Civil Liberties Committee, 1924), pp. 28–29. The house still stands, though it is no longer owned by the Vanzetti family.

20. John Silvestro, in *News-Bulletin* of the Sacco-Vanzetti National League, January 1929.

21. Ibid.; Roberta Strauss Feuerlicht, *Justice Crucified: The Story of Sacco and Vanzetti* (New York: McGraw-Hill, 1977), p. 14.

22. Luigi Botta, *Sacco e Vanzetti: Giustiziata la verità* (Cavallermaggiore: Gribaudo, 1978), p. 143. Of the Vanzetti children only Vincenzina, now a resident of Cuneo, remains alive.

23. Ralph Colp, Jr., "Bitter Christmas: A Biographical Inquiry into the Life of Bartolomeo Vanzetti," *The Nation*, December 27, 1958.

24. *The Letters of Sacco and Vanzetti*, pp. 207–208.

25. Ibid., pp. 101, 223.

26. Feuerlicht, *Justice Crucified*, p. 15.

27. Russell, *Tragedy in Dedham*, p. 73; *The Nation*, August 21, 1929.

28. Vanzetti, *The Story of a Proletarian Life*, p. 5; Feuerlicht, *Justice Crucified*, p. 15. Vanzetti's manuscript, "La mia vita," preserved in the Boston Public Library, gives the figure as forty-five lire.

29. Vanzetti, *The Story of a Proletarian Life*, p. 5; Vanzetti to his parents, August 23, 1901, in Vanzetti, *Non piangete la mia morte: Lettere ai familiari*, ed. Cesare Pillon and Vincenzina Vanzetti (Rome: Riuniti, 1962), pp. 37–38.

30. Not three years, as Vanzetti later said (*The Story of a Proletarian Life*, p. 5, and *The Sacco-Vanzetti Case*, II, 1690). His letters to his family show that he worked in Cavour from December 1902 to November 1904.

31. Vanzetti, *The Story of a Proletarian Life*, p. 5.

32. Vanzetti to his parents, June 10, 1903, in Vanzetti, *Non piangete la mia morte*, p. 39; Feuerlicht, *Justice Crucified*, p. 17.

33. Vanzetti, *The Story of a Proletarian Life*, p. 6; *The Sacco-Vanzetti Case*, II, 1690; Vanzetti, *Non piangete la mia morte*, p. 46.

34. Vanzetti, *The Story of a Proletarian Life*, p. 6.

35. Ibid.

36. *The Letters of Sacco and Vanzetti*, p. 211; Colp, "Bitter Christmas."

37. Vanzetti, *The Story of a Proletarian Life*, p. 6.

38. Ibid., p. 17.

39. Ibid.

40. *The Letters of Sacco and Vanzetti*, p. 220.

41. Vanzetti, *The Story of a Proletarian Life*, p. 17. De Amicis, now largely forgotten, was much admired by radicals and liberals of the period, including Vanzetti's mentor, Luigi Galleani. See G. Pimpino [Luigi Galleani], "Edmondo De Amicis, 1846–1908," *Cronaca Sovversiva*, March 21, 1908.

42. Vanzetti, *The Story of a Proletarian Life*, p. 17.

43. Ibid., p. 18. Cf. Evans, *Outstanding Features of the Sacco-Vanzetti Case*, p. 29.

44. Vanzetti, *The Story of a Proletarian Life*, p. 7.

45. *The Letters of Sacco and Vanzetti*, pp. 101, 128, 156; G. Louis Joughin and Edmund M. Morgan, *The Legacy of Sacco and Vanzetti* (New York: Harcourt, Brace, 1948), pp. 457–458.

46. Vanzetti, *The Story of a Proletarian Life*, p. 7.

47. Art Shields, *Are They Doomed? The Sacco-Vanzetti Case and the Grim Forces Behind It* (New York: Workers Defense Union, 1921), p. 9.

48. *The Sacco-Vanzetti Case*, V, 4911.

49. Vanzetti, *The Story of a Proletarian Life*, p. 7; Lyons, *The Life and Death of Sacco and Vanzetti*, p. 14.

50. *The Letters of Sacco and Vanzetti*, p. 10.

CHAPTER TWO
FREE COUNTRY

1. *The Letters of Sacco and Vanzetti*, p. 10; *The Sacco-Vanzetti Case*, II, 1818.

2. *The Sacco-Vanzetti Case*, II, 1869; *L'Agitazione*, December 1920.

3. Lyons, *The Life and Death of Sacco and Vanzetti*, p. 17; Dos Passos, *Facing the Chair*, p. 65.

4. *The Sacco-Vanzetti Case*, V, 5239; Lyons, *The Life and Death of Sacco and Vanzetti*, p. 17.

5. *The Sacco-Vanzetti Case*, II, 1627; telephone interview with Henry Iacovelli, Jr., Lake Ford, N.H., September 22, 1987.

6. *The Sacco-Vanzetti Case*, V, 5229–5530.

7. Ibid., II, 1627; telephone interview with Michael Sacco, September 26, 1987.

8. *The Sacco-Vanzetti Case*, II, 1617; interview with Joseph Moro, Haverhill, Mass., April 13, 1987; Shields, *Are They Doomed?*, pp. 12–13.

9. *The Sacco-Vanzetti Case*, II, 1932, 2120; Mary Heaton Vorse, *A Footnote to Folly: Reminiscences* (New York: Farrar & Rinehart, 1935), p. 333; Gardner Jackson, Oral History Project, Columbia University, pp. 208–209; Sinclair, *Boston*, p. 111.

10. Interview with Ralph Piesco, Brockton, Mass., October 9, 1987; telephone interview with Lucy Costello, Cotuit, Mass., September 22, 1987; interview with Gemma Diotalevi, September 19, 1987.

11. Francis Russell, *Sacco and Vanzetti: The Case Resolved* (New York: Harper & Row, 1986), pp. 71–72; telephone interviews with Dr. Joseph Murray, Wellesley, Mass., and William A. Murray, Jr., Milford, Mass., September 9, 1987; interview with Gemma Diotalevi, September 19, 1987.

12. Dos Passos, *Facing the Chair*, p. 66; interviews with Gemma Diotalevi, September 19, 1987, and Spencer Sacco, Cambridge, Mass., January 8, 1987.

13. Katherine Anne Porter, *The Never-Ending Wrong* (Boston: Little, Brown, 1977), p. 37; interview with Gemma Diotalevi, September 19, 1987. Elizabeth Glendower Evans describes her as "a lovely North Italian girl with Titian colored hair." *Outstanding Features of the Sacco-Vanzetti Case*, p. 26.

14. *The Letters of Sacco and Vanzetti*, pp. 12–13.

15. *The Sacco-Vanzetti Case*, II, 1820; Evans, *Outstanding Features of the Sacco-Vanzetti Case*, p. 27.

16. *The Letters of Sacco and Vanzetti*, pp. 11, 66; interview with Frank Paradiso, Springfield, Mass., September 19, 1987.

17. Nicola gave up the bakery in 1917 and went to work at the Milford Iron Foundry, and afterwards at the Draper Company in Hopedale, where he remained until his retirement. He died in Milford in 1973. Telephone interviews with Nicholas Sacco, Milford, Mass., September 25, 1987, and Michael Sacco, September 26, 1987.

18. Interview with Gemma Diotalevi, September 19, 1987, confirmed by Luigi Paradiso, Frank Paradiso, Ralph Piesco, and Henry Iacovelli, Jr., among others.

19. Eric Foner, "Sacco and Vanzetti: The Men and the Symbols," *The Nation*, August 20, 1977; John H. Scott, "Nicola Sacco," January 21, 1921, Massachusetts State Police archives, Boston; Lyons, "Torremaggiore."

20. *The Letters of Sacco and Vanzetti*, p. 45.

21. Ibid., pp. 9, 45, 68, 72.

22. Dos Passos, *Facing the Chair*, p. 65; Elizabeth Gurley Flynn, *The Rebel Girl, An Autobiography: My First Life (1906–1926)* (New York: International Publishers, 1973), p. 150.

23. Lyons, *The Life and Death of Sacco and Vanzetti*, pp. 32–33; Bartolomeo Vanzetti, *Background of the Plymouth Trial* (Boston: Road to Freedom Group, 1926), pp. 5–6.

24. *The Sacco-Vanzetti Case*, II, 1831–1833; interviews with Ralph Piesco, October 9, 1987, and Luigi Paradiso, Springfield, Mass., September 19, 1987. There were anarchists in Milford as early as 1904. See "Piccola Posta," *Cronaca Sovversiva*, February 27, 1904.

25. *The Letters of Sacco and Vanzetti*, pp. 8, 11, 17.

26. Ibid., p. 73.

27. *Cronaca Sovversiva*, August 2, 1913; Robert D'Attilio, "La Salute è in Voi: The Anarchist Dimension," in *Sacco-Vanzetti: Developments and Reconsiderations—1979* (Boston: Boston Public Library, 1982), p. 78.

28. Flynn, *The Rebel Girl*, p. 303; *The Letters of Sacco and Vanzetti*, pp. 56, 361; Max Shachtman, *Sacco and Vanzetti: Labor's Martyrs* (New York: International Labor Defense, 1927), p. 50.

29. Gardner Jackson, Oral History Project, Columbia University, p. 209.

30. *The Letters of Sacco and Vanzetti*, pp. 18–19, 69, 72.

31. William J. West to J. Edgar Hoover, August 15, 1927, FBI 61-126-798 (Federal Bureau of Investigation, Washington, D.C.); D'Attilio, "La Salute è in Voi," p. 84; Russell, *Sacco and Vanzetti*, p. 181.

32. Coldwell to Eugene Lyons, in Lyons, *The Life and Death of Sacco and Vanzetti*, p. 33.

33. *Boston Globe*, December 4, 1916; *Cronaca Sovversiva*, December 3, 1916; Dos Passos, *Facing the Chair*, p. 66.

34. *Cronaca Sovversiva*, January 6, 1917; D'Attilio, "La Salute è in Voi," p. 78.

35. BI OG (Old German files) 360257; U.S. Army, Military Intelligence Division 10110-193.

CHAPTER THREE
VANZETTI

1. *The Sacco-Vanzetti Case*, II, 1691. From Le Havre he sent greetings to his family in Villafalletto. Vanzetti, *Non piangete la mia morte*, p. 47.

2. Vanzetti, *The Story of a Proletarian Life*, pp. 8–9; *The Sacco-Vanzetti Case*, II, 1691; Vanzetti, *Non piangete la mia morte*, p. 49.

3. Vanzetti, *The Story of a Proletarian Life*, pp. 9–10; *Non piangete la mia morte*, p. 49. For an English translation of this important letter, see Feuerlicht, *Justice Crucified*, pp. 20–23.

4. Vanzetti, *The Story of a Proletarian Life*, p. 10; Russell, *Tragedy in Dedham*, p. 76.

5. Vanzetti, *The Story of a Proletarian Life*, p. 11.

6. Ibid., p. 12.

7. Ibid., p. 13.

8. Vanzetti, *Non piangete la mia morte*, pp. 49–50.

9. Vanzetti, *The Story of a Proletarian Life*, p. 13.

10. Ibid.

11. Shields, *Are They Doomed?*, pp. 9–10.

12. *The Sacco-Vanzetti Case*, II, 1693.

13. Ibid., II, 1738.

14. Foner, "Sacco and Vanzetti." In this instance, contrary to the popular stereotype, it was the southern Italian, Sacco, who made good in America, rather than the northern Italian, Vanzetti.

15. Vanzetti, *Non piangete la mia morte*, p. 49; Lyons, *The Life and Death of Sacco and Vanzetti*, pp. 20–21.

16. Art Shields, *On the Battle Lines, 1919–1939* (New York: International Publishers, 1986), pp. 33–34; *The Sacco-Vanzetti Case*, II, 1737.

17. *The Letters of Sacco and Vanzetti*, p. 100.

18. Vanzetti, *The Story of a Proletarian Life*, pp. 18–19.

19. Quoted in Theodore Schroeder, *Free Speech for Radicals*, enlarged ed. (Riverside, Conn.: Free Speech League, 1916), p. 7.

20. *The Letters of Sacco and Vanzetti*, p. 242.

21. Ibid., pp. 95, 109, 274. Here Vanzetti was echoing Bakunin: "To look for my happiness in the happiness of others, for my worth in the worth of all those around me, to be free in the freedom of others—that is my whole faith, the aspiration of my whole life." *The "Confession" of Mikhail Bakunin*, ed. Robert C. Howes and Lawrence D. Orton (Ithaca, N.Y.: Cornell University Press, 1977), p. 92.

22. Vanzetti, *The Story of a Proletarian Life*, p. 14.

23. *Cronaca Sovversiva*, November 30, 1912; *The Letters of Sacco and Vanzetti*, pp. 81, 105, 110, 143, 306, 323.

24. Ibid., pp. 256, 322.

25. Colp, "Bitter Christmas."

26. *The Letters of Sacco and Vanzetti*, p. 106; Upton Sinclair, Oral History Project, Columbia University, pp. 201–202.

27. *The Letters of Sacco and Vanzetti*, pp. 99, 116, 308.

28. Ibid., p. v; Vanzetti, *The Story of a Proletarian Life*, p. 5.

29. Interview with Lefevre Brini Wager, Plymouth, Mass., April 12, 1987. Brini, like Vanzetti, collected money for *Cronaca Sovversiva*. See, for example, the issue of May 5, 1917.

30. Interview with Beltrando Brini, Fort Lauderdale, Fla., March 14, 1987.

31. Interview with Lefevre Brini Wager, April 12, 1987; Lefevre Brini Wager to Signor Martinelli, November 6, 1962, Brandeis University Library; Feuerlicht, *Justice Crucified*, p. 24.

32. *The Sacco-Vanzetti Case*, II, 1963; interview with Lefevre Brini Wager, April 12, 1987.

33. Samuel E. Morison, *The Ropemakers of Plymouth: A History of the Plymouth Cordage Company, 1824–1949* (Boston: Houghton Mifflin, 1950), pp. 103–104.

34. Michael A. Musmanno, *After Twelve Years* (New York: Knopf, 1939), p. 47.

35. Vanzetti to William G. Thompson, August 2, 1927, Sacco-Vanzetti Letters, Harvard Law School Library.

36. *Cronaca Sovversiva*, March 11, 1916.

37. Vanzetti, *Background of the Plymouth Trial*, p. 6; Morison, *The Ropemakers of Plymouth*, pp. 113–114.

38. Vanzetti, *Background of the Plymouth Trial*, p. 6; Vanzetti, *The Story of a Proletarian Life*, p. 15.

39. Morison, *The Ropemakers of Plymouth*, pp. 113–114; Shields, *Are They Doomed?*, p. 13.

40. *The Sacco-Vanzetti Case*, II, 1695.

41. D'Attilio, "La Salute è in Voi," p. 79; "Summary of Files Relating to Nicola Sacco and Bartolomeo Vanzetti," FBI 61-126-789 (Federal Bureau of Investigation).

42. Edward Holton James, "The Story of Mario Buda Before the Jury of the World," typescript, Rome, February 21, 1928, Ehrmann Papers, Harvard Law School Library.

43. *The Letters of Sacco and Vanzetti*, p. 178; interview with Beltrando Brini, March 14, 1987; David Felix, *Protest: Sacco-Vanzetti and the Intellectuals* (Bloomington: Indiana University Press, 1965), p. 88.

44. Interview with Beltrando Brini, March 14, 1987.

45. *The Sacco-Vanzetti Case*, II, 1740, 1790; Gardner Jackson, Oral History Project, Columbia University, p. 206; Eugene Lyons, *Assignment in Utopia* (New York: Harcourt, Brace, 1937), p. 34; Matilda Robbins, "One of Ours," *The Industrial Pioneer*, July 1924.

46. *The Sacco-Vanzetti Case*, II, 1778, 1836; Vanzetti, *Non piangete la mia morte*, p. 52; interview with Lefevre Brini Wager, April 12, 1987.

47. Vanzetti, *Non piangete la mia morte*, p. 53; Feuerlicht, *Justice Crucified*, p. 25.

48. Joughin and Morgan, *The Legacy of Sacco and Vanzetti*, pp. 470–471; *The Letters of Sacco and Vanzetti*, p. 196.

49. *The Letters of Sacco and Vanzetti*, pp. 82, 363–364.

50. Ibid., p. 181.

51. Interview with Beltrando Brini, March 14, 1987.

52. Vanzetti, *The Story of a Proletarian Life*, p. 18.

53. Ibid., p. 14.

CHAPTER FOUR
ANARCHISTS

1. *The Letters of Sacco and Vanzetti*, p. 274; Vanzetti, *The Story of a Proletarian Life*, p. 20.

2. Peter Kropotkin, *Memoirs of a Revolutionist* (Boston: Houghton Mifflin, 1899), p. 394.

3. Max Nettlau, *Saverio Merlino* (Montevideo: Studi Sociali, 1948).

4. Carlo Molaschi, *Pietro Gori* (Milan: Il Pensiero, 1959), p. 15, gives a figure of three hundred meetings.

5. See Ugo Fedeli, *Giuseppe Ciancabilla* (Imola: Galeati, 1965).

6. On Malatesta's sojourn in America, see Max Nettlau, *Errico Malatesta: Vita e pensieri* (New York: Il Martello, 1922), pp. 255–256; Armando Borghi, *Errico Malatesta* (Milan: Istituto Editoriale Italiano, 1947), pp. 135–139; and Luigi Fabbri, *Malatesta* (Buenos Aires: Edizione Americalee, 1945), pp. 113–115.

7. For this account of Galleani's career I have drawn on Ugo Fedeli, *Luigi Galleani: Quarant'anni di lotte rivoluzionarie (1891–1931)* (Cesena: Antistato, 1956); "Luigi Galleani: Note biografiche," *L'Adunata dei Refrattari*, December 19, 1931; "Luigi Galleani: 12 agosto 1861–4 novembre 1931," *Studi Sociali*, January 10, 1932; "Luigi Galleani non è più," *L'Emancipazione*, December 15, 1931.

8. Paul Ghio, *L'Anarchisme aux Etats-Unis* (Paris: Armand Colin, 1903), p. 140.

9. *The Letters of Sacco and Vanzetti*, p. 104.

10. Luigi Galleani, *The End of Anarchism?*, tr. Max Sartin [Raffaele Schiavina] and Robert D'Attilio (Sanday, Orkney: Cienfuegos Press, 1982), p. 5.

11. Ibid., p. 48.

12. *Cronaca Sovversiva*, March 19, 1918; D'Attilio, "La Salute è in Voi," p. 81.

13. *Cronaca Sovversiva*, February 17, 1917.

14. Eugene Lyons, "Another Frame-Up Exposed," *Free Voice*, December 1, 1920.

15. Gori, "Vieni, O Maggio!" See Robert D'Attilio, "Primo Maggio: Haymarket as Seen by Italian Anarchists in America," in *Haymarket Scrapbook*, ed. Dave Roediger and Franklin Rosemont (Chicago: Charles H. Kerr, 1986), pp. 229–231; and Rudolph J. Vecoli, " 'Primo Maggio' in the United States," in Andrea Panaccione, ed., *May Day Celebration*, Quaderni della Fondazione G. Brodolini (Venice: Marsilio, 1988), pp. 55–83.

16. *Free Society*, September 24, 1899.

17. Errico Malatesta, *A Talk Between Two Workers* (Oakland, Calif.: Man!, 1933), p. iii.

CHAPTER FIVE
MEXICO

1. *Cronaca Sovversiva*, January 2, 1915.

2. Ibid., March 18, 1916; Vanzetti, *Non piangete la mia morte*, p. 54. For Vanzetti's criticism of the war, see also *L'Era Nuova*, June 19, 1915.

3. *The Sacco-Vanzetti Case*, II, 1877.

4. Mentana [Luigi Galleani], "Matricolati!," *Cronaca Sovversiva*, May 26, 1917. "Matricolati!" was also printed up in postcard format and circulated in large quantity.

5. Interview with Joseph Moro, April 13, 1987.

6. *The Sacco-Vanzetti Case*, II, 1827, 1923–1924.

7. Ibid., II, 1727.

8. *Un trentennio di attività anarchica (1914–1945)* (Cesena: Antistato, 1953), pp. 135–136.

9. *The Sacco-Vanzetti Case*, II, 1770; interview with Alberico Pirani, New York, March 20, 1975.

10. Estimates range from thirty to more than one hundred. An authoritative source, *Un trentennio di attività anarchica*, p. 135, gives the number as "several tens" (*alcune decine*).

11. United States Congress; House of Representatives; Committee on Rules, *Attorney General A. Mitchell Palmer on Charges Made Against Department of Justice by Louis F. Post and Others*, 66th Congress, 2d Session, 1920 (Washington, D.C.: Government Printing Office, 1920), p. 542; interview with William Gallo, Highland, N.Y., May 9, 1987.

12. INS 54379/329 (Immigration and Naturalization Service, Washington, D.C.); Emilio Coda, "Dai campi minerari," *L'Era Nuova*, February 12, 1910.

13. Bliss Morton, Cleveland, December 8, 1921, FBI 61-481-7; Lyons, quoted in Felix, *Protest*, p. 107.

14. R. W. Finch, Cleveland, February 4, 1918, FBI 61-481-1.

15. Finch, New York, April 5, 1918, BI OG 20713.

16. *L'Adunata dei Refrattari*, August 30, 1947.

17. Ibid.

18. Interviews with Fiorina Rossi, Needham, Mass., February 14, 1988; Charles Poggi, Flushing, N.Y., September 30, 1987; and Jenny Salemme, Malden, Mass., February 13, 1988.

19. INS 54616/214 (Immigration and Naturalization Service). "The Glories of America," Colarossi's last speech before departing for Mexico, was delivered in Lynn on April 15, 1917.

20. Enrico Gualtieri to Charles Poggi, October 16, 1981, courtesy of Charles Poggi; James, "The Story of Mario Buda."

21. James, "The Story of Mario Buda"; Mario Buda police file, Archivio Centrale dello Stato, Direzione Generale della Pubblica Sicurezza, Casellario Politico Centrale, Rome.

22. Ibid.; *Boston Globe*, September 26, 1916; *Un trentennio di attività anarchica*, pp. 132–133.

23. M. J. Davis, Boston, March 22, 1920, FBI 61-481-7.

24. *Cronaca Sovversiva*, March 24, 1917.

25. Giuseppe Sberna, in informant's report of January 19, 1920, BI 211793.

26. Interview with Valerio Isca, New York, June 30, 1988.

27. Lyons, *The Life and Death of Sacco and Vanzetti*, p. 37. According to Buda, however, neither Sacco nor Vanzetti could find work. James, "The Story of Mario Buda."

28. Valdinoci sometimes used "Carluccio" as his pen name in *Cronaca Sovversiva*.

29. Russell, *Sacco and Vanzetti*, p. 77; Paco Carlucci [Carlo Valdinoci] to Schiavina, September 4, 1917, Finch, April 5, 1918, BI OG 20713.

30. *The Sacco-Vanzetti Case*, II, 1820.

31. Vanzetti, *Non piangete la mia morte*, pp. 57–58.

32. BI OG 20713 and 72577; *Un trentennio di attività anarchica*, p. 137.

33. BI OG 20713; interview with Harry Richal, Needham, Mass., March 11, 1988.

34. *The Sacco-Vanzetti Case*, II, 1952.

35. Ibid., II, 1821–1822, 1919; Evans, *Outstanding Features of the Sacco-Vanzetti Case*, p. 26.

36. *The Sacco-Vanzetti Case*, II, 1606, and V, 5230–5231; Russell, *Sacco and Vanzetti*, p. 78.

37. *The Sacco-Vanzetti Case*, I, 870.

38. Ibid., V, 5231.

39. Ibid., II, 1606, 1859–1861; V, 5231.

40. Ibid., I, 851–852, and V, 5231; Evans, *Outstanding Features of the Sacco-Vanzetti Case*, p. 26. Sacco's address was 534 Park Street, Stoughton.

41. Interview with Joseph Moro, April 13, 1987; *The Letters of Sacco and Vanzetti*, pp. 12, 72.

42. *The Letters of Sacco and Vanzetti*, p. 57; Evans, *Outstanding Features of the Sacco-Vanzetti Case*, p. 27.

43. Interview with George T. Kelley, Worcester, Mass., January 9, 1987.

44. Dos Passos, *Facing the Chair*, p. 64; Evans, *Outstanding Features of the Sacco-Vanzetti Case*, pp. 26–27.

45. Interview with George T. Kelley, January 9, 1987. In 1923 Sacco told his doctors at the Boston Psychopathic Hospital: "I am soft-hearted. I cannot kill a chicken. I am kind, tender, I never killed anybody. I love my fellow man." Colp, "Sacco's Struggle for Sanity." Cf. George Kelley: "There never was a better fellow than Nick Sacco, nor one with a kinder heart. He couldn't kill a chicken." Evans, *Outstanding Features of the Sacco-Vanzetti Case*, p. 26.

46. Evans, *Outstanding Features of the Sacco-Vanzetti Case*, p. 26.

47. Sinclair, *Boston*, p. 39.

48. Vanzetti, *Non piangete la mia morte*, p. 58; *The Sacco-Vanzetti Case*, II, 1770.

49. Interview with Beltrando Brini, March 14, 1987.

50. Ibid.; *The Sacco-Vanzetti Case*, II, 1541–1542.

51. Ibid.; Vanzetti, *The Story of a Proletarian Life*, p. 15.

52. *The Sacco-Vanzetti Case*, II, 1548–1549, 1698; Dos Passos, *Facing the Chair*, p. 58.

53. Vanzetti, *The Story of a Proletarian Life*, p. 15.

54. Ibid.; *The Sacco-Vanzetti Case*, II, 1694–1699.

55. Interview with Joseph Moro, April 13, 1987.

56. Town of Plymouth permits to dig for clams were issued to Vanzetti on October 28, 1919, and May 1, 1920. Massachusetts Supreme Judicial Court archives, Boston.

57. Interview with Beltrando Brini, March 14, 1987; Felix, *Protest*, p. 88; Feuerlicht, *Justice Crucified*, p. 27.

CHAPTER SIX
FACE TO FACE WITH THE ENEMY

1. Horace C. Peterson and Gilbert C. Fite, *Opponents of War, 1917–1918* (Madison: University of Wisconsin Press, 1957), p. 14.

2. Ibid.

3. *The Letters of Sacco and Vanzetti*, p. 35.

4. "The Social Revolution in Court," *The Liberator*, September 1918.

5. Peterson and Fite, *Opponents of War*, p. 240.

6. William Young and David E. Kaiser, *Postmortem: New Evidence in the Case of Sacco and Vanzetti* (Amherst: University of Massachusetts Press, 1985), p. 15; Feri Felix Weiss, Boston, September 3, 1918, DJ 9-12-276.

7. *Cronaca Sovversiva*, June 9, 1917. For the cover design of *Pane e Libertà* see ibid., May 12, 1917.

8. *Cronaca Sovversiva*, June 16, 1917; DJ 186233-444; Finch, April 6, 1918, BI OG 20713.

9. *Cronaca Sovversiva*, February 24, 1917; Harry M. Bowen, Boston, July 18, 1917, FBI 61-481-1.

10. Inspector R. E. Nelson, November 26, 1917, FBI 61-481-1.

11. Charles H. Lane, Jr., Hartford, July 24, 1917, FBI 61-481-1; George W. Lillard, Hartford, May 9, 1918, FBI 61-481-2.

12. *Cronaca Sovversiva*, July 21, 1917; *Un trentennio di attività anarchica*, p. 136.

13. Weiss, September 3, 1918, DJ 9-12-276.

14. *Un trentennio di attività anarchica*, pp. 128–129, 167. See also Richard H. Frost, *The Mooney Case* (Stanford, Calif.: Stanford University Press, 1968), pp. 48–49.

15. Jean Maitron, *Le mouvement anarchiste en France*, 2 vols. (Paris: Maspero, 1975), II, 183–194; James Joll, *The Anarchists* (London: Eyre & Spottiswoode, 1964), pp. 114–115.

16. Clément Duval, *Memorie autobiografiche* (Newark, N.J.: L'Adunata dei Refrattari, 1929).

17. *Cronaca Sovversiva*, February 10, 1905, June 21, 1906; D'Attilio, "La Salute è in Voi," pp. 81–82; Fedeli, *Luigi Galleani*, p. 54. Galleani was Molinari's secretary in Paris in 1894.

18. Thomas J. Tunney, *Throttled! The Detection of the German and Anarchist Bomb Plotters* (Boston: Small, Maynard, 1919), pp. 53–54; *Cronaca Sovversiva*, December 26, 1908.

19. See Paul Avrich, *The Modern School Movement: Anarchism and Education in the United States* (Princeton, N.J.: Princeton University Press, 1980), pp. 183–213.

20. Tunney, *Throttled!*, p. 42.

21. Tunney, ibid., reproduces two pages from the handbook.

22. *L'Era Nuova*, July 31, 1915. Emma Goldman took the same view in *Mother Earth*, April 1915.

23. *L'Era Nuova*, April 10, 1915.

24. *Cronaca Sovversiva*, March 13, 1915.

25. Ibid.

26. Ibid., June 6, 1917; *Boston Globe*, December 7, 1916.

27. *Boston Globe*, December 18, 1916; *Cronaca Sovversiva*, January 6, 1917.

28. *Cronaca Sovversiva*, March 10, 1917.

29. Ibid., June 23, 1917.

30. D'Attilio, "La Salute è in Voi," p. 83.

31. Nasus [Buda] to Schiavina, September 4, 1917; Paco Carlucci [Valdinoci] to Schiavina, September 4, 1917, Finch, April 5, 1918, BI OG 20713.

CHAPTER SEVEN
CARLO AND ELLA

1. *Milwaukee Journal*, September 10, 1917; *Chicago Tribune*, September 10, 1917. According to the *Tribune*, the police also seized batteries, wire, and motorboat accessories, but the *Journal* makes no mention of these items.

2. *Milwaukee Journal*, November 25, 1917; *Chicago Tribune*, November 25, 1917. For Galleani's account of the incident, see *Cronaca Sovversiva*, November 24, 1917.

3. *Chicago Tribune*, November 25, 1917. Milwaukee detectives believed that the bombs had been made in Chicago. *Milwaukee Journal*, November 26, 1917.

4. Emma Goldman, "The Milwaukee Frame-up," *Mother Earth Bulletin*, January 1918.

5. *Milwaukee Journal*, December 27, 1917.

6. Ibid., December 12, 1917.

7. Ibid., December 27, 1917; *Mother Earth Bulletin*, January 1918.

8. Nicola Mosmacotelli [Sacco] to Pasquale Rossi, January 23, 1918, Finch, Cleveland, February 4, 1918, FBI 61-481-1.

9. *L'Internazionale*, April 1984; interview with Febo Pomilia, Miami, December 8, 1988. See also Lillard, January 29, 1918, FBI 61-481-1; and Antolini trial transcript, Chicago, October 21, 1918, FBI 61-481-4.

10. One document, however, dated November 15, 1909, states that he was a native of Italy. Edward J. Hickey, Hartford, December 16, 1919, FBI 61-481-6. U.S. officials rendered his surname variously as Segata, Segatta, Segatti, and Sicotti before settling, wrongly, on Segato; the correct spelling is Segata, as indicated in his marriage license, New Britain, May 1, 1916.

11. Lillard, January 29, February 6, and February 9, 1918, FBI 61-481-1.

12. Memorandum, October 10, 1919, FBI 61-481-5.

13. Gabriella Antolini to Elide Sanchini, August 10, 1978, courtesy of Elide Sanchini.

14. Antolini trial transcript, FBI 61-481-4.

15. Gabriella Antolini to her brother Luigi, n.d. [February 1918], FBI 61-481-1; H. S. Hibbard, Chicago, April 29, 1918, FBI 61-481-2.

16. Statement of Linda José [Gabriella Antolini], Chicago, May 9, 1918, FBI 61-481-2; Finch, February 4, 1918, FBI 61-481-1; Hibbard, May 15, 1918, FBI 61-481-2.

17. Finch, April 5, 1918, FBI 61-481-2.

18. Charles DeWoody to William M. Offley, January 31, 1918, FBI 61-481-1.

19. FBI 61-481-3.

20. S. T. Klawans, Detroit, February 14, 1918; David S. Groh, Chicago, January 26, 1918, FBI 61-481-1; Antolini trial transcript, FBI 61-481-4.

21. Antolini trial transcript, FBI 61-481-4; Linda José [Gabriella Antolini] to Carlo Rossini [Valdinoci], January 20, 1918, FBI 61-481-1.

22. Groh, January 22 and 30, 1918, FBI 61-481-1; Finch, April 6, 1918, BI OG 20713.

23. The play, *Juan José* by G. Dicenta, was performed in 1917 in Milford, Lynn, and other New England towns. *Cronaca Sovversiva*, February 14 and March 24, 1917. Years later, Ella was to name her only daughter Linda.

24. Clabaugh to A. Bruce Bielaski, Director of the Bureau of Investigation, January 18, 1918; Groh, January 30, 1918, FBI 61-481-1.

25. Hibbard, April 29, 1918, FBI 61-481-2.

26. Statement of Linda José, May 9, 1918, FBI 61-481-2.

27. Memorandum, October 10, 1919, FBI 61-481-5; *Cronaca Sovversiva*, February 2, 1918; telephone interview with Maria Rando, Boston, February 7, 1989.

28. *Chicago Tribune*, January 29 and 31, 1918; Joseph F. McDermott, Boston, September 22, 1919, BI 211793.

29. *Milwaukee Journal*, April 16–19, 1918.

30. Hibbard, May 15, 1918, FBI 61-481-2.

31. Antolini trial transcript, FBI 61-481-4.

32. Gabriella Antolini to Elide Sanchini, August 10, 1978, courtesy of Elide Sanchini.

33. Kate Richards O'Hare, *In Prison* (St. Louis, Mo.: Frank P. O'Hare, 1920), p. 11. Ella was admitted to the prison on November 22, 1918, prisoner number 21150. She gave her religion as "none." Missouri State Archives, RG 213, Series 3.

34. Emma Goldman, *Living My Life* (New York: Knopf, 1931), pp. 671, 692.

35. Kate Richards O'Hare, *Selected Writings and Speeches*, ed. Philip S. Foner and Sally M. Miller (Baton Rouge: Louisiana State University Press, 1982), pp. 206–209, 219; *Letters of Kate Richards O'Hare to Her Family*, typescript in library of Bowling Green State University, letter of October 2, 1919 (also in the Schlesinger Library, Radcliffe College, Cambridge, Mass., titled *Dear Sweethearts*).

36. O'Hare, *Letters*, June 6, 1919.

37. Ibid., May 3, 1919; O'Hare, *In Prison*, enlarged ed. (New York: Knopf, 1923), p. 55. Emma Goldman, in her memoirs, never mentions dynamite at all, saying only that Ella had been jailed "on a Federal charge." *Living My Life*, p. 671.

38. O'Hare, *Letters*, May 3, 1919.

39. Ibid., June 6, 1919; December 14, 1919.

40. Ibid., September 11, 1919.

41. Ibid., October 11, 1919.

42. Ibid., October 2, 1919; December 2, 1919.

43. Ibid., September 28, 1919.

44. Ibid., October 19, 1919; December 2, 1919. Regrettably, the manuscript has been lost.

45. Ibid., January 5 and 10, 1920.

46. Ibid., December 11, 1919.

47. Ibid., January 15 and April 11, 1920; O'Hare, *Selected Writings and Speeches*, pp. 28, 265–266.

48. Linda José to Carlo Rossini, January 20, 1918, FBI 61-481-1.

49. Finch, February 4, 1918, FBI 61-481-1.

50. Ibid.

51. Ibid.

52. Ibid.

53. Ibid.

54. Ibid.

55. DeWoody to Clabaugh, February 7, 1918, FBI 61-481-1.

56. Clabaugh to R. S. Judge, special agent in charge of the Pittsburgh office, January 26, 1918, FBI 61-481-1.

57. Finch, February 4, 1918, FBI 61-481-1.

58. DeWoody to Bielaski, January 29, 1918, FBI 61-481-1.

59. Hibbard, May 11, 1918, FBI 61-481-2; Morton, December 8, 1921; H. J. Lenon, Pittsburgh, March 29, 1922, FBI 61-481-7.

60. Fred H. Hessler, Detroit, February 19, 1918; Finch, April 5, 1918, FBI 61-481-2.

61. William P. Hazen to Frank Burke, Assistant Director of the Bureau of Investigation, December 16, 1919, FBI 61-481-6.

62. Vanzetti to his father, May 14, 1918, *Non piangete la mia morte*, pp. 58–59.

Chapter Eight
Deportations Delirium

1. Hibbard, May 20, 1918, FBI 61-481-2.

2. Finch, March 26, 1918, FBI 61-481-1.

3. Ibid. Cf. Clabaugh to DeWoody, January 30, 1918, FBI 61-481-1.

4. Finch, March 26, 1918, FBI 61-481-1.

5. Finch, April 5, 1918, BI OG 20713; Anthony Caminetti to H. J. Skeffington, May 13, 1918, INS 54379/353 (Immigration and Naturalization Service).

6. Raffaele Schiavina police file, Archivio Centrale dello Stato, Direzione Generale della Pubblica Sicurezza, Casellario Politico Centrale; INS 54391/81 (Immigration and Naturalization Service); Raffaele Schiavina, "Breve note autobiografiche," *L'Internazionale*, January–February 1988.

7. Finch, April 5, 1918, BI OG 20713.

8. *Cronaca Sovversiva*, January 6, February 3, July 14, 1917; Clifford, February 26, 1918, BI OG 72577.

9. McDermott, September 22, 1919; Finch, April 5, 1918, BI OG 20713.

10. Interview with Attilio Bortolotti, North Miami Beach, December 10, 1988.

11. BI OG 20713.

12. Caminetti to Skeffington, May 13, 1918, INS 54379/353 (Immigration and Naturalization Service).

13. Ibid.

14. Ibid.

15. Ibid. In April 1918 Finch had been transferred from Cleveland to the New York office of the Bureau of Investigation, from which he was now temporarily assigned to the Bureau of Immigration in Boston.

16. U.S. Army, Military Intelligence Division 10110-548 and 796; 10630.

17. *Cronaca Sovversiva*, October 6, 1917; Young and Kaiser, *Postmortem*, pp. 14–15.

18. INS 54235/33 (Immigration and Naturalization Service); Young and Kaiser, *Postmortem*, p. 16.

19. Young and Kaiser, *Postmortem*, p. 15.

20. *Revolutionary Radicalism: Its History, Purpose and Tactics*, 4 vols. (Albany, N.Y.: J. B. Lyon, 1920), I, 849; interview with Joseph Moro, April 13, 1987.

21. See Kate H. Claghorn, *The Immigrant's Day in Court* (New York: Harper, 1923); and Constantine M. Panunzio, *The Deportation Cases of 1919–1920* (New York: Federal Council of Churches of Christ, 1921).

22. William Preston, Jr., *Aliens and Dissenters: Federal Suppression of Radicals, 1903–1933* (Cambridge, Mass.: Harvard University Press, 1963), p. 212.

23. If an order to expel was given by the Secretary of Labor, it could be challenged in court on a writ of habeas corpus, but if there was the slightest evidence in the record to justify the administrative decision, the writ would be dismissed and the alien remanded for deportation. Louis F. Post, *The Deportations Delirium of Nineteen-Twenty* (Chicago: Charles H. Kerr, 1923), pp. 52–53.

24. Preston, *Aliens and Dissenters*, p. 12.

25. Ibid., p. 17; Zechariah Chafee, *Free Speech in the United States* (Cambridge, Mass.: Harvard University Press, 1942), p. 233.

26. Preston, *Aliens and Dissenters*, p. 83.

27. Leon Whipple, *The Story of Civil Liberty in the United States* (New York: Vanguard, 1927), pp. 301–303; E. P. Hutchinson, *Legislative History of American Immigration Policy, 1798–1965* (Philadelphia: University of Pennsylvania Press, 1981), p. 97.

28. Roy L. Garis, *Immigration Restriction: A Study of the Opposition to and Regulation of Immigration into the United States* (New York: Macmillan, 1927), p. 102; Schroeder, *Free Speech for Radicals*, p. 78.

29. Garis, *Immigration Restriction*, p. 104; Hutchinson, *Legislative History of American Immigration Policy*, p. 423.

30. Garis, *Immigration Restriction*, p. 126; Hutchinson, *Legislative History of American Immigration Policy*, pp. 444–445.

31. INS 54379/353 (Immigration and Naturalization Service).

32. William B. Wilson to Burnett and Hardwick, May 25, 1918, INS 54235/36A.

33. *Congressional Record*, 65th Congress, 2d Session, pp. 8109–8111, quoted in Richard Polenberg, *Fighting Faiths: The Abrams Case, the Supreme Court, and Free Speech* (New York: Viking, 1987), p. 159.

34. Abercrombie to Hardwick, July 1, 1918, INS 54235/36A. Abercrombie, Solicitor of the Department of Labor, served as Assistant Secretary to sign papers and perform other duties for Secretary Wilson.

35. Abercrombie to Hardwick, September 24, 1918, ibid.

36. William E. Borah to William B. Wilson, July 5, 1918, ibid.

37. Department of Labor memorandum, July 26, 1918, signed by H. McLelland of the department's Law Division, who attended the meeting, ibid.

38. Garis, *Immigration Restriction*, pp. 138–140. See also Panunzio, *Deportation Cases*, pp. 99–100. The law, as Garis puts it, went "as far as it is possible to go in providing for the exclusion of radical aliens."

39. *New York World*, February 11 and 12, 1919, quoted in Stanley Coben, *A. Mitchell Palmer: Politician* (New York: Columbia University Press, 1963), p. 199.

40. Vanzetti, *Background of the Plymouth Trial*, p. 11; Coda in *L'Agitazione*, November 20, 1921. See also *Il Martello*, April 26, 1919.

41. "The Boston Case," Bureau of Immigration, 1919, INS 54235/36C. See also United States Congress; House of Representatives; Committee on Immigration and Naturalization, *Communist and Anarchist Deportation Cases*, 66th Congress, 2d Session, 1920 (Washington, D.C.: Government Printing Office, 1920), p. 132.

42. INS 54379/351 (Immigration and Naturalization Service); *L'Adunata dei Refrattari*, January 22, 1927. His real name was Giovanni Balloni.

43. Fedeli, *Luigi Galleani*, p. 158; *L'Internazionale*, March 1984; INS 54235/33 (Immigration and Naturalization Service).

44. "The Boston Case," INS 54235/36C.

CHAPTER NINE
GO-HEAD!

1. U.S. Army, Military Intelligence Division 10110-1088; United States Congress; Senate Committee on the Judiciary, *Bolshevik Propaganda*, 65th Congress, 3d Session, 1919 (Washington, D.C.: Government Printing Office, 1919), pp. 1076, 1121–1122.

2. In addition to New England, copies were found near Iron River, Michigan, where Buda had taken refuge in the wake of the Youngstown affair. U.S. Army, Military Intelligence Division 10110-1088.

3. INS 54235/33 (Immigration and Naturalization Service).

4. *New York Times*, December 31, 1918; *Philadelphia Inquirer*, January 1, 1919; Paul Avrich, *An American Anarchist: The Life of Voltairine de Cleyre* (Princeton, N.J.: Princeton University Press, 1978), pp. 200–202.

5. McDermott, September 22, 1919, BI 211793; *Communist and Anarchist Deportation Cases*, p. 133; *Boston Herald*, March 1, 1919; *Boston Globe*, March 2, 1919; interview with Concetta Silvestri, Malden, Mass., February 13, 1988.

6. Charles A. Bancroft, Boston, June 28, 1922, FBI 61-381. According to Luigi Vella, a brother-in-law of the De Chellises, the men had been killed because of inaccuracies in Galleani's bomb manual, *La Salute è in voi!* Interview with Valerio Isca, New York, January 17, 1987.

7. BI 211793; Young and Kaiser, *Postmortem*, p. 132.

8. Interview with Concetta Silvestri, February 13, 1988. She and her sister-in-law Carmela (Eustachio's wife) were in fact listed for deportation, along with another Franklin anarchist, Antonio Capaldo, but the warrants were canceled. M. J. Davis, Boston, March 27, 1920, BI 211793.

9. Robert K. Murray, *Red Scare: A Study in National Hysteria, 1919–1920* (Minneapolis: University of Minnesota Press, 1955), pp. 63, 65.

10. *New York Times*, April 29 and 30, 1919; *New York World*, May 1 and 4, 1919. According to another version, the acid had leaked through the package, thus preventing an explosion from taking place.

11. *New York Times* and *New York World*, May 1, 1919.

12. *Washington Post*, April 29, 1919.

13. *New York Times* and *New York World*, May 1, 1919.

14. *Pittsburgh Press*, May 1, 1919; *New York Times*, May 2, 1919; Frost, *The Mooney Case*, p. 328. *The Chicago Tribune* warned: "BEWARE IF BOX COMES THROUGH MAIL–Do Not Open It–Call the Police Bomb Squad." Some worried citizens ruined legitimate packages by dousing them with water in fear that they contained explosives. Murray, *Red Scare*, p. 72.

15. *New York World* and *Cleveland Plain Dealer*, May 1, 1919.

16. *New York World, Washington Post, Pittsburgh Press, Boston Herald*, May 1, 1919.

17. *Washington Post*, May 2, 1919.

18. Julian F. Jaffe, *Crusade Against Radicalism: New York During the Red Scare, 1914–1924* (Port Washington, N.Y.: Kennikat Press, 1972), p. 88.

19. *A. Mitchell Palmer on Charges*, pp. 157–158. The name of Albert Johnson was omitted from the list of recipients compiled by the Department of Justice, but it appeared in the *Pittsburgh Press* of May 4, 1919. The figure of thirty-six bombs, given in some accounts, is apparently erroneous.

20. *New York Times*, May 2, 1919; Murray, *Red Scare*, p. 72.

21. *Washington Post*, May 1, 1919; *The Liberator*, July 1919; Murray, *Red Scare*, p. 73.

22. *New York World* and *Philadelphia Inquirer*, May 1, 1919.

23. *Cleveland Plain Dealer*, May 1, 1919; *Pittsburgh Press*, May 2, 1919; *New York World*, May 4, 1919; Murray, *Red Scare*, p. 73.

24. *Congressional Record*, 65th Congress, 2d Session, p. 8111. It is worth noting that *Cronaca Sovversiva* of May 1919, in an article entitled " 'Treat Them Rough'," justified the mailing of the package bombs.

25. Preston, *Aliens and Dissenters*, p. 76.

26. Donald Johnson, *Challenge to American Freedoms: World War I and the Rise of the American Civil Liberties Union* (Lexington: University of Kentucky Press, 1963), pp. 126–127; Patrick Renshaw, *The Wobblies: The Story of Syndicalism in the United States* (Garden City, N.Y.: Anchor Books, 1967), p. 173.

27. Jaffe, *Crusade Against Radicalism*, p. 187. *The New York World* of March 13, 1919, criticized the raid on the Union of Russian Workers as an "intolerable abuse of police power."

28. Polenberg, *Fighting Faiths*, pp. 163, 171.

29. *A. Mitchell Palmer on Charges*, p. 158.

30. Harry Weinberger to A. Mitchell Palmer, March 29, 1919, DJ 214242.

31. William M. Offley to I. H. McCarty, June 26, 1919, BI OG 20713.

32. Archibald E. Stevenson to R. W. Finch, June 23, 1919, Lusk Committee Papers, New York State Archives, Albany.

33. Vecoli, " 'Primo Maggio'," p. 75.

34. *Cleveland Plain Dealer*, May 2, 1919; Murray, *Red Scare*, pp. 74, 77.

35. *Boston Herald*, May 2, 1919; *Cleveland Plain Dealer*, May 2, 1919.

36. *Boston Globe*, May 8, 1919; *Boston Herald*, June 3, 1919.

CHAPTER TEN
PLAIN WORDS

1. U.S. Army, Military Intelligence Division 10110-1279.

2. Ibid.; *A. Mitchell Palmer on Charges*, p. 165.

3. William J. West, Boston, January 28, 1922, FBI 61-1003.

4. *Boston Globe* and *Boston Herald*, June 3 and 4, 1919.

5. Ibid. See also *Pittsburgh Press*, June 3, 1919; and *Philadelphia Inquirer*, June 4, 1919.

6. Young and Kaiser, *Postmortem*, p. 18.

7. *New York Times* and *New York World*, June 3, 1919; *Philadelphia Inquirer*, June 4, 1919.

8. The distinguished attorney Charles C. Burlingham, a future supporter of Sacco and Vanzetti, thought him "the finest criminal judge we'd ever seen in New York from the beginning of time." Oral History Project, Columbia University, p. 10.

9. *New York Call*, June 4, 1919.

10. *New York World*, June 3 and 4, 1919.

11. On the other hand, John J. Fitzgerald, secretary of the Paterson Chamber of Commerce and a strong opponent of radicals, had lived at the same address until a short time before, and some believed that he was the actual target.

12. *Paterson Press-Guardian* and *Paterson Evening News*, June 3, 1919; *Paterson Morning Call*, June 4, 1919. The owner of the house, Max Gold, is sometimes listed as the intended victim, but this is incorrect.

13. *Pittsburgh Press*, June 3, 1919; *Philadelphia Inquirer*, June 4, 1919.

14. *Pittsburgh Press*, June 3, 1919; *New York Times*, June 4, 1919. In Pittsburgh, as in Boston, New York, and Philadelphia, an automobile was observed speeding from the scene.

15. *New York Times*, September 19, 1920; *Un trentennio di attività anarchica*, p. 147.

16. *Cleveland Plain Dealer*, June 4, 1919; *Pittsburgh Press*, June 3, 1919.

17. *Washington Post*, June 3, 1919.

18. Coben, *A. Mitchell Palmer*, p. 206; *Pittsburgh Press*, June 3, 1919.

19. U.S. Army, Military Intelligence Division 10110-1279.

20. Ibid.; *New York Times*, June 4, 1919.

21. U.S. Army, Military Intelligence Division 10110-1279; *Philadelphia Inquirer*, June 4, 1919.

22. *New York World*, June 4, 1919.

23. U.S. Army, Military Intelligence Division 10110-1279.

24. *Philadelphia Inquirer*, June 5, 1919.

25. *Washington Post*, June 5, 1919.

26. U.S. Army, Military Intelligence Division 10110-1279. The Italian-English dictionary and Philadelphia hatter likewise pointed to an Italian identification.

27. Department of Labor, Bureau of Immigration, BI OG 20713.

28. Undercover report, New York, January 19, 1920, BI 211793; interview with Spencer Sacco, January 8, 1987.

29. West, January 28, 1922, FBI 61-1003.

30. Interview with Fiorina Rossi, February 14, 1988.

31. Nicola Recchi police file, Archivio Centrale dello Stato, Direzione Generale della Pubblica Sicurezza, Casellario Politico Centrale; William E. Hill, Boston, April 3, 1920, BI 211793. Some of the bombs were made at the home of Luigi Falsini, 183 Leyden Street, East Boston.

32. Whether all of the bombs were manufactured in Boston or some by collaborators on the spot is not known. Given their similar construction, however, the former seems more likely.

33. Undercover report, New York, February 15, 1920, BI 211793; Dante DiLillo, Boston, December 23, 1921, FBI 61-481-7; *A. Mitchell Palmer on Charges*, p. 36. Other members of Gli Insorti were Gemma Mello, Pietro Muccini, Luigi Martinelli, and F. Scalera. In *Cronaca Sovversiva* of March 17, 1917, the group declared: "Forward! It depends on ourselves alone, on our own fervor, to make Paterson what Gori and Malatesta, Bresci and Galleani, earlier made of it: the center of every great revolutionary activity."

34. DiLillo, September 1, 1921, DJ 202600-2513.

35. Undercover report, January 19, 1920, BI 211793; *Cleveland Plain Dealer*, June 4, 1919.

36. *The Letters of Sacco and Vanzetti*, p. 119.

37. Ibid., pp. 151, 169.

38. James, "The Story of Mario Buda"; Davis, March 22, 1920, FBI 61-481-7; West, November 9, 1922, FBI 61-1003; interview with Spencer Sacco, January 8, 1987.

39. Gardner Jackson, Oral History Project, Columbia University, p. 209.

40. *The Letters of Sacco and Vanzetti*, pp. 57, 69; Aldino Felicani, Oral History Project, Columbia University, p. 65.

41. Interview with Beltrando Brini, March 14, 1987. Cf. Lefevre Brini Wager, April 12, 1987: "He was a gentle soul. There was not a bit of meanness in him. I never saw him angry. That man didn't know how to be mean."

42. Peggy Lamson, *Roger Baldwin: Founder of the American Civil Liberties Union* (Boston: Houghton Mifflin, 1976), p. 169.

43. James, "The Story of Mario Buda."

44. Thomas O'Connor to Upton Sinclair, June 6, 1928, Sinclair Papers, Lilly Library, Indiana University; Sinclair, *Boston*, p. 546.

45. Upton Sinclair, *Autobiography* (New York: Harcourt, Brace, 1962), p. 240.

46. Ibid., p. 241; Leon Harris, *Upton Sinclair: American Rebel* (New York: Crowell, 1975), p. 244.

47. Sinclair to Hill, July 12, 1928, Houghton Library, Harvard University.

48. Sinclair, *Autobiography*, p. 240; Sinclair to Hill, July 12 and August 9, 1928, Houghton Library.

49. Sinclair to Hill, July 20, 1928, Houghton Library. See also Sinclair to Herbert B. Ehrmann, June 12, 1928, Ehrmann Papers, Harvard Law School Library; and Fred Moore to Lola Darroch Moore, February 21, 1928, Sinclair Papers, Lilly Library.

50. Harris, *Upton Sinclair*, p. 244.

51. Sinclair to Hill, July 12, 1928, Houghton Library.

52. *The Road to Freedom*, June 1929.

53. Interview with Joseph Moro, April 13, 1987.

54. Interview with Concetta Silvestri, February 13, 1988.

CHAPTER ELEVEN
MANHUNT

1. *Cleveland Plain Dealer*, June 4, 1919.

2. *Philadelphia Inquirer*, June 5, 1919.

3. Murray, *Red Scare*, p. 80; Jaffe, *Crusade Against Radicalism*, p. 94; *New York Times*, June 4, 1919.

4. *Philadelphia Inquirer*, June 4, 1919.

5. Post, *Deportations Delirium*, pp. 49–50.

6. Johnson, *Challenge to American Freedoms*, p. 130.

7. *New York World*, June 19, 1919.

8. Athan G. Theoharis and John Stuart Cox, *The Boss: J. Edgar Hoover and the Great American Inquisition* (Philadelphia: Temple University Press, 1988), pp. 6–7.

9. Post, *Deportations Delirium*, p. 46; Coben, *A. Mitchell Palmer*, p. 207; Frank J. Donner, *The Age of Surveillance: The Aims and Methods of America's Political Intelligence System* (New York: Knopf, 1980), p. 35.

10. Donner, *The Age of Surveillance*, p. 34. The phrase "anarchistic and similar classes" derives from the October 16, 1918, immigration law.

11. *New York Times*, June 5, 1919.

12. Ibid., June 7, 1919, quoted in Polenberg, *Fighting Faiths*, p. 172.

13. Richard G. Powers, *Secrecy and Power: The Life of J. Edgar Hoover* (New York: Free Press, 1987), p. 66.

14. *A. Mitchell Palmer on Charges*, pp. 159–160; Hoover to Brigadier General M. Churchill, May 24, 1920, DJ 9-12-276.

15. West, June 21, 1919; Emmett T. Drew, Paterson, May 16, 1920, BI 211793. A Roxbury police captain told Special Agent Feri Felix Weiss that he had not the slightest doubt that "Galleani and his gang of Italian anarchists" had planted the bomb in Judge Hayden's house. Weiss, September 5, 1919, ibid.

16. M. R. Valkenburgh, Boston, June 23, 1919, BI 211793.

17. S. Busha, Philadelphia, August 4, 1919; E. J. Wheeler, Pittsburgh, October 7, 1919, FBI 61-481-4.

18. *New York Times*, May 4, 1920.

19. Ibid.; U.S. Army, Military Intelligence Division 10110-1279.

20. *A. Mitchell Palmer on Charges*, pp. 159–161.

21. Chief Inspector John A. McGarr to Superintendent Raymond W. Pullman, June 6, 1919; John B. Hanrahan, Boston, June 24, 1919, BI 211793. The clerk who sold the automatic, Lincoln Wadsworth, was later to testify at the Sacco-Vanzetti trial.

22. West, October 7, 1919, DJ 9-12-276.

23. U.S. Army, Military Intelligence Division 10110-1279.

24. DJ 9-12-276.

25. Weiss, September 19, 1919, BI 211793. Cf. George F. Lamb to Todd Daniels, March 1, 1920, ibid.

26. Valkenburgh, July 18 and 21, 1919; Weiss, October 10, 1919, BI 211793.

27. *New York Times*, May 4, 1920; undercover report, New York, January 14, 1920, BI 211793.

28. *A. Mitchell Palmer on Charges*, p. 163.

29. West, January 28, 1922, FBI 61-1003.

30. Ibid.

31. West, November 9, 1922, FBI 61-1003.

32. A. Mitchell Palmer, "The Case Against the 'Reds'," *Forum*, February 1920; Osmond K. Fraenkel, *The Sacco-Vanzetti Case* (New York: Knopf, 1931), p. 5.

33. Richard Gambino, *Blood of My Blood: The Dilemma of Italian-Americans* (Garden City, N.Y.: Doubleday, 1974), p. 118; *A. Mitchell Palmer on Charges*, p. 7; Coben, *A. Mitchell Palmer*, p. 198.

34. William E. Leuchtenburg, *The Perils of Prosperity, 1914–32* (Chicago: University of Chicago Press, 1958), p. 66; John Higham, *Strangers in the Land: Patterns of American Nativism, 1860–1925*, revised ed. (New York: Athenaeum, 1971), p. 228; Murray, *Red Scare*, p. 206.

35. INS 54235/36C.

36. *Washington Post* and *New York World*, June 19, 1919; *New York Times*, June 18, 1919; Coben, *A. Mitchell Palmer*, p. 211.

37. *A. Mitchell Palmer on Charges*, pp. 166–167.

38. Palmer, "The Case Against the 'Reds'."

39. Murray, *Red Scare*, pp. 197, 213–215.

40. Coben, *A. Mitchell Palmer*, p. 221.

41. United States Congress, Senate, Committee on the Judiciary, *Charges of Illegal Practices of the Department of Justice*, 66th Congress, 3d Session,

1921 (Washington, D.C.: Government Printing Office, 1921), p. 573; David Williams, "The Bureau of Investigation and Its Critics, 1919–1921: The Origins of Federal Political Surveillance," *Journal of American History* 68 (December 1981): 562–563.

42. *Baltimore Sun*, September 13 and 27, 1920.

43. Frederic C. Howe, *Confessions of a Reformer* (New York: Scribner, 1926), p. 276.

44. National Popular Government League, *To the American People: Report upon the Illegal Practices of the United States Department of Justice* (Washington, D.C.: National Popular Government League, 1920), p. 4.

45. Post, *Deportations Delirium*, p. 97; Murray, *Red Scare*, p. 250.

46. *A. Mitchell Palmer on Charges*, p. 6; Murray, *Red Scare*, pp. 247–249.

47. *Charges of Illegal Practices of the Department of Justice*, p. 582.

48. J. H. Wigmore, "Freedom of Speech and Freedom of Thuggery," *Illinois Law Review*, March 1920; William R. Roalfe, *John Henry Wigmore: Scholar and Reformer* (Evanston, Ill.: Northwestern University Press, 1977), p. 151.

CHAPTER TWELVE
THE SPY

1. *Sacco e Vanzetti a sessant'anni dalla morte: Atti del convegno di studi, Villafalletto, 4–5 settembre 1987* (Cuneo: Istituto Storico della Resistenza in Cuneo e Provincia, 1988), p. 39.

2. *Il Martello*, October 1 and December 1, 1920; *New York Times*, July 14, 1948; Becker to Flynn, March 17, 1920, BI 211793.

3. *Il Martello*, May 1, 1920; *New York Call*, June 14, 1920. See also statement of Carlo Tresca, May 12, 1927, Sinclair Papers, Lilly Library.

4. Undercover reports of January 14 and 19, 1920, BI 211793. See also J. Edgar Hoover, "Memorandum for Files," March 13, 1920, FBI 61-481-7.

5. Undercover report, February 17, 1920, BI 211793.

6. *New York Times*, February 16, 1920; *A. Mitchell Palmer on Charges*, pp. 11, 182, 536–537. Among those whose warrants were voided were Pietro Baldiserotto, Serafino Grandi, Franz Widmer, and Alberto Guabello, all veteran members of the group.

7. *Il Martello*, February 15, 1920.

8. Ibid., May 1, 1920.

9. "Statement of Carlo Tresca," November 3, 1922, Sophia Smith Collection, Smith College, Northampton, Mass.; Dorothy Gallagher, *All the Right Enemies: The Life and Murder of Carlo Tresca* (New Brunswick, N.J.: Rutgers University Press, 1988), p. 77.

10. Vanzetti to Felicani, March 26, 1920, MS. SV 7B5, Boston Public Library.

11. Davis, March 20, 1920, BI 211793.

12. *New York Times*, February 16 and 17, 1920; United States Congress, House of Representatives, Committee on Immigration and Naturalization, *Communist Labor Party Deportation Cases*, 66th Congress, 2d Session 1920

(Washington, D.C: Government Printing Office, 1920), p. 40; *A. Mitchell Palmer on Charges*, p. 541.

13. Frank R. Stone, Newark, February 25, 1920, FBI 61-260-2 (Federal Bureau of Investigation); J. Edgar Hoover, "Memorandum to Mr. Flynn," March 8, 1920, BI 211793.

14. DJ 202600-418.

15. Gaspare Cannone to Roberto Elia, April 17, 1920, FBI 61-260-3 (Federal Bureau of Investigation); *A. Mitchell Palmer on Charges*, p. 704.

16. Hoover, "Memorandum to Mr. Flynn," March 8, 1920, BI 211793.

17. Stone, February 25, 1920, FBI 61-260-2 (Federal Bureau of Investigation). Stone also telephoned Bureau of Investigation headquarters in Washington, and Hoover and Flynn were informed. M. J. Davis, "Memorandum for Mr. Hoover," February 16, 1920, ibid.

18. Joseph A. Barbera, New York, February 25, 1920, FBI 61-260-2 (Federal Bureau of Investigation); *A. Mitchell Palmer on Charges*, p. 162.

19. V. J. Valjavec, New York, February 28, 1920, FBI 61-260-2 (Federal Bureau of Investigation); *The Sacco-Vanzetti Case*, V, 4983.

20. Statement of Roberto Elia at Raymond Street Jail, Brooklyn, N.Y., February 28, 1920, FBI 61-260-2 (Federal Bureau of Investigation); Barbera, March 2, 1920, ibid.

21. Charles J. Scully, New York, May 22, 1920, FBI 61-260-3 (Federal Bureau of Investigation); National Popular Government League, *To the American People*, pp. 21–22; *The Sacco-Vanzetti Case*, V, 4983–4984.

22. Statement of Roberto Elia, Ellis Island, May 7, 1920, FBI 61-260-3 (Federal Bureau of Investigation); *The Sacco-Vanzetti Case*, V, 4984.

23. *The Sacco-Vanzetti Case*, V, 4984.

24. Scully, May 22, 1920, FBI 61-260-3 (Federal Bureau of Investigation); *New York Call*, June 10, 1920; Fedeli, *Luigi Galleani*, p. 100; *Un trentennio di attività anarchica*, pp. 144–145.

25. Statement of Roberto Elia, May 7, 1920, FBI 61-260-3 (Federal Bureau of Investigation); *L'Ordine*, October 31 and December 1, 1919.

26. *The Sacco-Vanzetti Case*, V, 4984–4985; Statement of Roberto Elia, May 7, 1920, FBI 61-260-3 (Federal Bureau of Investigation).

27. Frank Francisco, New York, May 24, 1920, FBI 61-260-3 (Federal Bureau of Investigation); *A. Mitchell Palmer on Charges*, p. 163.

28. National Popular Government League, *To the American People*, pp. 11–27; Murray, *Red Scare*, p. 214.

29. National Popular Government League, *To the American People*, pp. 31–32; Barbera, March 16, 1920, BI 211793; *Il Martello*, July 15, 1920.

30. George F. Lamb, May 24, 1920, FBI 61-260-3 (Federal Bureau of Investigation); *New York Call*, June 10, 1920; *Cronaca Sovversiva* (Turin), July 31, 1920.

31. George F. Lamb to Frank Burke, May 11, 1920, FBI 62-18674 (Federal Bureau of Investigation).

32. *The Sacco-Vanzetti Case*, V, 4985.

33. Scully, May 22, 1920, FBI 61-260-3 (Federal Bureau of Investigation);

A. Mitchell Palmer on Charges, pp. 41–42, 162. Canzani's fifteen-year-old daughter Elvira told agents that Salsedo had asked her to proofread the original setting.

34. *The Sacco-Vanzetti Case*, V, 4985; FBI 61-260-2 (Federal Bureau of Investigation).

35. *The Sacco-Vanzetti Case*, V, 4986; Statement of Roberto Elia, May 7, 1920, FBI 61-260-3 (Federal Bureau of Investigation); *A. Mitchell Palmer on Charges*, pp. 162–163. Deportation warrants were issued for Elia and Salsedo on February 20 and March 10, 1920, respectively.

36. "Memorandum re Bomb Plot of June 2, 1919," BI 211793.

37. *A. Mitchell Palmer on Charges*, p. 162; *New York Times*, May 4, 1920.

38. Lamb, May 24, 1920, FBI 61-260-3 (Federal Bureau of Investigation).

39. Lamb to Burke, May 11, 1920, FBI 62-18674 (Federal Bureau of Investigation).

40. *The Sacco-Vanzetti Case*, V, 4986.

41. Ibid.; Lamb to Burke, May 11, 1920, FBI 62-18674 (Federal Bureau of Investigation); William R. Palmera, New York, May 24, 1920, FBI 61-260-3 (Federal Bureau of Investigation).

42. Statement of Roberto Elia, May 7, 1920, FBI 61-260-3 (Federal Bureau of Investigation).

43. *The Sacco-Vanzetti Case*, V, 4986.

Chapter Thirteen
Death of Salsedo

1. Lyons, *The Life and Death of Sacco and Vanzetti*, p. 45; Russell, *Sacco and Vanzetti*, p. 84.

2. Aldino Felicani, Oral History Project, Columbia University, p. 47.

3. Vanzetti to Felicani, April 17, 1920, MS. SV 7B7, Boston Public Library. See also Ronald Creagh, *Sacco et Vanzetti* (Paris: La Découverte, 1984), p. 127.

4. *The Sacco-Vanzetti Case*, II, 1705–1710, 1849; *The Story of the Sacco-Vanzetti Case* (Boston: Sacco-Vanzetti Defense Committee, 1921), p. 41.

5. *The Sacco-Vanzetti Case*, II, 1831–1833, 2049–2050.

6. Aldino Felicani, Oral History Project, Columbia University, p. 69.

7. *L'Era Nuova*, July 3, 1915; Tresca to Schiavina, September 25, 1917, Finch, March 27, 1918, BI OG 20713; *Il Martello*, July 20, 1919.

8. Nunzio Pernicone, "Carlo Tresca and the Sacco-Vanzetti Case," *Journal of American History* 66 (December 1979):540; Gallagher, *All the Right Enemies*, p. 76.

9. Statement of Carlo Tresca, May 12, 1927, Sinclair Papers, Lilly Library; Lamb, May 24, 1920, FBI 61-260-3 (Federal Bureau of Investigation).

10. Luigi Quintiliano, "Preludii alla tragedia di Dedham," *Controcorrente*, August 1958. The title of the defense committee varied: Comitato Italiano per la Difesa delle Vittime Politiche and Comitato Italiano Pro Vittime Politiche. After the arrest of Sacco and Vanzetti it evolved into the Comitato Italiano Pro

Vittime Politiche: Pro Sacco e Vanzetti. *Il Martello*, January 1 and July 15, 1920.

11. *New York Times*, April 1, 1937; *The Sacco-Vanzetti Case*, II, 1982–1983, 2048; Walter Nelles, *A Liberal in Wartime: The Education of Albert DeSilver*, ed. Lewis Gannett (New York: Norton, 1940), pp. 14–15, 121.

12. One of his partners, Swinburne Hale, was a signer of the National Popular Government League report of 1920, which condemned the Justice Department's illegal practices. Nelles himself assisted in the preparation of the report. He was also the author of a pamphlet on *Espionage Act Cases* (1918).

13. *New York Times*, April 1, 1937.

14. *The Sacco-Vanzetti Case*, II, 1982–1983.

15. Ibid., II, 2074. Vanzetti's receipt is preserved in the Sacco-Vanzetti Case Papers, Harvard Law School Library.

16. *The Sacco-Vanzetti Case*, II, 1809; Aldino Felicani, Oral History Project, Columbia University, p. 47.

17. *The Sacco-Vanzetti Case*, II, 1705–1710.

18. Evans, *Outstanding Features of the Sacco-Vanzetti Case*, p. 23; Herbert B. Ehrmann, *The Case That Will Not Die: Commonwealth vs. Sacco and Vanzetti* (Boston: Little, Brown, 1969), p. 48.

19. "Memorandum re Bomb Plot of June 2, 1919," BI 211793; Lamb to Burke, May 11, 1920, FBI 62-18674 (Federal Bureau of Investigation).

20. *New York Call*, May 4, 1920; *The Sacco-Vanzetti Case*, V, 4986.

21. *New York Call*, June 10, 1920; *The Sacco-Vanzetti Case*, V, 4987.

22. Statement of Roberto Elia, May 7, 1920; Palmera, May 24, 1920, FBI 61-260-3 (Federal Bureau of Investigation).

23. *New York Times*, May 4, 1920; Scully, May 22, 1920, FBI 61-260-3 (Federal Bureau of Investigation).

24. *The Sacco-Vanzetti Case*, V, 4986–4987.

25. *New York Times*, May 4, 1920; Lamb to Burke, May 11, 1920, FBI 62-18674 (Federal Bureau of Investigation); Dotzert, New York, May 24, 1920, FBI 61-260-3 (Federal Bureau of Investigation).

26. *L'Agitazione*, November 20, 1921; DiLillo, November 26, 1921, FBI 61-481-7.

27. *Cronaca Sovversiva*, June 12, 1920; Vanzetti to Governor Fuller, *The Letters of Sacco and Vanzetti*, p. 383. At his trial Vanzetti declared: "The papers say he jump down, but we don't know." *The Sacco-Vanzetti Case*, II, 1808. Fifty years later, Italian anarchists saw a parallel between the fate of Salsedo and that of Giuseppe Pinelli, who plunged to his death in 1969 from the window of police headquarters in Milan. See "Una defenestrazione di cinquant'anni fa," *L'Internazionale*, March 15, 1970. This incident inspired Dario Fo's play, *Accidental Death of an Anarchist*.

28. Post, *Deportations Delirium*, pp. 278–282.

29. *A. Mitchell Palmer on Charges*, pp. 162–163. According to George Lamb, Salsedo had more than once told Donato that he would commit suicide. Lamb to Burke, May 11, 1920, FBI 62-18674 (Federal Bureau of Investigation).

30. Nelles, *A Liberal in Wartime*, p. 194.

31. "Maria Salsedo v. A. Mitchell Palmer, William J. Flynn, George F. Lamb, Charles J. Scully, and John Francisco, the name 'John' being fictitious, the real Christian name of the defendant being unknown to the plaintiff" [it was Frank], DJ 213479.

32. Ibid.; Jaffe, *Crusade Against Radicalism*, p. 223.

33. *New York Call*, June 10, 1920.

34. Post, *Deportations Delirium*, p. 200.

35. INS 54809 (Immigration and Naturalization Service); *Il Martello*, August 30, 1924.

36. *Un trentennio di attività anarchica*, p. 62; FBI 61-126-602 (Federal Bureau of Investigation).

37. Vanzetti wrote Elia a get-well letter shortly before his death. Vanzetti to Elia, July 9, 1924, MS. SV 7B47, Boston Public Library.

CHAPTER FOURTEEN
THE ARREST

1. Davis, March 22, 1920, FBI 61-481-7; West, November 9, 1922, FBI 61-1003; interview with Fiorina Rossi, February 14, 1988. Among the others who departed were Amleto Fabbri, John Scussel, and Domenico Ricci, all of whom later returned to the United States.

2. *A. Mitchell Palmer on Charges*, pp. 21, 36; *Una trentennio di attività anarchica*, p. 141; J. Edgar Hoover, "Memorandum for Files," July 12, 1921, DJ 202600-2342.

3. Sberna, according to Agent Drew of Paterson, had "full information concerning the bomb plot of June 2nd." Drew, May 16, 1920, BI 211793.

4. *The Sacco-Vanzetti Case*, V, 4501.

5. Ibid., II, 2006.

6. *A. Mitchell Palmer on Charges*, p. 712; West, January 12, 1921, DJ 202600-143; Davis, March 22, 1920, BI 211793.

7. *The Sacco-Vanzetti Case*, II, 1933.

8. Vanzetti, *Background of the Plymouth Trial*, p. 10; *Non piangete la mia morte*, p. 61; Feuerlicht, *Justice Crucified*, p. 50.

9. *The Sacco-Vanzetti Case*, II, 1833–1834, 1927.

10. *Boston Herald* and *New York Times*, May 4, 1920.

11. Felix Frankfurter, *The Case of Sacco and Vanzetti: A Critical Analysis for Lawyers and Laymen* (Boston: Little, Brown, 1927), pp. 45–46.

12. Edward Holton James, "New Light Coming on the Sacco-Vanzetti Case," *Unity*, August 15, 1932.

13. Felicani Collection, Boston Public Library; *The Sacco-Vanzetti Case*, II, 2120.

14. *The Sacco-Vanzetti Case*, I, 752; Vanzetti, *The Story of a Proletarian Life*, p. 16.

15. James, "The Story of Mario Buda"; Russell, *Tragedy in Dedham*, p. 54.

16. *New Bedford Standard-Times*, August 23, 1952; Thomas O'Connor,

"The Origin of the Sacco-Vanzetti Case," *Vanderbilt Law Review* 14 (June 1961).

17. *The Sacco-Vanzetti Case*, VI, 382.

18. Memorandum of Michael E. Stewart, May 31, 1921, Massachusetts State Police; Stewart, "Commonwealth vs. Nicola Sacco and Bartolomeo Vanzetti," Sacco-Vanzetti Case Papers, Harvard Law School Library.

19. Memorandum of Michael E. Stewart; Stewart, "Commonwealth vs. Nicola Sacco and Bartolomeo Vanzetti"; Russell, *Tragedy in Dedham*, pp. 58–59.

20. *The Sacco-Vanzetti Case*, I, 842–851; III, 3387–3389.

21. The Sacco-Vanzetti Case Papers, Harvard Law School Library.

22. *The Sacco-Vanzetti Case*, IV, 3514.

23. Sinclair to Hill, July 20 and August 9, 1928, Houghton Library. See also Fred Moore to Sinclair, March 6, 1928, Sinclair Papers, Lilly Library; Sinclair, *Boston*, pp. 453, 459; and D'Attilio, "La Salute è in Voi," p. 88.

24. Vorse, *A Footnote to Folly*, pp. 333–334. Cf. Shields, *Are They Doomed?*, p. 10.

25. James, "The Story of Mario Buda."

26. *New York Times* and *New York World*, September 17, 1920. See also *New York Call*, September 17, 1920; and Edmund Gilligan, "The Wall Street Explosion Mystery," *The American Mercury*, September 1938, pp. 63–67.

27. *New York Times*, September 18, 1920; Jaffe, *Crusade Against Radicalism*, p. 226.

28. Murray, *Red Scare*, pp. 257–259; Jaffe, *Crusade Against Radicalism*, pp. 226–227; *New York Times*, September 18, 1920.

29. *New York Times*, September 19, 1920.

30. Ibid., September 18, 1920; *New York Call*, September 19, 1920.

31. Young and Kaiser, *Postmortem*, pp. 126–127.

32. Gilligan, "The Wall Street Explosion Mystery"; *New York Daily News*, August 25, 1921. That Buda was the Wall Street bomber cannot be proved; documentary evidence is lacking. But it fits what we know of him and his movements. I have it, moreover, from a reliable source and believe it to be true.

CHAPTER FIFTEEN
EPILOGUE

1. James, "The Story of Mario Buda."

2. Ibid.; *Umanità Nova*, January 13, 1921.

3. Interview with Charles Poggi, September 30, 1987.

4. Outlawed in the United States, *Cronaca Sovversiva* was smuggled in and distributed clandestinely under the title *A Stormo!* Among its articles (August 7, 1920) was a report by Schiavina on Vanzetti's conviction in the Bridgewater case, which he denounced as a frame-up.

5. *La Frusta*, December 19, 1919; DiLillo, December 23, 1921, FBI 61-381.

6. DiLillo, February 27, 1922, FBI 61-381.

7. Luigi Galleani police file, Archivio Centrale dello Stato, Direzione Generale della Pubblica Sicurezza, Casellario Politico Centrale.

8. *Pensiero e Volontà*, June 1, 1926, in Vernon Richards, ed., *Errico Malatesta: His Life and Ideas* (London: Freedom Press, 1965), p. 34.

9. Fedeli, *Luigi Galleani*, pp. 189–190; Max Nettlau, "Luigi Galleani (1861–1931)," *Die Internationale*, January 1932.

10. Interview with Charles Poggi, May 19, 1988 (for Schiavina's meeting with Buda in Rimini). For Schiavina's visit to his native town (San Carlo), I am indebted to Professor Nunzio Pernicone, who got the story from Schiavina.

11. Lyons, *Assignment in Utopia*, p. 24; Ferruccio Coacci police file, Archivio Centrale dello Stato, Direzione Generale della Pubblica Sicurezza, Casellario Politico Centrale.

12. Recchi police file, Archivio Centrale dello Stato; Osvaldo Bayer, *Anarchism and Violence: Severino Di Giovanni in Argentina, 1923–1931* (London: Elephant Editions, 1985), pp. 141–142; *Un trentennio di attività anarchica*, p. 107; *L'Internazionale*, October 20, 1975.

13. In 1925 the police confiscated in his home copies of the anarchist journal *Fede!*, published in Rome by Gigi Damiani. Buda police file, Archivio Centrale dello Stato.

14. Interview with Charles Poggi, September 30, 1987.

15. James, "The Story of Mario Buda" and "New Light Coming on the Sacco-Vanzetti Case."

16. Buda police file, Archivio Centrale dello Stato. See also Hugo Rolland, "Il Caso Sacco e Vanzetti: Nella storia e nella leggenda," manuscript, International Institute of Social History, Amsterdam; and Creagh, *Sacco et Vanzetti*, p. 166.

17. *The Letters of Sacco and Vanzetti*, pp. 214–215.

18. *Protesta Umana*, June 1926; D'Attilio, "La Salute è in Voi," p. 89.

19. *The Road to Freedom*, August 1929; Felix, *Protest*, p. 90; *The Letters of Sacco and Vanzetti*, pp. 119–120, 151, 315.

20. *The Road to Freedom*, June 1927; *The Letters of Sacco and Vanzetti*, p. 69.

21. *Boston Traveler*, June 1, 1926; *Boston Evening Transcript*, May 14, 1927; *Boston Globe*, August 17, 1927. Apparently McHardy was chosen as a target because he had opposed the governor's appointment of an advisory committee to review the case.

22. *Un trentennio di attività anarchica*, pp. 162, 167; Russell, *Tragedy in Dedham*, p. 456. Elliott was the country's most active and famous executioner. In 1939 he was to electrocute Bruno Richard Hauptmann, the kidnapper of the Lindbergh baby. Jim Fisher, *The Lindbergh Case* (New Brunswick, N.J.: Rutgers University Press, 1987), p. 392.

23. John P. Diggins, *Mussolini and Fascism: The View from America* (Princeton, N.J.: Princeton University Press, 1972), p. 130; Gallagher, *All the Right Enemies*, pp. 131–133. See also *The Lantern*, January and February 1928.

24. Raffaele Schiavina, *Sacco e Vanzetti: Cause e fini di un delitto di Stato* (Paris: Jean Bucco, 1927); Schiavina, "Breve note autobiografiche." See also Paul Berman, "The Torch and the Axe: The Unknown Aftermath of the Sacco-Vanzetti Affair," *The Village Voice*, May 17, 1988.

25. Interview with Valerio Isca, Brooklyn, N.Y., January 25, 1988; interview with Galileo Tobia, New York, March 9, 1988.

26. Giuseppe Fiori, *L'anarchico Schirru, condannato a morte per l'intenzione di uccidere Mussolini* (Milan: Mondadori, 1983), pp. 159–175; Berman, "The Torch and the Axe." See also Marcus Graham, ed., *Man! An Anthology of Anarchist Ideas, Essays, Poetry and Commentaries* (London: Cienfuegos Press, 1974), pp. 510–518; and Charles F. Delzell, *Mussolini's Enemies: The Italian Anti-Fascist Resistance* (Princeton, N.J.: Princeton University Press, 1961), pp. 107–108.

27. *Un trentennio di attività anarchica*, p. 167.

28. Interview with Fiorina Rossi, February 14, 1988. Schiavina, himself a fugitive, went under the name of Bruno Rossi.

29. Financial Report of the Committee for Sacco and Vanzetti, Detroit, 1920–1925, Labadie Collection, University of Michigan.

30. Ella Antolini to Emma Goldman, March 27, 1940, courtesy of Federico Arcos. Goldman did not recover, dying on May 14, 1940.

31. *L'Adunata dei Refrattari*, January 12, 1946; interviews with Fiorina Rossi and Louis Tarabelli, Needham, Mass., February 14, 1988.

32. *L'Adunata dei Refrattari*, August 30, 1947; *Un trentennio di attività anarchica*, p. 140.

33. Interview with Attilio Bortolotti, December 10, 1988.

34. Raffaele Schiavina to Febo Pomilia, January 10, 1984, courtesy of Febo Pomilia.

35. Interview with Caira Tarabelli, Needham, Mass., August 10, 1988.

36. *New York Times*, August 23, 1977.

37. *L'Adunata dei Refrattari*, June 15, 1963; *L'Internazionale*, October 20, 1975.

38. Interview with Aurora Magliocca, Brooklyn, N.Y., September 27, 1988. The information regarding Hoover comes from Professor Nunzio Pernicone, who interviewed Schiavina.

39. Galleani, *The End of Anarchism?*, introduction.

Bibliography

The literature on Sacco and Vanzetti is so vast that a comprehensive list of sources would fill a volume in itself. The present bibliography makes no claim to completeness. It confines itself, rather, to works that, by shedding light on the lives of Sacco and Vanzetti and their place in the Italian anarchist movement in America, have been especially helpful in preparing this book. Sacco and Vanzetti materials are to be found in many libraries and archives. The principal repositories, however, are the Boston Public Library; the Harvard Law School Library; the Labadie Collection of the University of Michigan; the National Archives, Washington, D.C.; the Archivio Centrale dello Stato, Rome; and the International Institute of Social History, Amsterdam.

BOOKS AND PAMPHLETS

Gli anarchici in Puglia dal 1872 al 1892. Poggibonsi: Lalli Editore, 1986.
Avrich, Paul. *Anarchist Portraits*. Princeton, N.J.: Princeton University Press, 1988.
————. *The Haymarket Tragedy*. Princeton, N.J.: Princeton University Press, 1984.
Bayer, Osvaldo. *Anarchism and Violence: Severino Di Giovanni in Argentina, 1923–1931*. London: Elephant Editions, 1985.
Bettini, Leonardo. *Bibliografia dell'anarchismo*. 2 vols. Florence: CP Editrice, 1972–1976.
Botta, Luigi. *Sacco e Vanzetti: Giustiziata la verità*. Cavallermaggiore: Edizioni Gribaudo, 1978.
Claghorn, Kate H. *The Immigrant's Day in Court*. New York: Harper, 1923.
Coben, Stanley. *A. Mitchell Palmer: Politician*. New York: Columbia University Press, 1963.
Cook, Fred J. *The FBI Nobody Knows*. New York: Macmillan, 1964.
Creagh, Ronald. *Sacco et Vanzetti*. Paris: Editions La Découverte, 1984.
Delzell, Charles F. *Mussolini's Enemies: The Italian Anti-Fascist Resistance*. Princeton, N.J.: Princeton University Press, 1961.
Diggins, John P. *Mussolini and Fascism: The View from America*. Princeton, N.J.: Princeton University Press, 1972.
Dos Passos, John. *Facing the Chair: Story of the Americanization of Two Foreignborn Workmen*. Boston: Sacco-Vanzetti Defense Committee, 1927.
Drinnon, Richard. *Rebel in Paradise: A Biography of Emma Goldman*. Chicago: University of Chicago Press, 1961.
Duval, Clément. *Memorie autobiografiche*. Newark, N.J.: L'Adunata dei Refrattari, 1929.
Ehrmann, Herbert B. *The Case That Will Not Die: Commonwealth vs. Sacco and Vanzetti*. Boston: Little, Brown, 1969.

Evans, Elizabeth Glendower. *Outstanding Features of the Sacco-Vanzetti Case*. Boston: New England Civil Liberties Committee, 1924.

Fedeli, Ugo. *Luigi Galleani: Quarant'anni di lotte rivoluzionarie (1891–1931)*. Cesena: Antistato, 1956.

Felix, David. *Protest: Sacco-Vanzetti and the Intellectuals*. Bloomington: Indiana University Press, 1965.

Fenton, Edwin. *Immigrants and Unions, A Case Study: Italians and American Labor, 1870–1920*. New York: Arno, 1975.

Feuerlicht, Roberta Strauss. *Justice Crucified: The Story of Sacco and Vanzetti*. New York: McGraw-Hill, 1977.

Fiori, Giuseppe. *L'anarchico Schirru, condannato a morte per l'intenzione di uccidere Mussolini*. Milan: Mondadori, 1983.

Flynn, Elizabeth Gurley. *The Rebel Girl, An Autobiography: My First Life (1906–1926)*. New York: International Publishers, 1973.

Fraenkel, Osmond K. *The Sacco-Vanzetti Case*. New York: Knopf, 1931.

Frankfurter, Felix. *The Case of Sacco and Vanzetti: A Critical Analysis for Lawyers and Laymen*. Boston: Little, Brown, 1927.

Frost, Richard H. *The Mooney Case*. Stanford, Calif.: Stanford University Press, 1968.

Gallagher, Dorothy. *All the Right Enemies: The Life and Murder of Carlo Tresca*. New Brunswick, N.J.: Rutgers University Press, 1988.

Galleani, Luigi. *The End of Anarchism?* Tr. Max Sartin [Raffaele Schiavina] and Robert D'Attilio. Sanday, Orkney: Cienfuegos Press, 1982.

———. [Mentana, pseud.]. *Faccia a faccia col nemico: Cronache giudiziarie dell'anarchismo militante*. East Boston: Edizione del Gruppo Autonomo, 1914.

Gambino, Richard. *Blood of My Blood: The Dilemma of Italian-Americans*. Garden City, N.Y.: Doubleday, 1974.

Goldman, Emma. *Living My Life*. New York: Knopf, 1931.

Graham, Marcus, ed. *Man! An Anthology of Anarchist Ideas, Essays, Poetry and Commentaries*. London: Cienfuegos Press, 1974.

Guadagni, Felice. *Il Caso Sacco-Vanzetti: Una mostruosità giudiziaria: Esposizione sintetica dei fatti più importanti inerenti al caso*. Boston: Comitato Centrale di Difesa [Sacco-Vanzetti Defense Committee], 1924.

Harris, Leon. *Upton Sinclair: American Rebel*. New York: Crowell, 1975.

Higham, John. *Strangers in the Land: Patterns of American Nativism, 1860–1925*. Revised ed. New York: Athenaeum, 1971.

Jaffe, Julian F. *Crusade Against Radicalism: New York During the Red Scare, 1914–1924*. Port Washington, N.Y.: Kennekat Press, 1972.

Johnson, Donald. *Challenge to American Freedoms: World War I and the Rise of the American Civil Liberties Union*. Lexington: University of Kentucky Press, 1963.

Joll, James. *The Anarchists*. London: Eyre & Spottiswoode, 1964.

Joughin, G. Louis, and Edmund M. Morgan. *The Legacy of Sacco and Vanzetti*. New York: Harcourt, Brace, 1948.

Lowenthal, Max. *The Federal Bureau of Investigation*. New York: William Sloane Associates, 1950.

Lyons, Eugene. *Assignment in Utopia*. New York: Harcourt, Brace, 1937.

———. *The Life and Death of Sacco and Vanzetti*. New York: International Publishers, 1927.

Martellone, Anna Maria. *Una Little Italy nell'Atene d'America: La comunità italiana di Boston dal 1880 al 1920*. Naples: Guida Editori, 1973.

Montgomery, Robert H. *Sacco-Vanzetti: The Murder and the Myth*. New York: Devin-Adair, 1960.

Murray, Robert K. *Red Scare: A Study in National Hysteria, 1919–1920*. Minneapolis: University of Minnesota Press, 1955.

National Popular Government League. *To the American People: Report upon the Illegal Practices of the United States Department of Justice*. Washington, D.C.: National Popular Government League, 1920.

O'Hare, Kate Richards. *In Prison*. St. Louis, Mo.: Frank P. O'Hare, 1920.

———. "Letters of Kate Richards O'Hare to Her Family." Typescript, Bowling Green State University, Bowling Green, Ohio.

Omaggio alla memoria imperitura di Carlo Tresca. New York: Il Martello, 1943.

Panunzio, Constantine M. *The Deportation Cases of 1919–1920*. New York: Federal Council of Churches of Christ, 1921.

Parrish, Michael E. *Felix Frankfurter and His Times: The Reform Years*. New York: The Free Press, 1982.

Peterson, Horace C., and Gilbert C. Fite. *Opponents of War, 1917–1918*. Madison: University of Wisconsin Press, 1957.

Polenberg, Richard. *Fighting Faiths: The Abrams Case, the Supreme Court, and Free Speech*. New York: Viking, 1987.

Post, Louis F. *The Deportations Delirium of Nineteen-Twenty*. Chicago: Charles H. Kerr, 1923.

Powers, Richard G. *Secrecy and Power: The Life of J. Edgar Hoover*. New York: The Free Press, 1987.

Preston, William, Jr. *Aliens and Dissenters: Federal Suppression of Radicals, 1903–1933*. Cambridge, Mass.: Harvard University Press, 1963.

Revolutionary Radicalism: Its History, Purpose and Tactics. 4 vols. Albany, N.Y.: J. B. Lyon, 1920.

Russell, Francis. *Sacco and Vanzetti: The Case Resolved*. New York: Harper & Row, 1986.

———. *Tragedy in Dedham: The Story of the Sacco-Vanzetti Case*. New York: McGraw-Hill, 1962.

Sacco, Nicola, and Bartolomeo Vanzetti. *The Letters of Sacco and Vanzetti*. Ed. Marion Denman Frankfurter and Gardner Jackson. New York: Viking, 1928.

Sacco e Vanzetti a sessant'anni dalla morte: Atti del convegno di studi, Villafalletto, 4–5 settembre 1987. Cuneo: Istituto Storico della Resistenza in Cuneo e Provincia, 1988.

Sacco-Vanzetti: Developments and Reconsiderations—1979. Boston: Boston Public Library, 1982.

The Sacco-Vanzetti Case: Transcript of the Record of the Trial of Nicola Sacco and Bartolomeo Vanzetti in the Courts of Massachusetts and Subsequent Proceedings, 1920–7. 6 vols. New York: Henry Holt, 1928–1929.

The Sacco-Vanzetti Case Papers. Microfilm, 23 reels, Frederick, Md.: University Publications of America, 1986.

The Sacco-Vanzetti Defense Committee. *Financial Report of the Sacco-Vanzetti Defense Committee, from the Date of Organization, May 5, 1920, to July 31, 1925.* Boston: Sacco-Vanzetti Defense Committee, 1925.

La Salute è in voi! n.p., n.d. [1905?]

Salvatore, Nick. *Eugene V. Debs: Citizen and Socialist.* Urbana: University of Illinois Press, 1982.

Schiavina, Raffaele. *Sacco e Vanzetti: Cause e fini di un delitto di Stato.* Paris: Jean Bucco, 1927.

Shields, Art. *Are They Doomed? The Sacco-Vanzetti Case and the Grim Forces Behind It.* New York: Workers Defense Union, 1921.

Sinclair, Upton. *Boston: A Documentary Novel of the Sacco-Vanzetti Case.* 2 vols. New York: Albert and Charles Boni, 1928. Reprint, Cambridge, Mass.: Robert Bentley, 1978.

The Story of the Sacco-Vanzetti Case. Boston: Sacco-Vanzetti Defense Committee, 1921.

Theoharis, Athan G., and John Stuart Cox. *The Boss: J. Edgar Hoover and the Great American Inquisition.* Philadelphia: Temple University Press, 1988.

Un trentennio di attività anarchica (1914–1945). Cesena: Antistato, 1953.

Tunney, Thomas J. *Throttled! The Detection of the German and Anarchist Bomb Plotters.* Boston: Small, Maynard, 1919.

United States Congress, House of Representatives, Committee on Rules. *Attorney General A. Mitchell Palmer on Charges Made Against Department of Justice by Louis F. Post and Others.* 66th Congress, 2d Session, 1920. Washington, D.C.: Government Printing Office, 1920.

United States Congress, Senate, Committee on the Judiciary. *Bolshevik Propaganda.* 65th Congress, 3d Session, 1919. Washington, D.C.: Government Printing Office, 1919.

U.S. Military Intelligence Reports: Surveillance of Radicals in the United States, 1917–1941. Microfilm, 34 reels, Frederick, Md.: University Publications of America, 1985.

Vanzetti, Bartolomeo. *Autobiografia e lettere inedite.* Ed. Alberto Gedda. Florence: Vallecchi, 1977.

———. *Background of the Plymouth Trial.* Boston: Road to Freedom Group, 1926.

———. *Lettere sul sindacalismo.* Cesena: Antistato, 1957.

———. *Non piangete la mia morte: Lettere ai familiari.* Ed. Cesare Pillon and Vincenzina Vanzetti. Rome: Editori Riuniti, 1962.

———. *The Story of a Proletarian Life.* Tr. Eugene Lyons. Boston: Sacco-Vanzetti Defense Committee, 1923.

Vecoli, Rudolph J., ed. *Italian American Radicalism: Old World Origins and New World Developments.* Staten Island, N.Y.: American Italian Historical Association, 1973.

Vorse, Mary Heaton. *A Footnote to Folly: Reminiscences.* New York: Farrar & Rinehart, 1935.

Woodcock, George. *Anarchism: A History of Libertarian Ideas and Movements.* Cleveland: World, 1962.

Young, William, and David E. Kaiser. *Postmortem: New Evidence in the Case of Sacco and Vanzetti.* Amherst: University of Massachusetts Press, 1985.

ARTICLES

Bagdikian, Ben H. "New Light on Sacco and Vanzetti." *The New Republic,* July 13, 1963.

Beffel, John N. "Eels and the Electric Chair." *The New Republic,* December 29, 1920.

————. "Felicani—A Fighter for Freedom," *Freedom.* June 24, 1967.

Berman, Paul. "The Torch and the Axe: The Unknown Aftermath of the Sacco-Vanzetti Affair." *The Village Voice,* May 17, 1988.

Calese, Robert S. "John Nicholas Beffel, Radical Journalist: 1887–1973." *Industrial Worker,* October 1973.

Candeloro, Dominic. "Louis F. Post and the Red Scare of 1920." *Prologue* 11 (September 1979):46–49.

Cappelli, Roberto. "La fondazione della 'Cronaca sovversiva'." *Volontà,* September–October 1972, pp. 190–200.

Carey, George W. " 'La Questione Sociale,' an Anarchist Newspaper in Paterson, N.J. (1895–1908)." In Lydio F. Tomasi, ed., *Italian Americans: New Perspectives in Italian Immigration and Ethnicity,* pp. 289–298. New York: American Italian Historical Association, 1985.

————. "The Vessel, the Deed, and the Idea: Anarchists in Paterson, 1895–1908." *Antipode: A Radical Journal of Geography* 10–11 (1979):46–58.

Cerrito, Gino. "Sull'emigrazione anarchica italiana negli Stati Uniti d'America." *Volontà,* July–August 1969, pp. 269–276.

Colp, Ralph, Jr. "Bitter Christmas: A Biographical Inquiry into the Life of Bartolomeo Vanzetti." *The Nation,* December 27, 1958.

————. "Sacco's Struggle for Sanity." *The Nation,* August 16, 1958.

Cook, Fred J. "The Missing Fingerprints." *The Nation,* December 22, 1962.

D'Attilio, Robert. "Primo Maggio: Haymarket as Seen by Italian Anarchists in America." In Dave Roediger and Franklin Rosemont, eds., *Haymarket Scrapbook,* pp. 229–231. Chicago: Charles H. Kerr, 1986.

————. "La Salute è in Voi: The Anarchist Dimension." In *Sacco-Vanzetti: Developments and Reconsiderations–1979,* pp. 75–89. Boston: Boston Public Library, 1982.

De Monte, Matteo. "Il Caso Sacco e Vanzetti [interview with Sabino Sacco]." *Il Messaggero,* February 1, 1976.

Eastman, Max. "Is This the Truth About Sacco and Vanzetti?" *The National Review,* October 21, 1961.

Felicani, Aldino. "Sacco-Vanzetti: A Memoir." *The Nation,* August 14, 1967.

Foner, Eric. "Sacco and Vanzetti: The Men and the Symbols." *The Nation,* August 20, 1977.

Gilligan, Edmund. "The Wall Street Explosion Mystery." *The American Mercury,* September 1938.

Gold, Michael [Irwin Granich]. "Anarchists in Plymouth." *Revolt*, February 5, 1916.

Grossman, James. "The Sacco-Vanzetti Case Reconsidered." *Commentary*, January 1962.

James, Edward Holton. "New Light Coming on the Sacco-Vanzetti Case." *Unity*, August 15, 1932.

———. "The Story of Mario Buda Before the Jury of the World." Typescript, Rome, February 21, 1928, Harvard Law School Library.

Lyons, Eugene. "Torremaggiore: A Glimpse of Sacco's Birthplace." *The World Tomorrow*, September 1921.

Martellone, Anna Maria. "Italian Mass Immigration to the United States, 1876–1930: A Historical Survey." *Perspectives in American History*, N.S., 1 (1984):379–423.

O'Connor, Thomas. "New Light on an Old Story." *The Nation*, September 22, 1926.

———. "The Origin of the Sacco-Vanzetti Case." *Vanderbilt Law Review* 14 (June 1961):987–1006.

Pernicone, Nunzio. "Carlo Tresca and the Sacco-Vanzetti Case." *Journal of American History* 66 (December 1979):535–547.

Sinclair, Upton. "The Fishpeddler and the Shoemaker." *Institute of Social Studies Bulletin* 2 (Summer 1953):13, 23–24.

Starrs, James E. "Once More Unto the Breech: The Firearms Evidence in the Sacco and Vanzetti Case Revisited." *Journal of Forensic Science*, April 1986, pp. 630–654; July 1986, pp. 1050–1078.

Vanzetti, Bartolomeo. "Events and Victims." *The Industrial Pioneer*, September 1924.

———. "Last Letters Home." Tr. Norman Thomas Di Giovanni, *The Nation*, August 24, 1963.

———. "The Work of a Fool or a Fakir." *The Road to Freedom*, August 1929.

Vecoli, Rudolph J. " 'Free Country': The American Republic Viewed by the Italian Left, 1880–1920." In Marianne Debouzy, ed., *In the Shadow of the Statue of Liberty: Immigrants, Workers and Citizens in the American Republic, 1880–1920*, pp. 35–56. Saint-Denis: Presses Universitaires de Vincennes, 1988.

———. " 'Primo Maggio' in the United States: An Invented Tradition of the Italian Anarchists." In Andrea Panaccione, ed., *May Day Celebration, Quaderni della Fondazione G. Brodolini*, pp. 55–83. Venice: Marsilio Editori, 1988.

Williams, David. "The Bureau of Investigation and Its Critics, 1919–1921: The Origins of Federal Political Surveillance." *Journal of American History* 68 (December 1981):560–79.

PERIODICALS

L'Adunata dei Refrattari. New York, 1922–1971.
L'Agitazione. Boston, 1920–1925.

L'Allarme. Chicago, 1915–1917.
L'Anarchico. New York, 1918.
La Comune. Philadelphia, 1910–1915.
Controcorrente. Boston, 1938–1967.
Cronaca Sovversiva. Barre, Vt.; Lynn, Mass.; Turin, Italy, 1903–1920.
La Difesa per Sacco e Vanzetti. Paris, 1923.
Il Diritto. New York, 1918–1919.
Domani. Brooklyn, N.Y., 1919.
L'Era Nuova. Paterson, N.J., 1908–1917.
La Frusta. Pesaro and Fano, Italy, 1919–1922.
L'Internazionale. Ancona, Italy, 1966–present.
La Jacquerie. Paterson, N.J. 1919.
The Labor Defender. New York, 1926–1927.
The Lantern. Boston, 1927–1929.
Liberación. Boston, 1923.
The Liberator. New York, 1918–1924.
Man! San Francisco, 1933–1940.
Il Martello. New York, 1916–1946.
Il Monito. Paris, 1925–1928.
The Official Bulletin of the Sacco-Vanzetti Defense Committee. Boston, 1925–
    1930.
L'Ordine. Brooklyn, N.Y., 1919–1920.
Protesta Umana. Boston, 1926–1927.
La Questione Sociale. Paterson, N.J., 1895–1908.
Il Refrattario. New York, 1919.
La Riscossa. Brooklyn, N.Y., 1916–1917.
La Rivolta degli Angeli. New York, 1923–1926.
The Road to Freedom. Stelton, N.J.; New York, 1924–1932.
Sacco-Vanzetti Bulletin. Boston, 1924.
The Sacco-Vanzetti Dawn. New York, 1927.

Index